The Satirist

The Satirist

His Temperament, Motivation, and Influence

Leonard Feinberg

The Citadel Press
New York

About the Author

LEONARD FEINBERG is professor of English at Iowa State University, where he has taught since taking his Ph.D. at the University of Illinois in 1946. In 1955 he made, for the Fund for Adult Education, a series of lectures on satire which were shown on educational television stations under the title "Man and Laughter." In 1957–1958 he was Fulbright lecturer in American Literature at the University of Ceylon. He has written for *The Atlantic, College English,* and other periodicals, has had radio plays produced on NBC, and is co-author with his wife of an English handbook-workbook published by Oxford University Press.

First paperbound edition, February, 1965

Published by The Citadel Press
222 Park Avenue South, New York 3, N.Y.

For Lilian, Ellen, and my mother

Preface 𝕏

For more than two thousand years men have written about the satirist. Satirists themselves, scholars, critics, and psychologists have speculated about the satirist's reasons for writing, his temperament, his place in society. The conclusions they reached are sometimes contradictory, sometimes complementary, sometimes outlandish. I have tried to bring together the significant theories that have been expressed about the satirist, to provide in one book a summary of the problems which specialists have examined intensively in numerous books and articles.

In Part One, I list the major theories about the motivation of the satirist, and then express my own belief that "adjustment" comes most closely to answering that question. The personality of the satirist — the apparently paradoxical elements of his nature, the problem of why so many great humorists are sad men, the contributions of psychoanalysts — all this is discussed in Part Two, where I imply that the satirist is not as abnormal as he has sometimes been made to seem, and that if he is a neurotic he has a good deal of company. In Part Three, I examine the beliefs of satirists and their relation to the environment within which they function. I stress the ubiquitousness of the satirist and suggest that there are a great many people with satiric temperaments who fail to attain literary expression.

I hope that this book will serve as an introduction, and that the reader will be sufficiently stimulated by the evidence of how much has been said about the satirist — and how little of it is conclusive — to investigate the subject further in some of the excellent books listed in the Reading List. A handbook of this kind is necessary because each proponent of a special theory has, naturally enough, applied his own point of view to the satirist he studied.

Whenever possible I have quoted verbatim, to keep the flavor of the writers' statements and to avoid distorting their remarks. In addition to summarizing the traditional and the psychoanalytic speculations, I have from time to time expressed my own opinions, trying to indicate clearly when those opinions differ from the conventional literary theories and the unconventional psychoanalytic interpretations.

For reading the manuscript and offering helpful suggestions I am very grateful to four of my colleagues at Iowa State University — Albert L. Walker, Keith Huntress, Robert Orlovich, and Norris Yates.

LEONARD FEINBERG

Table of Contents 𝒳

Part One ✿

Motivation

Creativity

There is an embarrassingly large number of theories which explain why a writer writes. The most popular answer is perhaps the least satisfactory one: he is driven by an irresistible compulsion. According to this somewhat imprecise theory, writers are "divinely" or "mysteriously" inspired, or forced to write without themselves understanding what inspired or forced them. One of the things that got Socrates into his final predicament was asking poets how they went about their work. They told him that they didn't really know; the gods inspired them, and the poets simply carried out divine instructions.

In some respects, we are not much further ahead than Socrates' contemporaries. A "creative impulse" of some sort has been generally accepted as a suitable motivation — for writers other than satirists. But many critics reject the concept that the creative impulse which motivates other writers is the same force that motivates the satirist. They

> *the creative impulse in the artist,*
> *springing from the tendency to*
> *immortalize himself*
> — Dr. Otto Rank

have chosen to attribute to him different stimuli from those of other writers. Nonetheless, the satirist is a writer. His being a writer may be inconvenient for theorists, or in somewhat bad taste, but there it is. He may be working the other side of the street from the poet, for instance, but he resembles the poet in many ways. It is only fair that a satirist be examined primarily as a writer.

The ancient theory of "creative inspiration" is supported to some extent in the psychology-conscious twentieth century not only by philosophers and mystics but by three fairly eminent psychoanalysts. According to Dr. Jung, "Art is a kind of *innate* drive that seizes a human being and makes him its instrument. The artist is not a person endowed with free will, who seeks his own end, but one who allows art to realize its purpose through him. . . . As an artist he is 'man' in a higher sense — he is 'collective man' — one who carries and shapes the unconscious psychic life of mankind."

Dr. Otto Rank, representing another coterie, is in essential agreement. "Creation is itself an experience of the artist, perhaps the most intense possible for him or for mankind in general. . . . Even in spite of a clear original conception, the work turns during production into something other than the artist had originally planned."

A spokesman for a third clique, Dr. S. Freud, wrote, "Wit shows in a most pronounced manner the character of an involuntary 'inspiration' or a sudden flash of thought. A moment before one cannot tell what kind of a joke one is going to make . . . one usually experiences something indefinable which I should like most to compare to an absence, or sudden drop, of an intellectual tension; then all of a sudden the witticism appears." The process that Freud is here describing he calls the creating of "tendentious" wit — that is, wit at the expense of somebody or something. That, of course, is what satire is.

Juvenal's remark, "It is difficult *not* to write satire," has usually been interpreted as proof of morality being the motivation of the satirist. Juvenal was writing in the first century A.D., a period when Rome was corrupt, decadent, and immoral, even by liberal standards of morality. However, at the very time that Juvenal made this statement, hundreds of Roman writers found it not at all difficult to keep from writing satire; they wrote epics and lyrics instead. The supporters of the "aesthetic drive" theory are convinced that Juvenal would have written satire whenever he lived. They believe that the satirist is motivated simply by the desire for self-expression, and the drive he responds to is similar in its spontaneity to the impulse that makes poets write lyrics and musicians compose music. It is a drive that may have been conditioned differently from the musical and poetical drives, but which manifests itself in essentially the same way — as aesthetic expression. The satirist's motivation for writing satire, then, would be this internal, personal, subjective compulsion.

Perhaps the most vigorous spokesman for the theory that the satirist is motivated by an aesthetic drive is Wyndham Lewis. Lewis may or may not be correct in saying, "The artistic impulse is more primitive than the ethical," but he is certainly correct in saying that satire can exist for its own sake as well as anything else can exist for its own sake. Lewis contends that although satire often is moral and an expression of a desire to reform, it is also frequently amoral and an expression of an aesthetic drive.

At this stage it would be helpful to agree on a working definition of satire. Unfortunately, no universally accepted definition exists. It is generally agreed that both criticism and humor have to be present in a work before it can be called satiric. But even the criticism-plus-humor formula is not wholly adequate, for much of Juvenal's and Swift's satire is too bitter to be humorous, and in Orwell's *1984*, Twain's *Mysterious Stranger,* and Waugh's *Loved One* there is a good deal of material which is satiric but certainly not comical. Professor Edgar Johnson suggests that "unmasking" or exposing is the indispensable characteristic of satire, and he is right; but this won't do as a definition for there exists an enormous amount of "unmasking" and exposing which cannot by the widest stretch of the imagination be called satire. What detectives and the F.B.I. and congressional investigating committees expose rarely falls under the category of satiric communication.

The following definition will be used in this book: The technique of the satirist consists of a *playfully critical distortion of the familiar.* The word "playfully" here is intended to stress the element of "pretense" rather than of jollity, although pure jollity does sometimes appear in satire.

Like other arts and philosophy, satire is primarily concerned with the nature of reality. Unlike other arts and philosophy, which emphasize what *is* real, satire emphasizes what *seems* to be real but isn't. It rejects man's naive acceptance of other men and institutions at face value. That rejection may be expressed in amused terms or in bitter terms, but the essence of satire is persistent revelation and exaggeration of the contrast between reality and pretense. And the persistent revelation and exaggeration of that contrast requires a particular kind of personality. The satirist has it.

Another popular explanation of the writer's motivation is the "escape" theory. The hypothesis that writers create literature in order to escape from reality has a long history, but refinements have been offered by recent theorists, such as Albert Camus: " 'No artist can tolerate the real,' said Nietzsche. This is true; but no artist can do without the real. Creation is a demand for unity and a refusal of the world." W. H. Auden, explaining why nonsense poetry is written, calls it "an attempt to find a world where the divisions of class, sex, occupation did not operate." And David

Worcester suggests: "Irony offers an escape from mental pain, as morphine offers an escape from physical pain. . . . The inveterate ironist escapes from the paralysis of the mind only to fall a victim to paralysis of the will."

Haakon Chevalier agrees that the ironic attitude is a dangerous philosophy. "In actual experience," he quips, "irony characterizes the attitude of one who, when confronted with the choice of two things that are mutually exclusive, chooses both. Which is but another way of saying that he chooses neither." Chevalier applies his theory: "Anatole France insists upon illusion because he wants illusion. He cannot escape the obsession because he does not want to: the Freudian pleasure-principle. He seeks illusion — beauty, a dream-world, fairyland. He feels an urgent need to escape actuality, which does not satisfy him." France once said, "A lasting illusion has the attributes of truth."

Dr. A. A. Brill, a psychoanalyst, lists Swift, Poe, Emily Dickinson, and "perhaps Hawthorne and Melville" as writers who considered "their dream-creations more real than the actual world." Professor J. G. Frederick adds Cabell, Dunsany, and Blake, each a writer escaping to "a world which he likes better than the world about him." And Aldous Huxley thinks that both Swift's *Gulliver* and Shelley's *Prometheus Unbound* originate in the authors' refusal to accept the physical reality of the world. (But Rabelais, Huxley says, accepts the world — and Rabelais too is a satirist.)

According to Donald Ogden Stewart, "When a

humorist feels deep down inside him that there is no outlet to his life, that he is surrounded by blind alleys, then his humor becomes mad, fantastic; then in his utter despair he creates illogical dream worlds." And in *Pierre,* Melville explains what he means by "demoniac" humor: "If fit opportunity offer in the hour of unusual affliction, minds of a certain temperament find a strange, hysterical relief in a wild, perverse humorousness, the more alluring from its entire unsuitableness to the occasion."

The woman who was Sinclair Lewis' wife during his most productive and successful years recalls his constant restlessness — he always had to keep moving, to new houses and new cities; only writing a book relaxed and anchored him. As soon as he finished it, he felt impelled to move on again.

Some critics believe that under certain conditions the ironic attitude is a healthy one. "Well-integrated souls like Socrates or Sophocles," says A. R. Thompson, "may use irony constantly, but with them it is a weapon of offense. The man who suffers inner conflicts uses it in defense against himself." And, defending the daydreamer, James Thurber writes, "In a triumphant daydream, it seems to me, there is felicity and not defeat. You can't just take a humiliation and dismiss it from your mind. . . . The thing to do is to visualize a triumph over the humiliator, so vividly and so insistently that it becomes, in effect, an actuality."

Presumably, if writers turn to writing as an escape from reality, they regard the process as a pleasant alternative, or at least a more pleasant alternative than facing reality. James Thurber so regards it. "You have to enjoy humorous writing while you're doing it," he says. "Anybody who says he doesn't is lying (he may, of course, not like to start). You've got to be enjoying it. You can't be mad, or bitter, or irate. If you are it will be no good."

Mark Twain also seemed to find that kind of pleasure in writing. While working on *The Prince and the Pauper,* he wrote to his wife, "I take so much pleasure in the story, I am loath to hurry, not wanting to get it done." Five months after the death of his daughter Suzy, Twain, in a letter to his friend Twitchell, said: "I am working, but it is for the sake of the work — the 'surcease of sorrow' that is found there. . . . This book will not long stand between trouble and me, now; but that is no matter, I have many unwritten books to fly to for my preservation."

But other satirists and humorists have not found writing a pleasant escape. Wilson Mizner said, "Writing is too damned lonesome," and Irvin S. Cobb called writing "the loneliest job in the world." Finley Dunne was so expert in procrastinating, and so ingenious in finding excuses to avoid writing, that his editor once locked him in the office with orders to write; an hour later, the editor found Dunne happily counting the squares on the wallpaper to pass the time; he had not written a word. And Dorothy Parker, ordered to stay in her office until she turned in the copy that she was always late in producing, took the MEN sign off the washroom and put it outside her door.

Anatole France's dislike for the actual process of writing has been noted by several biographers. "Obviously," points out Chevalier, "he did not write forty volumes under protest. But the labor of composition was in the nature of an unpleasant necessity."

In addition to the conventional explanations of why writers write, a few surprising motivations have been suggested. To Franz Kafka, "Writing is a form of prayer." As far as Samuel Johnson was concerned, "No man but a block-head ever wrote, except for money." Replying to a questionnaire, Knut Hamsun said that he wrote to kill time.

Alva Johnson inverted a popular idea when he wrote: "Psychoanalysts build a false science on the theory that millions of people are maladjusted lovers; a better knowledge of the world would teach that they are maladjusted writers." Another reversal of the usual point of view was offered by Dr. Jung: "The work in process becomes the poet's fate and determines his psychic development. It is not Goethe who created *Faust,* but *Faust* which creates Goethe."

The wish for immortality is the basic reason for the creative urge, according to Dr. Otto Rank; every human being has a tremendous desire, conscious or subconscious, for immortality; or, failing that, for leaving some mark of his personality, some product made by him, as evidence of his existence on earth and as an extension of his individuality. This is "the creative impulse in the artist, springing from the tendency to immortalize himself," and it is only through this "will-to-self-immortalization" that we can understand the interrelationship of artistic production and suffering.

Man's desire for immortality in a special form has been suggested by S. N. Behrman as the reason for Duveen's phenomenal success in selling masterpieces to millionaires who had no aesthetic interest at all in paintings. Man's wish for immortality has also been credited, or charged, with his desire to have children, establish foundations, and get streets or buildings named after him.

A number of writers have offered a motivation quite different, at least superficially, from the desire for immortality. Logan Pearsall Smith wrote: "Every author, however modest, keeps a most outrageous vanity chained like a madman in the padded cell of his breast." William Bolitho went further in calling a man "immoderately vain or sensitive or obstinate (three names for the same thing)."

There is no coyness in Bernard Shaw's announcement: "I am a master of comic irony." H. G. Wells described Shaw as "fantastically vain. He was ruled by a naked, unqualified, ego-centered, devouring vanity." And Aretino announced proudly, "Medals of me have been struck in gold, in silver," and "My head is engraved on combs . . . like that of Alexander, Caesar, and Scipio." Chevalier sees in Anatole France's subjectivity "evidence of a fundamental and inescapable egotism." And Pope was being much more honest than usual when he wrote:

> Yes, I am proud; I must be proud to see
> Men not afraid of God, afraid of me.

Edith Sitwell, an enthusiastic admirer of Pope, admits that vanity was "the one grave fault in his character." And Charles Rolo quotes a friend of Evelyn Waugh's saying, "Evelyn is so frightfully witty and so fearfully rude. Terribly conceited, of course."

Dr. Pannenborg's statistics (described in Chapter 5) have only limited value, based, as they are, on an insufficient number of examples and attempting, as they do, to measure intangibles. Still, for what they are worth, these figures claim that 71 per cent of the satirists are vain, compared to 36 per cent of the general public, and that 86 per cent of the satirists are "proud," compared to a 47 per cent average.

The notion that satirists may be writing simply in order to have fun has also been expressed. Byron said of his *Don Juan* that his purpose was to be "a little quietly facetious about everything," and Thomas Mann believed that the artist is usually concerned with enjoyment. Sinclair Lewis, speaking of his own *Main Street* and Upton Sinclair's *Jungle,* said: "I suspect that the authors of both these books wrote them — whatever reasons they

may have given to their earnest, perfect selves —
essentially because it tickled their sense of mis-
chief to write thus, and that later, when they
found their fulminations perfectly ineffective, they
have gone on to other manners and themes with no
vast grieving."

DeVoto tells about a letter Mark Twain wrote
to his friend Twitchell, in which Twain "made
the medieval men and women use the kind of
'frank indelicacies of speech permissible in that
ancient time.'" Twain gloated: "I put into the
Queen's mouth, and into the mouths of those other
people, grossnesses not to be found outside of Rabelais, perhaps . . . and all this was charming to
me — delightful, delicious."

More support for fun as the motivation in writing comes from psychoanalyst Ernst Kris, who, referring to Freud's recognition of children's play
as "the forerunner of the comic," suggests: "To
my mind it is the *starting point* for the comic we
see in others . . . the tendentious joke of the
adult has its roots in the child's idea of fun."

An unusual theory is offered by Professor Rice,
who says that "Byronic despair or laughter springs
from a curiosity that has been at once too rabid
and too easily satisfied, a curiosity satisfied entirely
by experience." Rice concludes that "it is not a
philosophy; it is a failure to be a philosophy rising . . . into impassioned self-interest or impassioned satire."

There is one more explanation of why writers
write which is probably too simple to be worth

mentioning. In the struggle for survival there are always people to whom writing seems an occupation preferable to doing physical labor, or handling mechanical gadgets, or trying to sell things. Writing involves hard work, but it is a different kind of work and it permits a privacy which some people find highly desirable.

For many reasons one must be wary of accepting at face value people's statements about their motivations. Vanity, rationalization, cowardice, ignorance may embellish the truth. And, in the case of satirists, whimsy or mischievousness may influence their opinions. Nevertheless, there is some value in examining relevant remarks by satirists themselves.

Anatole France, writing in 1889 concerning the surprising candidacy of Emile Zola for the French Academy, said, "this election would satisfy the innate need of disrespect, that taste for irony which I feel within me." The important word for our purposes is "innate," revealing France's belief that he was born with this attitude. France may, of course, have been wrong.

The possibility that the satiric attitude toward life is subconsciously motivated is also supported by the famous nineteenth-century clown, Grock: "Ever since I can remember, all kinds of inanimate objects have had a way of looking at me reproachfully and whispering to me in unguarded moments: ' . . . take us now, and turn us into something different.' . . . transforming the little, everyday annoyances, actually *transforming* them into something strange and terrific."

H. L. Mencken claimed that his primary purpose in writing was to "attain that feeling of tension relieved and function achieved which a cow enjoys on giving milk." Granting Mencken his usual license for exaggeration and playfulness, this attitude is very similar to that described by other satirists, and other creative writers.

Robert Benchley was a nondrinking, highly moral, earnest young man who had visions of becoming a social worker and of some day writing morally earnest, serious prose. But, as William L. Miller put it, "his sense of humor somehow overcame it all. It was, as his admirers would doubtless say, the triumph of his better instinct over his conscience."

Herman Melville marked this passage in his copy of Balzac's *Bureaucracy*: "he aspired to something better, but the fatal demon hiding in his wit hindered him from acquiring the gravity which imposes on fools." And of Melville himself Rosenberry said, "When Melville sat down to write, always at his knees stood that chosen emissary of Satan, the comic spirit: a demoniac familiar never long absent from his pages."

Frances Russell, assuming that a man who has a critical sense of humor will satirize, wrote: "In the province of satire the real internal stimulus is temperament." And Edgar Johnson, speaking of Byron, said: "Although Byron tells us that satiric derision is for him only a refuge from melancholy . . . his readers cannot feel that any such depth of gloom animated the frisky passages of *Don Juan* . . . such as . . . Julia berating her husband for his base suspicions of her chastity while Don Juan almost smothers . . . between her thighs."

Explaining the satirist's ability to make artistic use of grotesque material, Worcester said, "Where common souls react to a situation with moral feelings, he sees only aesthetic values." Worcester's suggestion can be extended. It is not only grotesque situations that arouse in the satirist "aesthetic" rather than "moral" reactions.

Morality

Sydney Smith, called by his contemporaries the wittiest Englishman who ever lived, said, in reply to the question "Why do you write?" "I write for three reasons: first, because I really wish to do good; secondly, because if I don't write, I know nobody else will; and thirdly, because it is in the nature of the animal to write, and I cannot help it."

The idea that morality is the basic motivation of the satirist has a good deal to be said for it, and a good deal has been said for it, often by satirists themselves and sometimes after quoting Mark Twain's remark: "Humor must not professedly teach, and it must not professedly preach, but it must do both if it would live forever. By forever, I mean thirty years. . . . I have always preached. That is the reason that I have lasted thirty years." Twain, who spent his life denouncing conven-

Ask you what Provocation I have had?
The strong Antipathy of Good to Bad.
When Truth or Virtue an Affront endures,
The Affront is mine, my Friend, and
    should be yours . . .
O sacred Weapon! Left for Truth's defense,
Sole dread of Folly, Vice, and Insolence!
— Alexander Pope

tional morality, may seem to be an unexpected spokesman for sweetness and light. But so are Bernard Shaw, Will Cuppy, and D. H. Lawrence.

When Bernard Shaw, rarely regarded by orthodox moralists as a kindred soul, said, "All great art and literature is propaganda," he was not speaking of propaganda on behalf of conventional morality, but he was insisting that his purpose was "to chasten morals with ridicule." The author of *How To Tell Your Friends From the Apes*, Will Cuppy, says: "I can't imagine myself hitting anybody, even in a dream, but I want the world to be what I want it to be, and if I didn't I wouldn't write. Humor is meant to blow up evil and make fun of the follies of life." And D. H. Lawrence, ignoring the American Post Office Department's suspicion that *Lady Chatterley's Lover* was immoral, wrote, "The essential function of all art is moral. Not aesthetic, not decorative, not pastime and recreation. But moral."

Nicholas Boileau took his duties as a moralist so seriously that his last words were: "It is a great consolation to a poet at the point of death, that he has never written a line injurious to good morals." Joseph Hall, having informed his Elizabethan contemporaries that he was going to imitate Juvenal and become England's first poetic satirist, expressed his view of satire's duty:

> The satyre should be like the Porcupine,
> That shoots sharp quills out in each angry line,
> And wounds with blushing cheeke, and fiery eye
> Of him that heares, and readeth guiltily.

G. K. Chesterton, writing in twentieth-century England, agreed that the purpose of satire is to make the victim improve his behavior.

Pope apparently felt that he qualified as a fine moral advocate. In "Epilogue to the Satires" he wrote:

> Ask you what Provocation I have had?
> The strong Antipathy of Good to Bad.
> When Truth or Virtue an Affront endures,
> The Affront is mine, my Friend, and should be yours. . . .
> O sacred Weapon! Left for Truth's defense,
> Sole dread of Folly, Vice, and Insolence!

In addition to satirists who proclaimed a moral mission, many critics have also agreed that a primary purpose of the satirist is to moralize. Edgar Johnson, discussing Swift, says: "The *saeva indignatio* he shares with Juvenal is even deeper, for Juvenal's indignation is civic, whereas Swift's is human." A. R. Thompson believes that "all his life Ibsen was a moralist, the stern searcher of souls, the searcher above all of his own soul." Wyndham Lewis (who prefers amoral satire himself) describes William Faulkner as "a fierce moralist, who operates upon the satiric plane, armed with corn cobs and such like sardonic weapons of aggression, to insult the victims of his epical rage." Dr. Pannenborg set up a separate category for satirists motivated by "noble indignation" — and put Vondel and Victor Hugo into that group.

Other critics have gone further and demanded not only that the satirist serve this noble moral purpose, but that he ought himself be a fine specimen of moral philosophy and noble behavior. Although their satire sometimes reaches a high level of morality, such personal excellence as Rebecca West requested has rarely been exhibited by satirists. Miss West said, "The first necessary condition which the satirist must fulfill. . . . He must fully possess, at least in the world of the imagination, the quality, the lack of which he is deriding in others."

Humbert Wolfe's standards would also frighten the average satirist. According to Wolfe, the satirist is halfway between a preacher and a wit; he has the purpose of the former, uses the weapon of the latter. He is motivated by hatred of wrong and injustice as much as love of the right and the just. Not only that, but the task of the satirist is ascetic; he must be an anchorite in spirit, and free himself of the vices that he satirizes. And Professor Bredvold regards the satirist as a noble moralist, insisting that the satirist complains not on his own account but for the sake of humanity, and that his indignation is altruistic rather than selfish.

John Shand maintains that the indignation of such writers as Swift and Voltaire proves that they have high ideals; the satirist is optimistic and believes in the potential goodness of man, otherwise he would not be angered at our deviation from his ideal, nor would he attempt to improve us; our weaknesses and wickedness are exposed by the satirist not to show us that we are bad, but to make us better; the satirist keeps his ideals and his faith in humanity intact.

Strindberg has been described as "a born moralist." Gogol's "tendency to preach" has been noted. In "Miscellaneous Observations" Samuel Butler said that satire should be moral: "A Satyr is a kinde of Knight Errant that goe's upon Adventures, to Relieve the Distressed Damsel Virtue, and Redeeme Honor. . . . And opprest Truth, and Reason out of the Captivity of Giants and Magitians." Juvenal is often cited as the model of the moral satirist, and Gilbert Cannan's remark about him is typical: "Juvenal's morality is not exactly profound or noble, but it is . . . sound enough. With a higher morality he would not have been a satirist, but a poet, content to leave Rome to stew in its own juices." Of Ibsen and Shaw, Seiger said: "Both were moralists, attacking outworn ideals of conventions on the basis of a more spiritual concept of morality." And David Worcester suggested that the satirist's purpose is to make "his readers comprehend and remember that criticism and adopt it as their own."

"A humorist," said Bergson, "is a moralist disguised as a scientist." Phillips Brooks wrote that "All satire must keep sight of man's greatness." And Ellen Leyburn, in her study of satiric allegory, concludes that the satirist's "purpose can only be described as moral." Assuming that morality is the motivating force in both cases, she suggests that when "the impetus that disturbs the author into writing is a single fault of man," the satirist may dispose of his victim in a single episode, as in Dryden's *Mac Flecknoe;* or, "if the loss of values by a whole society is what troubles him," the satirist may imagine a new society in which to express his criticism, as in *Brave New World* and *1984*. Satire, she says, is as didactic as any other kind of writing. Its art is "the delivering of a moral judgment," and its objective is not to degrade man but to show him how he has degraded himself.

It has frequently been pointed out by skeptical critics that many satirists who proclaimed morality as their satiric motivation were not themselves especially moral. Alexander Pope, for instance, whose sanctimonious virtue we have just seen expressed in his last epilogue, was called by Leslie Stevens "the most untruthful man of his age." Pope published his own letters surreptitiously, pretending that they had been pirated; he made anonymous attacks on specific individuals, pretending to be completely innocent; he was in many ways a despicable and contemptible individual. But it would be difficult to learn that fact from the moral views that he poetically professed.

Cervantes' Don Quixote is the prototype of the idealist, the truthful man in a materialistic world. But Cervantes himself was sent to jail for withholding money as collector of revenue. Byron, who also spoke out for morality and virtue, had one daughter by his half-sister, another daughter by a friend of the family, Claire Clairmont. He, too, kept up the pose of morality.

Heinrich Heine, the wittiest of German satirists, says in his confession: "One needs no palms and camels to be good, and goodness is better than beauty." Heine may have been sincere, but what he meant by goodness did not quite coincide with Judeo-Christian morality, as far as his own relationships with women went. Erasmus was called (by an unsympathetic biographer) "a very uncharitable man" and "malicious." The morality of Holberg seemed to one critic "a utilitarian morality." Aretino's biographer accuses him of libel and blackmail: "his house was a harem." Charles Churchill is described in one study as possessing an "appetite for debauchery."

This tendency of satirists to pose as moral individuals working for the good of society has irritated some scholars. Max Eastman complains: "I do not know why people who spend half their free time enjoying experiences for their own sake, and the other half talking about them, should, when they come to write essays, have to pretend that every worthwhile thing in human life has some moral purpose." And William Lee Miller, ridiculing the remark about Benchley, "His lamp pierced more shams than all the preachment of the indignation boys and do-gooders," says: "I am at a loss to explain why people who write about humor and humorists get all choked up and sober about it, and always try to say that humor is absolutely the best method of exposing folly and piercing shams and attacking foibles. (There is always a lot about foibles.)"

Frances Russell believes that the real stimulus of the satirist is his temperament, not his morality.

"But the declared motives are for the most part ethical and altruistic, a lineage much more presentable and worthy of high command. . . . This human tendency to justify its instinctive behavior by *ex post facto* morality produced much serious writing to prove the noble purpose of satire. Horace was honest enough to say that he wrote satire because he couldn't write epics. But from Juvenal on, the satirists claimed great moral missions."

Lewis Carroll, into whose work psychoanalysts have read numerous sexual symbols, frequently wrote letters to the press protesting about indecent lines he had heard in the theater. Mark Twain described a painting of Titian as "the foulest, the vilest, the obscenest picture the world possesses"; he circulated his own pornographic writing only among friends.

Until we have a society in which there is considerably more agreement as to precisely what morality is, we will have to admit the possibility that there are satirists who are moral, satirists who are amoral, and satirists who are immoral. All of these definitions are, of course, relative but except for their opposition to "evil" there is little that satirists agree on. Yet they all regard themselves as moral, even when they contradict each other.

For the moment, then, we may assume that satire may be moral, as in Juvenal; amoral, as in H. L. Mencken; and perhaps immoral, as in Rochester, Bernard Mandeville, and Machiavelli. Sinclair Lewis has been regarded by some critics as a moralist and by others as an immoral critic of sacred and traditional beliefs. E. M. Foerster, however, as early as 1930 wrote: "Lewis has nothing of the aseptic awfulness of the seer. Neither for good nor evil is he lifted above his theme; he is neither a poet nor a preacher, but a fellow with a camera, a few yards away."

The quality of morality is strained by Swift's sharp distinction between the spoken and the written word. He confined his scatological remarks to paper, never saying a filthy word aloud. Dr. Greenacre, a psychoanalyst, suggests that such a distinction indicates "the anal stamp of his character." And there is a special irony about notions of absolute morality if it is true (as Dr. Greenacre believes) that children, like Swift, who believe in anal birth, often derive their ideas of "bad and good, dirty and godly" from their interest in toilet activities. She interprets Swift's "personal immaculateness" and "stubborn vengefulness in righteous causes" as evidences not of a moral but of a typically "anal" personality, usually apparent only in children who had been subjected to premature and overharsh toilet training. The "morality" of Jonathan Swift, Dr. Greenacre tells us, may simply be the result of training by an overly conscientious nurse who left "this stamp of the nursery morals of the chamber pot forever on his character."

Psychoanalysis provides a *reductio ad absurdum* for the morality of Swift; sociology offers a *reductio ad absurdum* for the morality of Restoration dramatists. Andrew Schiller suggests that their morality was "an unconscious burlesque of Calvinism," reversing the effects of Election and Predestination so that the "elect" turn out to be the amoral, whereas the "damned" are the pious. Furthermore, since the elect are irrevocably "saved," they may behave as immorally as they like; but the pious cannot get to heaven even if their conduct has been exemplary.

A further complication in the definition of morality is the distinction Louis Kronenberger makes between "humanity" and "society": Shaw, he suggests, is concerned with the latter, not the former. Daiches agrees: "Shaw wasn't concerned with the pity of it; he was concerned to diagnose sham and release vitality."

Critics who emphasize the "moral" element in a satirist's work tend to ignore the fact that "morality" is a significant characteristic of almost every literary form. The detective story, the melodrama, the western movie, the fairy tale — all provide rewards for the "good" and punishment for the "bad." Almost all adventure and conflict fiction expresses, in the terms of its own culture's morality, the struggle between "right" and "wrong," and almost always permits "right" to win. Yet critics do not pretend that writers of detective, adventure, and western fiction are primarily motivated by a moral drive.

The terminology is vague. Freud calls humor "good" and satire "bad," but he never satisfactorily distinguishes between overlapping forms of humor and satire. And skeptical intellectuals, from Heraclitus to Colin Wilson, have considered the possibility that good and evil are complementary and indispensable components, incapable of absolute identification.

There is a large number of satirists whose works cannot be easily fitted into the category of morality, in the conventional sense of that term. The mysticism of Aldous Huxley is not "morality"; it is an impersonal concept, detached from interest in or concern for others. Wyndham Lewis says: "I am a satirist, but I am not a moralist." One may dispute Mr. Lewis' first assertion, but not the second.

Nor is it easy to accept morality as Evelyn Waugh's motivation. Waugh certainly feels that he is on the right side, but for the majority of twentieth-century readers the morality of Waugh is a negative morality, emphasizing hatred and criticism of contemporary institutions rather than Christian love or a genuine belief in the virtues of the past.

In the conventional sense, Mencken is certainly not a "moral" satirist. He ridicules Christianity, democracy, our social system, most of the values which our morality regards as desirable. Is he amoral? Immoral? Were the Restoration playwrights Wycherley and Congreve moral? Immoral? They were expressing the morality of the dominant group at King Charles' court. They were certainly immoral by Puritan standards, and by modern middle-class standards.

Was Lucian moral or immoral? Lucian was so skeptical about the existence of gods in the second century that he wasn't indignant about them, he just teased them. By the standards of twentieth-century monotheism, in rejecting a belief in mythological gods he was being "moral"; but by the standards of his own time he was immoral. When we read Lucian, we do not find him objectionable on that count. Is Lucian then an immoral writer who has finally become moral?

Nor do we find agreement on the morality of Voltaire. From the point of view of the upper classes and the clergy of eighteenth-century France, he was shockingly immoral. But from the point of view of the twentieth century, his fight for individual liberty and his attempt to practice the humanitarian teachings of Jesus make him a paradigm of morality.

A perspicacious critic of Jane Austen, Professor Mudrick, stresses the amorality of her approach. Even when she was very young, he notes, "Jane Austen's first choice [was] to treat life, even in her letters, as material for comedy: not sentimentally, not morally . . . with a detached discrimination among its incongruities."

Samuel Butler's *Erewhon* was criticized when it appeared because it ridiculed many of the values of Victorian England. Yet today we praise it as a book which pointed out existing evils and hypocrisy. Was Butler immoral? Was he moral in *The Way of All Flesh*? He delayed publication of the book until after his death; it is a strong indictment of what was conventionally regarded as a very high type of morality. Yet millions of modern readers regard *The Way of All Flesh* as moral, and the values it attacks as immoral.

Where in the category of morality does Bernard Shaw belong? Shaw certainly felt that he was a moralist. He called himself one. He said that if it weren't for preaching what he regarded as necessary truths, he would never have written a word. And yet people have called Shaw "the apostle of the devil" and "the most dangerous intellectual influence of the twentieth century." Shaw, it is true, was not especially disturbed, but apart from Shaw's own view of the matter (he was sure he was moral) —and the views of his critics (they were sure he was immoral) — where does he fit in the category of morality? Unless we make that a very wide category — almost an all-inclusive one — we would have difficulty in passing off such diverse types as Shaw and Samuel Johnson as "typical" satirists.

Then there is Mandeville, with his outright defense of the pragmatic point of view, with his outright admission that uneducated men are necessary in society to provide cheap labor, with his assumption that conflict and envy are desirable social qualities because they stimulate competition and aggressive originality. If Mandeville is immoral, does he stop being a satirist? And how about Oscar Wilde? Certainly Wilde disparaged (sometimes childishly in his paradoxes) most of the values, virtues, and traditions of his time. Was he then immoral? Or was he, because he was exposing the hypocrisy and artificiality of his society, a moral writer? And what of Norman Douglas? In *South Wind* Douglas inverts the usual values of society. He makes the "good" seem priggish and childish. He makes the "bad" seem desirable and civilized. Isn't that immoral? And if we put Douglas with the satirists — and we can hardly keep him out — does he belong in the same moral category with such serious religious satirists as C. S. Lewis? Finally, it is hard to visualize Max Beerbohm, brilliant satirist though he is, in the company of conventionally moral satirists.

Addison went so far as to accuse satirists of immorality. "If the talent of ridicule were employed to laugh men out of vice and folly," he wrote, "it might be of some use to the world; but instead of this, we find that it is generally made use of to laugh men out of virtue and good sense, by attacking everything that is solemn and serious, decent and praiseworthy in human life."

"The moralist," says Mencken, "at his best, can never be anything save a sort of journalist. Moral values change too often to have any serious validity or interest; what is virtue today is a sin tomorrow." The satirist is very much aware of the problem of relative morality: that what is right in one society (polygamy, for instance) is wrong in another; what is correct in a society at one time (killing in battle) is wrong in the same society at another time (killing in peacetime); even simultaneously, at different levels in the same society, one kind of behavior is morally acceptable, another kind is not (behavior among aristocrats and bourgeoisie).

No unanimous agreement can be reached on the question of morality; the conventional view is that what a society calls moral, *is* moral for that society. On the other hand, there is the view of Mencken: "In the struggle for existence an act is never actually moral or immoral but only (in the broadest sense of the words) profitable or unprofitable." We may not agree with Mencken's Nietzschean attitude, but it is an attitude accepted by at least some of the writers who have written satire.

Another point about the relativity of moral values, in reference to satire, is made by Wyndham Lewis: "As far as laughter is concerned, either everyone should be laughed at, or no one should be. Why call some laughter cruel, when all of it is at someone's expense? In general, people laugh at spiritual or mental shortcomings in men, but not physical. Yet it is no more pleasant to be a fool than a cripple." Again, we need not share Lewis' attitude but we have to admit that some people who create satire hold unconventional views of morality.

Furthermore, what is immoral, illegal, or criminal for an individual is often fully justified for a state. War, going in debt, diplomatic lying, and many similar activities are indispensable for governments which forbid exactly the same procedures on the part of individual citizens.

From another aspect, the whole business of giving the satirist credit for being a moralist is naive. Almost every human being regards his own actions as morally justified. Even the criminal ordinarily does not think of himself as being immoral or wicked; he tends to rationalize that it is society, by its unfair treatment of him, that has forced him to do what he is doing in self-defense, and with a self-righteous attitude. Few people genuinely regard themselves as immoral; they may think that others have a distorted morality, but they usually think that they themselves have the correct one. There is no special virtue, from this particular vantage point, in calling a satirist a moralist if most human beings, nonsatirists as well as satirists, also regard themselves as moralists.

One might say that the satirist lays claim to being a moralist. We have seen that a number of satirists have spoken of themselves proudly as spokesmen for morality in an immoral world. Still, there is no more reason to accept the personal evaluation of the satirist than there is to accept the personal chest-thumping of a politician or movie star or any other performer. There may be no less reason to do so, but there isn't any more. And unless we assume that whatever anyone claims on his own behalf is necessarily true, there is no real reason to believe that because the satirist lays claim to morality, he should be believed any more than anyone else is.

When a satirist asserts that he is a moralist he implies that he is doing the work of a reformer. It is relevant, then, to examine the psychology, the temperament, of the reformer. What is the reformer trying to reform? Chesterton, who defined a "puritan" as "a person who pours righteous indignation into the wrong things," had no doubt that the righteous indignation he himself was pouring went into the right things. How sure can we be that the reform a particular satirist undertakes is a reform of the "right" kind? Do we regard the "small-time" reformers in our own community as noble, altruistically motivated moralists, or are we sometimes irritated and sometimes revolted by a literal application of moral laws? Is the reformer really a moralist or is he, as some social psychologists believe, simply a maladjusted individual who has chosen a particular form of "dedicated" behavior to work out his personal adjustment to society? "There is a guilty conscience," says Eric Hoffer, "behind every manifestation of self-righteousness."

Is the Marxist, or Stalinist, or post-Stalinist reformer, who believes that the end justifies the means, a moralist? Was Machiavelli, when he urged the Renaissance prince to accept an end-justifies-means philosophy, a moralist? Was the anti-Christian Nazi who devoutly practiced Hitler's pagan morality, a moralist? Yet satire has been written in defense of all of these positions, and against all of these positions. The satires have not been equal in literary value, but that is not the relevant point. The fact is that satirists have written on all sides of morality.

What is the effect of the satirist's "moral" efforts, as far as he himself is concerned? Is he actually satisfied when change takes place? Does he shift his position from criticism of what had previously been wrong to approval of what has now been improved? As a general rule, no. The satirist, when one thing has been changed, loses interest in it and shifts his critical and satiric attention to some other aspect of society which requires criticism rather an approval. He rarely runs out of subjects which require criticism in the nonutopian society of his particular time.

In an article about W. H. Auden, Professor Spears says, "The satirist, being realistic, has usually little hope of reform through literature; his purpose — or his compulsion — is to unmask, to reveal men to themselves and to their souls as they are, not as they pretend to be." Professor Spears' remark indicates that satirists not only do not achieve, but do not really expect to achieve, much moral reform.

Satirists themselves have often confessed this. Sinclair Lewis admitted that *Main Street* had no effect on provincialism in the small town, nor did his *Babbitt* improve the habits of American middle-class businessmen. H. L. Mencken freely admitted that he did not think his criticism had much effect, but that he had to keep writing satire nevertheless. Byron said that he laughed in order to prevent weeping, which may be a personally helpful device but hardly a moral one. Swift, the greatest of the English satirists, said that the reason satire is accepted by society is that each man sees in the satiric portrait the face of his neighbor. And Lewis Carroll used his satiric powers to amuse little girls.

"The plain fact," says Worcester, bluntly and truthfully, "is that no way of 'overawing vice' exists in literature."

A satirist's opinion of what he is achieving sometimes differs from the conventional view. Sinclair Lewis told me that he felt satire can be moral, amoral, or immoral, and cited Mencken as an amoral satirist; but Lewis refused to apply the word "amoral" to himself. "I am a hedonistic missionary," he said. "I am irritated by the fact that people could be so much happier than they are." This irritation, Lewis said, and his constant impulse to expose hypocrites, made him write satire.

Voorhees suggests a somewhat unusual source for George Orwell's morality: "Like Chesterton, Orwell thought that a good deal of sloppiness was necessary for a healthy society and considered that the motive of many a socialist was simply an excessive sense of order."

Jonathan Swift, as an orthodox Anglican clergyman and Dean of St. Paul's, presumably represents conventional Christian morality. But whether Swift's morality coincides with the morality preached by Jesus is open to question. The moral position which Swift reached has been described as "a morality which defines virtuous conduct in terms of an enlightened self-interest." And Swift himself wrote: "Now, human nature is so constituted that we can never pursue anything heartily but upon the hope of a reward." When Swift wrote this he was not being cynical (certainly he did not think that he was being cynical); he said it is perhaps a good thing that human passions frequently outweigh human reason because sometimes, as a result of those passions, good ends are achieved for the wrong reasons. This may not be orthodox morality, this may not be a system of "pure" ethics, but this is the morality which Swift believed in while he was writing brilliant satire.

The morality of Jane Austen is also of a limited kind, if one accepts Mudrick's statement: "The thesis of *Mansfield Park* is severely moral: that one world, representing the genteel orthodoxy of Jane Austen's time, is categorically superior to any other." And there is a good deal of doubt about the quality of the dramatists whom Cazamian had in mind when he wrote: "The Restoration satirists . . . generally speaking, . . . are not very sure whether they are writing in the name of morality and its defense, or against it, against the notion others have formed of it."

Internal and external evidence supports the conclusion that the satirist is motivated by morality no more, and no less, than other writers are. The internal evidence is that most satirists show the satiric temperament, the inclination for critical distortion, while they are still youngsters — long before they have any genuine concern with morality. And the influence of environment in making writers pretend to possess a great interest in morality is suggested by Alan Watts, a former Anglican priest who became a Zen Buddhist. Watts feels that most Anglo-Saxons are unable to purge themselves of the need for self-justification. The

Westerner finds it very difficult to "come to terms with the Lord God Jehovah and with his Hebrew-Christian conscience so that he can take it or leave it without fear of rebellion. He must be free of the itch to justify himself."

Superficially, there has always seemed to be reason to assume that the satirist is a noble moralist dedicated to improving people and conditions: the material used by satirists often exposes immorality. But there is an excellent reason why satirists choose that kind of material. It is not necessarily because they are interested in moral reform. Instead, it is usually because the violations of morality (by institutions which pretend to be altruistic and by individuals who pose as virtuous citizens) are flagrant examples of hypocrisy — and hypocrisy is the greatest single source of satiric material.

Satiric literature is critical literature. In order to do his work, the satirist has to find things to criticize. By trial and error he learns that the easiest things to criticize in society are hypocrisy, vanity, and folly. In civilized society, hypocrisy enters into almost every activity because society expects from its members an adherence to a high moral code — a code which most individuals find it impossible to adhere to, at least part of the time. And fools pretend to be wise. The immoral element happens to be inseparable from this hypocrisy and this pretense. So hypocrisy and pretense provide precisely the kind of incongruity that is suitable for the satiric method — *not necessarily because they are immoral but certainly because they are incongruous.*

There is reason to suppose that the subject matter of *Jurgen, Candide, Penguin Island,* and *Brave New World* appealed to Cabell, Voltaire, France, and Huxley in the same spontaneous way that quite different materials appealed to other writers. Dumas and Scott chose adventure and romance to work with, whereas Swift and Cervantes chose instead those elements which were most appropriate for their purposes. Appropriateness, rather than moral fervency, is often the difference.

In this sense the vehemence of Mencken is comparable to the vehemence of Van Gogh. Mencken's is an aesthetic choice, not a moral one, any more than the choice of colors by Van Gogh is a moral choice. Having the attitude of a satirist, and *using the devices most suitable for satire,* the satirist usually writes in order to satisfy a personal need rather than to reform by moralizing.

The satirist expresses himself in criticism which is socially acceptable. Inasmuch as he wants people to read his satire (the satirist is not working in a vacuum — he does want an audience) he must choose material with which his audience is familiar, and an attitude with which it is sympathetic. In most civilized communities the "moral" position, the assumption or at least the pretence that right is preferable to wrong, is accepted by the satirist's audience. So the satirist, in choosing material which involves ethics and morality, is choosing material with which his particular audience is familiar. Because he chooses this socially acceptable kind of criticism, his satire is likely to appear "moral"; but morality is usually incidental to his aesthetic intention, peripheral to it, and motivated to a large extent by purely technical requirements. It is no more fair to assume that satirists have greater moral motivation than other writers, than it would be to credit pharmacists with being more moral businessmen than other retailers, simply because the merchandise druggists sell is more directly related to the improvement of health than is the merchandise sold by other businessmen. Nor, of course, is it fair to assume that satirists are less motivated by morality than are other writers.

If the satirist is in most ways like other men (except for his special talent for distortion) and like other writers, there is no reason to suppose that he is any more or any less moral than most other men and most other writers are. There is reason to suppose that he chooses the exposing of immorality and hypocrisy as his subject matter not because he is a reformer, nor because he is especially interested in improving things. He may, and usually does, have little thought of alternatives or substitutes. He is obeying an irresistible impulse to show absurdities which he sees very clearly. Usually, his immediate purpose is to satirize, not to improve; his object in showing the ridiculous is to criticize, not to correct. If as a result of his attack conditions are improved, he does not object. If beneficial reform takes place, he may be pleased. But all this is secondary. His primary purpose is to satirize.

The satirist, then, functions as an artist, not as a moralist, *using for his material the moral values accepted by his society because satire deals with deviations from a norm* — an actual or a pretended norm. He is a "professional" in the same way that a career soldier, a boxer, or a salaried football player is a professional. It is no more necessary for him personally to hate the objects of his satire than it is for the soldier, boxer, or football player personally to hate his opponents. There are of course soldiers and athletes who, naively or uniquely, make a mission of their jobs; and there are satirists who, naively or uniquely, are genuine moralists and make missions of their jobs.

Compensation

We have seen that some critics offer the "aesthetic drive" as the primary motivation of the satirist, while others suggest that "morality" is the spur.

A number of other attempts to explain why the satirist writes satire can be loosely grouped in a third category: "compensation." All of the variations on this theory assume that the satirist is striking back at society because it has either neglected him for being inadequate or punished him for being obstreperous. This compensation is expressed in one, or a combination, of the following forms: rebellion and revenge, protective laughter, perverted self-criticism, and perverted frustration.

Rebellion and Revenge

"I was born for opposition," said Byron. Lucian announced, "I profess hatred of pretension and imposture, lying and pride." Edmund Wilson sees

> *The satirist attacks in others*
> *the weaknesses and temptations*
> *that are really within himself.*
> — Kenneth Burke

in Dickens a partially conscious, life-long rebellion against the institutions which had embittered his childhood. Aldous Huxley's initial protest, Floyd Matson suggests, was against conflicting traditions in his own family — the Victorian morality of Thomas Arnold, the scientific materialism of Thomas Huxley, and the aesthetics of his aunt, Mrs. Humphrey Ward. Walter Lippmann feels that Sinclair Lewis was a half-baked rebel, uncertain even in rebellion. G. K. Chesterton defied modern society, calling its leaders "heretics" and his own medieval economics "orthodoxy." And all of Evelyn Waugh's satiric novels reflect a violent rebellion against the values — political, humanitarian and religious — held by the majority of his contemporaries.

Rebellion of this kind is regarded by Freud as "a defense against reality." According to Freud, absurdity in dreams is an expression of bitter criticism; similarly, the method of the satirist is a form of attack on institutions and persons whose authority or actions the satirist resents. If Freud is right, distortion in dreams as a means of criticism, and distortion in satire as a technique, are closely related.

Freud's theory, however, ignores the simple fact that society is sometimes corrupt and individuals often misbehave; at such times not only neurotic and oversensitive individuals, but "normal," honest, courageous people, having no pretensions to art or literature, ought to criticize the existing state of affairs. Freud can hardly have believed that all the societies in which satirists lived were Utopias, criticism of which would be proof of maladjustment. He knew, better than most, that there is no perfect society, and that criticism, whether it comes from a clergyman, a reformer, a social worker, or a satirist, is often not only permissible but highly desirable. If one follows the reasoning of the psychoanalyst, all criticism, whether of evil societies and evil men, or good societies and good men, is unjustifiable because the criticism may be motivated by personal maladjustment rather than objective evaluation. But on that basis no criticism of any kind should ever be allowed.

In his study of Ambrose Bierce, Paul Fatout traces Bierce's life-long rebellion against society, his extreme suspicion of all people, his hatred of families, to a childhood lacking in normal affection and oppressed by stern religious training. Edgar Johnson sees in Samuel Butler's early rebellion against his father, the Reverend Thomas Butler, the source of Butler's eventual rebellion against the father-symbol everywhere in the world, as represented by authority, vested interest, religion, science, and other conventional institutions. "If the world glorified Beethoven," Johnson says, Butler "would enthrone Handel. If he had to admire Homer, he would . . . insist the Odyssey was really written by a woman . . . He would fight singlehanded against Darwin and the embattled biologists: their observations doubtless were correct, but their interpretations were wrong." Butler planned to spend his life "throwing bricks in the middle of them."

Voorhees thinks that the school which prepared George Orwell for Eton was responsible for his permanent rebellion against society; the tyranny of the masters and the bullying of the older boys aroused in Orwell the resentment against authority which was to permeate all of his subsequent writing. Orwell's bitter hatred of religion, the Bible, the upper classes, Voorhees suggests, began in his violent reaction against the form of religion and the attitude of the upper classes with whom he came in contact at this school. Later Orwell served as a policeman overseas, and the experience made him bitter against civil authority of that kind for the rest of his life. He had no particular love for the laborer, "but when I see an actual flesh and blood worker in conflict with his natural enemy, the policeman, I do not have to ask myself which side I am on." In spite of this, however, Voorhees concludes that the basic motivation of Orwell's writing was not rebellion but "his sense of responsibility. Responsibility, indeed, was the mainspring of Orwell's career."

Chevalier offers a counterbalance to the need for rebellion when he points out that "there is in everyone a basic craving for some order and harmony." Anatole France, he believes, perversely based the pattern of his rebellion against society on this craving for order. By organizing his life "antithetically to his father," France did everything in the opposite way from the way his father had done it. To his father's political conservatism he offered his own political (although inconsistent) radicalism. In adjusting himself to his father, a

France character says, "I became pessimistic and joyous, as he was optimistic and melancholy. In everything, instinctively I opposed myself to him." There is no evidence available from France's early life to explain why he should have so turned against the father whom he seemed at first to love and imitate. But there is a good deal of evidence that he was unhappy at school, where he was constantly exposed to contact with children from an environment far wealthier and more sophisticated than his own.

The rebellious attitude against society expressed in the work of Bernard Shaw and Oscar Wilde is obvious. Less obvious is the intended effect of Jane Austen. "Her books," D. W. Harding suggests, "are as she meant them to be, read and enjoyed by precisely the sort of people she disliked; she is a literary classic of the society which attitudes like hers, held widely enough, would undermine." Harding calls his essay, "Regulated Hatred: An Aspect of the Work of Jane Austen."

Rebellion may be justified, can be noble, is sometimes desirable. Revenge, however, is generally felt to be a despicable quality, and satirists have frequently been accused of being motivated not by rebellion against an evil or unjust society, but by revenge against individuals whom they disliked.

The theory that revenge is the motivation of the satirist was implied by Proust when he said, "The rule — which of course has its exception — is that harsh men are in reality weak ones whom originally no one liked." Some psychiatrists believe that a man's personality is shaped by the presence or absence of love in the family when he was a child: he grows up to be an affectionate adult if he was loved as a child; he grows up to hate people, to want revenge, if he was not loved as a child.

There is a clue to the personality, as well as to the art, of W. C. Fields in an anecdote that Gene Fowler tells. "I believed in Christmas until I was eight years old," said Fields. "I had saved up some money . . . and was going to buy my mother a copper-bottomed clothes-boiler for Christmas. . . . My father found the money. He did exactly what I would have done in his place. He stole it. And ever since then I've remembered nobody on Christmas, and I want nobody to remember me either."

George Meredith, who made a sharp and unconvincing distinction between the humorist and the satirist, believed that "The satirist is a moral agent, often a social scavenger, working on a storage of bile." Ronald A. Knox, having written some excellent satire himself, said: "The impulse to write satire usually comes from disappointment — and because many satirists have been disappointed in love, they have satirized women." Samuel Johnson agreed: "Personal resentment, though no laudable motive to satire, can add great force to general principles. Self-love is a busy prompter." Gilbert Cannan felt that satire is literary revenge, and cited Swift and the second Samuel Butler as examples.

"The talent of turning men into ridicule,"

wrote Addison, "is the qualification of little, un-generous tempers . . . what an absurd thing it is to pass over all the valuable parts of a man, and fix our attention on his infirmities? . . . We therefore very often find that persons the most accomplished in ridicule are those who are very shrewd at hitting a blot without exerting anything masterly in themselves. . . . By this means these unlucky little wits often gain reputation in the esteem of vulgar minds, and raise themselves above persons of much more laudable characters."

Voltaire constantly complained about being attacked and persecuted, yet was himself described as a man who "persecuted others with more virulence and acrimony" than any other writer. Analyzing the personal vexation in Melville's late satires, Rosenberry asks, "How sick was the author of *Pierre* and *The Confidence Man*? Was he, as legend has it, almost psychopathically alienated from the outer and inner worlds that had fed his early popularity?" And Kronenberger notes that Pope "seldom lashed out in the heat of anger; he knew how to bide his time, how to age his resentments." In avenging himself, Pope was harsh and persistent. "Sometimes, as with Hervey or Lady Mary, the repayment went on, in this poem and that, for years."

A good case can be made for revenge as Saki's motivation. He was brought up by maiden aunts whom he hated, and in many of his stories a child serves as the means of humiliating an adult, or ridiculing a person in authority. The behavior of these young triumphant characters in Saki's stories is often brutal and callous, presumably expressing the behavior Saki would have enjoyed.

In his essay on satire, Dryden admitted that he was tempted to be personally vindictive; but he laid claim to a record of moderation which must have amazed the victims of his satiric attacks. Said Dryden: "I have seldom answered any scurrilous lampoon, when it was in my power to have exposed my enemies; and, being naturally vindictive, have suffered in silence, and possessed my soul in quiet." Swift, too, admitted a propensity for vigorous attack:

> Hated by fools, and fools to hate,
> Be that my motto and my fate.

A number of critics have suggested that Anatole France was getting revenge. In his analysis of France's short story, "Our Lady's Juggler," Dr. Theodor Reik says, "His hatred for those persons and institutions became so intense only because he had once loved them so much." Reik believes that France's attack on religion and clergymen was motivated by his early experiences with the church. "He ingeniously seeks out their weakest and most vulnerable spots, because his sensitive nature had once been so deeply hurt." France's *Penguin Island* was called by one biographer "the burial of an illusion," implying that in that book France got revenge for the ideals he had lost.

T. K. Whipple thought that Sinclair Lewis' satire was motivated by Lewis' hatred of his environment, a hatred intense enough to make him lose the detachment that a good satirist must have. "Of one thing there can be no doubt; that he has hated his environment with a cordial and malignant hatred. That detestation has made him a satirist, and has barbed his satire and tipped it with venom." (It is only fair to Lewis to point out that other critics, such as Calverton, suggest that precisely the opposite quality, excessive sympathy for his early environment, is responsible for the weakness of Lewis' satire.) Sherwood Anderson also accounted for the "sense of dreary spiritual death" in Lewis' novels as a form of revenge. "To one who is himself afraid to live," said Anderson, "there is, I am sure, a kind of inverted joy in seeing other men as dead."

Revenge as Aldous Huxley's motivation is implied in Edgar Johnson's analysis: "Huxley's real animus is sharply emotional. And that emotion is hatred . . . of the ignorant and squalid poor, of the stodgy middle class, of the snobbish, vulgar, and cowardly rich."

Revenge was Swift's motivation too, Middleton Murry believes. Young Swift tried to make Temple a substitute for the father he never knew; Temple's lack of emotional response made Swift feel that he had been betrayed, and turned him to satire for compensation.

Personal satire appears in the work of many satirists. Quevedo ruthlessly attacked his victims with cruel, obvious satire. For Strindberg, said Bjornson, "a cause is . . . only persons. Bring them out, whip them." The satires of Charles Churchill were clearly motivated by personal grievances. And biographers have identified personal revenge as the motivation of Heine, Byron, Pope, Bierce, W. S. Gilbert, and many other satirists.

However, there are many people who have suffered disappointment without becoming satirists. And many disappointed writers (*all* writers, if one accepts the psychoanalytic interpretation, are disappointed) became not satirists but "optimistic" writers.

Closely related to the theory of rebellion, which is sometimes justified, and revenge, which is familiar enough to seem normal, is the possibility of sadism. Sadism is clearly an element in the work of an ironist such as Swift who, in Thompson's words, sympathizes with his victims "only in the sense that he must imagine the pain he inflicts in order to enjoy his act." And Anatole France, according to Chevalier, "makes it clear that he considers ironic expression to be grounded in malice," although France does not feel that the irony he himself invokes is cruel.

In his analysis of humor, Freud distinguishes between what he calls "harmless" wit and what he calls "tendency-wit." The motivation for creating "harmless" wit, he believes, is the relatively innocuous desire to show off. But the satirist, who belongs in the "tendency-wit"-making group, is motivated by a very different impulse: "Persons having a powerful sadistical component in their sexuality, which is more or less inhibited in life, are most successful with the tendency-wit of aggression."

Parsons accuses Mark Twain of sadism: "When Clemens lost an idea he suffered for it himself and, through satire and irony, he made others suffer too . . . entering into Satan, he does a cruel thing. He perseveringly demonstrates to the boys of Eseldorf that life is utterly miserable." The first smashing success young Sam Clemens experienced as a humorous storyteller occurred when he described an awkward young man falling off the roof into a taffy-pull. Twain immensely enjoyed the anecdote and its effect on listeners. And Gogol recollected, as the most delightful incident he had ever observed, a cat burning to death on a roof, "screeching and hopping from one redhot rafter to another." The recollection of this scene always sent Gogol into spasms of laughter.

Richard B. Sheridan, for whose own humor the statement is certainly true, felt that it was not possible to be witty "without a little ill-nature." Joseph Addison agreed that theoretically "the kind of laughter resulting from ridicule" could be usefully employed to chastise men for their vices and follies, and improve them; but in actual practice, "it is more likely to be directed against virtue and good sense," and to identify "little ungenerous tempers" who, not having special talents of their own, compensate for that lack by criticizing the shortcomings of others. Another satirist who vehemently "crowed in triumph" over his victims was Nashe. And H. G. Wells accused Shaw of inflicting pain as "a method of self-assertion."

About Ring Lardner there is a difference of opinion. Clifton Fadiman had written that Lardner hated himself and his characters, and that his characters hated each other. Lardner's biographer, Elder, vehemently disagrees; he points out that Lardner was so hurt by Fadiman's remark that he signed a letter "A Born Hater." Delmore Schwartz, agreeing with Elder, says, "Lardner was actually, of course, a born lover."

It is possible to defend the satirist against the charge that he is a sadist. For one thing, the satirist usually convinces himself that the objects of his criticism badly deserve it, and that what he is doing is a socially necessary rather than a personally satisfying task. Max Eastman, having made a careful survey of the attitudes humorists and satirists hold concerning their craft, concluded, "We find among professional humorists and comedians an extremely small number who have any tolerance for the derision theory." Most of the writers whom Eastman questioned said that they did not believe sadism or superiority to be an important factor.

Humbert Wolfe also denies that satirists get personal revenge through their satire. Wolfe notes that Horace had thrown away his shield but his satire is not limited to soldiers; Pope the cripple satirizes other people than healthy ones; Voltaire, beaten by a nobleman, satirizes much more than the nobly born; and Byron attacks many others than those who contributed to his departure from England.

Sinclair Lewis and John P. Marquand admire many of the characters and types whom in their novels they satirize. The satirist, says Edgar Johnson, "is not someone who hates happiness and beauty, and tries to spoil them for you by finding fault when you have been enjoying yourself"; rather by exposing falsehood and artificiality, the satirist is serving a useful purpose.

Having made an arbitrary division of satirists into "schizothymes" and "sanguines," Dr. Pannenborg concludes that the former are more vengeful than the latter. The "sanguine" or extrovert type is more likely, he says, to satirize situations and groups than to attack individuals.

Protective Laughter

Dr. Ernst Kris tells about a psychiatric patient who always played the part of a clown in public. This young man, having been outstripped by his brother, decided to adopt the pose of a "humorist, a clown." When people discussed political or social matters, he, the buffoon, concentrated on making jokes. "His wit could be spiteful and aggressive." Because he wanted to avoid competing with a stronger rival, he distorted his own personality. "Psycho-analysis teaches us the outcome of such an attitude," Dr. Kris concludes. "The clown will not remove his cap and bells until he has conquered his anxiety."

The theory of "protective laughter" as the stimulus for creativity is not limited to psychiatrists. Thyra Samter Winslow says, "We who write . . . have a number of traits in common. We are, as a class, conceited, dictatorial . . . this conceit . . . usually arises from an unconscious feeling of inferiority — but over-compensation though it is, it nearly always exists in a marked degree, no matter what the cause."

"Great comedists," A. R. Thompson writes, "see in the world around them far more sources of laughter than other men do. This comic perception is an armor against bitterness." Hesketh Pearson, having written several biographies of humorists and satirists, says, "No one dislikes ridicule more than the man who practices it." And Sydney Harris remarks: "The chronic wisecracker is usually a frightened man who is scared of seriousness and uses humor as a barrier against self-knowledge."

In an article entitled "Kidding," Dr. Oberndorf uses the psychoanalyst's terminology. "Inveterate kidders seem to be projecting an intolerance of their super-egos to their own childishness upon objects less capable of defending themselves." Oberndorf, after developing this thesis, concludes: "Such 'kidders' usually take kidding badly . . . and in analysis . . . it developed that unconsciously they often invited and relished the kidding."

According to the "protective-laughter" theory, the satirist (more "sensitive" or more "neurotic" than other people) is subconsciously forestalling the possibility of being hurt. Familiar expressions of this point of view are Byron's

> And if I laugh at any mortal thing,
> 'Tis that I may not weep.

and Heine's

> And when the heart in the body is torn,
> Torn and bleeding and broken,
> We still have laughter beautiful and shrill.

Heine recalled that when, during nights in his youth, he was afraid, "to fight off this fear I whistled the impudent tones of a satiric verse." Freud was convinced that Heine used satire for self-protection even more than as a weapon of offense.

Gogol was an ugly, unprepossessing child. His biographer, Lavrin, believes that the only thing that kept Gogol from becoming the butt of his class was his devastating sarcasm; the boy's vicious tongue protected him from being ridiculed. At a later stage in his career Gogol wrote, "The cause of the gaiety in my first writing was to be sought in my own inner need. I become prey to fits of melancholy which were beyond my comprehension. In order to get rid of them, I imagined the most comic things; funny characters in the funniest situations one could think of."

"My own humor," says Donald Ogden Stewart, "is the product of inferiority. The first manifestation came when as a boy I was persecuted — called 'Duck-Lip' by the other boys. I found out that I could kid. I began calling myself 'Duck-Lip' before they could get to it, and then I turned the kidding on them too."

"I laugh," said Abe Lincoln, "because I must not cry — that's all, that's all." David Worcester wrote: "Democritus, likewise, and his disciple, Burton, and Peacock, and Fielding, and Evelyn Waugh turned to satire as an escape from the sort of sensibility that Shelley felt." Chevalier called Anatole France "a sensitive child . . . particularly sensitive to ridicule. As frequently happens, this made him quick to detect the ridiculous in others." A (presumably) autobiographical character in France's *La Vie en Fleur* confesses, "Perhaps I should have fallen ill with grief in that atrocious school if a gift, which I have kept all my life, had not saved me, the gift of seeing the comic in things."

Pope had "a mania for suspicion," and sometimes took "deadly offense for some utterly inexplicable reason." Strindberg had "a bottomless distrust of everyone." Erasmus was supersensitive and delicate. Parsons suggests that for Mark Twain, too, protective laughter may have been the source of humor: "The Twainian humor may also be domestic in origin, for Sam soon learned that a smart jest turneth away wrath, that a pun can placate the strong and protect the weak."

Of Jane Austen, Mudrick says: "Irony and social convention turn out to be Jane Austen's defenses, not only against the world, but against herself, against the heart of passion. Irony is her defense as an artist . . . and convention is her defense as the genteel spinster when the artist is overcome." Her "earliest, and always her characteristic, defense is irony."

Ibsen wrote: "I know it to be a defect in me that I am incapable of entering into close and intimate relations with people who demand that one should yield oneself up entirely and unreservedly. . . . I can never bear to strip myself completely. . . . I have something of the same feeling as the Skald in the *Pretender*."

Several critics have applied the protective-laughter theory to Thackeray. "The clue to Thackeray's personality," says Dodds in a recent biography, "is his acute nervous sensibility, which not all his bluff heartiness, his love of the ridiculous . . . could hide." Professor Ennis agrees: Thackeray's "particular aggressive counterattack was aimed at tearing the shells from the inner personalities of other people. . . . This counterattack had a three-fold purpose: it helped him ward off unexpected treachery; it gave him the assurance that he was not uniquely weak since he could find shortcomings in others; and it averted their scorn from his weakness by placing them on the defensive."

Such apparent callousness as Swift's rejection of sick friends is interpreted by Dr. Greenacre as "part of his absorption in himself and his strong system of self-defense by denial of feeling." Whenever Swift was hurt in his relations with women he tried "to heal his wounded pride, by finding recognition in the world rather than by looking for some other woman whom he might love." Even Swift's becoming a clergyman, after his break with Temple, seems to Dr. Greenacre an attempt to find "security," as well as "a less personal kind of father, and also a retreat," by a man who was "chronically anxious, and at times frantic."

Her psychoanalysis of Lewis Carroll convinces Dr. Greenacre that Charles Dodgson's "outer life seems to have been impoverished in emotional attachments and in achievements, and his reality sense cramped and invaded by the prohibitions against his hostile fancies which terrified him, until they became masked in humor."

Again, Dr. Pannenborg's chart offers interesting material, but must be taken with extreme caution because his categories are arbitrary and the statistics questionable.

Finally, Steve Allen believes that most of his

	Satirists per cent	Humorists per cent	Average per cent
Shy	71	25	17
"Closed" character	57	12	23
Like large groups	0	—	9
Dislike large groups	43	—	17
Sensitive	86	—	54
Little sensitivity	0	—	11
Touchy	100	15	29
Good-tempered	0	80	19
Vehement	71	25	38
Equanimity	0	5	14
Tolerant	7	95	20
Intolerant	71	0	12
Hard to reconcile	64	0	9
Easy to reconcile	14	75	25
Suspicious	86	0	15
Credulous	0	50	14

fellow-comedians have a "great sensitivity that led them to erect a humorous defense. Far from being the overconfident buffoons the layman might think, most of the leading comedians are shy, pessimistic worriers, whose greatest fault is a lack of confidence."

Perverted Self-Criticism

A number of scholars think that the satirist perverts self-criticism and self-contempt into a criticism of society. By transforming his irritation with himself and his disgust with his own inadequacy into criticism of other people, the satirist compensates for his dissatisfaction by writing satire. Gilbert Cannan suggests that the satirist is a poet who has realized either that his imagination is not of a first-rate quality, or that he is unlucky. "Driven to despair by the apparent sterility of his imagination . . . the unhappy poet is only saved by the discovery of laughter. . . . He can laugh at himself, at his own misery, at his own aspirations, at the lives and misery and the aspirations of all men. Everything he will measure by his untried vision, and everything he will find small and fit only for derision. . . . His unsatisfied and unsatisfiable love feeds his indignation and drives him on to destroy and cleanse and purge."

Edgar Johnson ascribes this motivation to the "conscience" of the satirist: "this inward censorship may enable the satirist to diminish a private burden of guilt by projecting upon the world the weaknesses he feels within himself. Ridicule and self-ridicule, hatred and self-hatred, love and loathing, are intertwined." Kenneth Burke adds: "The satirist attacks in others the weaknesses and temptations that are really within himself . . . such a socialization of losses [explains the] . . . twisted tragedy behind Swift's satire, whereby he uses such thinking, not to lift himself up, but to pull all mankind down." And Frank M. Colby had a similar process in mind when he wrote, "Satire is a lonely and introspective occupation, for nobody can describe a fool to the life without much patient self-inspection."

According to psychoanalyst Edmund Bergler, "The humorist is a psychical masochist, an individual who bewails his misfortune and enjoys it unconsciously at the same time." The humorist, in this view, is a cowardly individual who gets pleasure out of punishing himself and finds in humor a perverse way of expressing both his fear and anxiety on the one hand, and his indirect, cowardly aggression against society on the other. "This is the reason why individuals with free aggression at their command which can be directed at objects are never humorous." Certain types of neurotics, according to Bergler, have a compulsion to prove that admired individuals and respected institutions are actually fraudulent or corrupt.

Dr. Otto Rank suggests that the predicament is not limited to the satirist, but faced by all creative artists. "The fundamental problem is *individual difference,* which the ego is inclined to interpret as inferiority unless it can be proved by achievement to be superiority." All artists are, in Rank's opinion, insecure and uncertain, and need the product of their creative drive to reassure them.

George Mikes, a humorist who has written a book about humorists, remarks, "A person who is too ironical . . . is often a coward. He knows that he is a constant loser on the so-called battlefields of life and tries to console himself by laughing at love and beauty. . . . A sense of humor . . . may be the flower of a balanced nature and a wise general outlook, but it may equally easily spring from bitterness, frustration, hatred, and cowardice."

Satirists themselves have been aware of the part self-criticism plays in their work. Gogol had a talent for getting people to laugh with him, a procedure which helped him get rid of undesirable characteristics: "Taking some bad feature of mine, I present it under a different name and in a different role, trying to make it appear in my eyes as a deadly enemy . . . so I persecute it with irony and malice, with anything I can lay my hands on . . . I have already freed myself from several nasty features by projecting them into my characters, by laughing at them and making others laugh at them."

Other satirists have, directly or by implication, expressed similar opinions. A character in Anatole France's *La Vie en Fleur* says: "I must tell you that, though I have been a mocker in all the ages of my life, I have never made fun of anyone so cruelly as of myself, nor with such great delight."

Irvin S. Cobb writes, "I concluded that a man who can't laugh and doesn't laugh — fundamentally — at himself, is not a humorist in the full sense." Mark Twain confessed that Byron "despised the human race because he despised himself. I feel as Byron did, and for the same reason." In his *Notebook* Twain wrote that "no man, deep down in the privacy of his heart, has any considerable respect for *himself*."

Long before modern psychology came into vogue, in an eighteenth-century discussion of ridicule, the Abbe Bellegard described a type of person who frequently makes insulting or sarcastic remarks. The Abbe urged sympathy for that person. "It was not with design to affront you," that the sardonic individual makes his remarks, "but he has a fund of maggotry, which makes him insupportable, even to himself: everything disgusts him, and he is not master of his spleen: the offensive language he utters, escapes him without thinking of it."

Robert Benchley directly and James Thurber indirectly deprecate themselves in their writing. Gilbert Cannan feels that "Heine . . . fundamentally could mock at nothing but the discordant trinity in himself," and that "Just such another was Sterne, the razor of whose wit never cut into anything more real than his own sentimentality, as Byron was forever raging and tearing at the bonds of his own rhetoric." And Battenhouse calls Byron "a guilty man wanting to be an innocent child, a prodigal wanting to come home."

Clifton Fadiman feels that in Dickens "self-revulsion . . . had always underlain his apparent self-complacence." "Brand, whom Ibsen called 'myself in my best moments' . . . is at the end condemned for lacking love," says A. R. Thompson. Thomas Mann suggests that Lessing's self-punishment took the form of "critical self-surrender and self-irony." Cartoonist Milt Gross says, "The really great humorists laugh at themselves. Look at Chaplin." And Mikes says of Evelyn Waugh: "The unbridgeable gap between his actual personality and the one he desires drives him to Catholicism and makes him hate humanity instead of hating himself."

The desire for self-punishment was so strong in George Orwell, says V. S. Pritchett, that Orwell retired after the success of *1984* to a Scotch island, "seeking punishment, not respite. It was a gesture . . . and it killed him." Isaac Rosenfeld agrees: not only did Orwell's retirement to the island lead to his death, but it was intended to do so; the gesture was a suicidal protest against the horrors of modern times. Voorhees, however, dissents vigorously; such a gesture would be a violation of all Orwell's life and work. Orwell believed, according to Voorhees, that "it was the duty of the writer, as citizen, to engage in all those things which, as writer, he pointed out to be wrong. And so Orwell fought in the Spanish Civil War."

Obviously, satirists are not the only people who are tempted to pervert self-criticism into criticism of others. In accounting for the behavior of a very different personality-type, the fanatic, Eric Hoffer finds precisely the same motivation: "Unreasonable hatreds . . . are an expression of a desperate effort to suppress an awareness of our inadequacy, worthlessness, guilt. . . . Self-contempt is here transmuted into hatred of others — and there is a most determined and persistent effort to mask this switch."

Perverted Frustration

The "frustrated-idealist" theory assumes that the satirist is a man who at one time had a high and noble vision of what society should be and how men ought to behave. Having seen what society actually is and how men do behave, he has become irritated and dissatisfied; he expresses this dissatisfaction by writing satire. That is why George Agassiz calls satire "the soured milk of human kindness." Potts says: "Great satirists are, of course, more than merely angry, bitter, or disappointed men; they are usually baffled idealists. They compare life as it is with life as they would have it be; and being unable or unwilling to reconcile the two, they attack that which is less dear to them."

The same idea is expressed by A. R. Thompson. "But the reason that the ironist's soul is sick is that he has visions of a better world than the existing one, and the destruction of present evils gives opportunity for future good. . . . He is acutely unhappy about man's fate because he is highly idealistic. If he were less so, he might sink into cynical apathy."

A number of satirists have been called frustrated idealists. Eric Bentley feels that Bernard Shaw's "is the formula of an exasperated idealist." Most critics feel that the satire of Erasmus expresses his earnest desire for an improved society. Parsons says: "Clemens' paradoxes arise from partially frustrated love of humanity . . . there was much of the Titan in Samuel Clemens. A Promethean protest against human limitations issued constantly from his lips."

Of Sinclair Lewis, Sherwood Anderson wrote: "Here is a man writing who, wanting passionately to love the life about him, cannot bring himself to do so, and who wanting perhaps to see beauty descend upon our lives like a rainstorm has become blind to the minor beauties our lives hold . . . fighting terrifically and ineffectually for a thing about which he really does care." Carl Van Doren thought that Sinclair Lewis "had by nature and by instinct always burningly demanded that human life be beautiful and splendid; always been disappointed that he could not everywhere find what his passion looked for; always offset his anger at stupidity by his delight in comedy." And Blankenship described Lewis as "fundamentally a socially minded idealist who states his idealism obliquely by means of realism and satire."

In his biography of Anatole France, Shanks wrote, "It is the charm of ironical detachment, the mask so often adopted by the disillusioned idealist." And a man who knew him well said that the irony of France "was, it seemed to us, the expression of an early disappointment, of a skepticism which grew out of a disenchantment, of a mocking doubt sprung from the soil of an early belief." Elder speaks of Ring Lardner's "longing for an ideal world where the rules, if observed, guaranteed the triumph of merit." Fatout tells of Ambrose Bierce's attempt, as a special agent for a mining company, to expose the confidence men and racketeers who had been fleecing the stockholders and workers; Bierce himself was made to appear dishonest.

Not all satirists, however, impress their readers as frustrated idealists. Evelyn Waugh, for example, was described by Joan Griffith in the following terms: "Nor does Waugh conform to the old adage of the satirist as disillusioned idealist. The ideas he postulates . . . are too limited and partisan. . . . Waugh's values are dead things."

It has been suggested that the level of one's frustrated idealism helps determine whether a satirist becomes as great as Voltaire or as superficial as, presumably, Evelyn Waugh. There is some evidence to support that position. But there is also evidence to indicate that it is not the level of his idealism that determines a satirist's greatness but rather his technical skill. Until one can decide whether Jonathan Swift was driven by frustrated idealism or by one of the many other motivations ascribed to him (ranging from the physiological to the psychoanalytic) — until we agree that idealism *is* an invariable element in the makeup of the satirist — it is dangerous to state dogmatically that the level of the satirist's idealism determines the greatness of his satire.

Related to the "frustrated-idealist" theory is the concept that the satirist is really a frustrated sentimentalist. According to this view, the satirist is actually a very tender, very sentimental person who tries to cover his softness and gentleness by pretending to be brusque and bitter; he directs this brusqueness and bitterness against "bad" things, things that a sentimental and gentle person would object to. Meredith had this in mind when he said, in his *Essay on Comedy,* humorists are "as in the case of Sterne, given to be sentimental; for with them the feelings are primary."

It is difficult to conceive of a less sentimental writer than Wilson Mizner. When told by his brother Addison that another brother, Lansing, had just been killed in an automobile accident, Mizner replied, "Why didn't you tell me before I put on a red tie?" Informed that his mistress had jumped out of an eleventh-floor hotel room to her death, he hurried off to the race-track to bet on Number Eleven. Yet the same Wilson Mizner, Alva Johnson tells us, couldn't keep from crying whenever his mother's name was mentioned, years after her death.

Whether the satirist is more sentimental than the average man will be discussed later. There is, however, considerable evidence that sentiment, if not sentimentality, is fairly profuse among humorists and satirists.

The sentimental element in the work of Dickens, Thackeray, Goldsmith, Lewis, Burns, Sterne, and Galsworthy is, of course, easy to recognize and well known. Less well known, perhaps, is a statement like Oscar Wilde's: "Where there is sorrow there is holy ground." Anatole France wrote, "Grief is sacred: the holiness of tears lies at the bottom of all religions. Unhappiness alone would be enough to make a man august to man." And Mark Twain wrote, "People that carry grief in their hearts know how to comfort others' griefs."

Sydney Smith, who once described an essay as "long but vigorous, like the penis of a jackass," was sensitive enough to say on another occasion: "I never go to tragedies; my heart is too soft; there is too much real misery in life." Once, when Smith had written a noncommittal review of a book which Jeffrey, the editor, had expected Smith to ridicule, Sydney excused himself in these words: "I think the book very ill done; still, it is done by an honest worthy man who has neither bread nor butter. How can I be true under such circumstances?"

Heinrich Heine, discussing "the toothache in my heart," recollected an incident from his childhood: "I soon recognized the dear face and asked, laughing, why little Veronica was so still, and Ursula said: 'Death does that.'"

François Villon's activities, including robbery

and manslaughter or murder, do not indicate an excessively sentimental man. But his most famous line is "where are the snows of yesteryear?" And in poem after poem, such as "Death of His Lady," "Fragment on Death," and "Epitaph in Form of a Ballad," Villon is sentimental, tender, and melancholy.

Aldous Huxley stresses the fact that Swift's misanthropy (caused, Huxley thinks, by Swift's inability to have sexual relations) "is accompanied, as often occurs, by a sentimentality of the worst kind." Professor Ennis believes that "the most important of all Thackeray's 'ambivalences' . . . is the opposition within him of cynicism and sentimentality."

Juvenal is often described as the poet of "savage indignation." His furious denunciation of contemporary Roman misbehavior is cited as indignation at a high level. But tough Juvenal himself, in Satire 15, says, "Tenderness is the best quality in man. . . . It is at nature's behest that we weep when we meet the bier of a full grown maiden. . . . For what good man . . . believes that any human woes concern him not?"

In a letter written shortly before he died, Byron told Augusta Leigh about some Turkish prisoners whose release he had arranged and whose expenses he had taken care of. One of those prisoners was "a pretty little girl of nine years of age . . . she has expressed a strong wish to remain with me, or under my care, and I have nearly determined to adopt her."

Voltaire, in 1776, did adopt a girl, eighteen years old, the daughter of a penniless army officer living in his neighborhood. The following year the girl married a marquis and was later helpful to Voltaire in Paris. Jore had printed an illegal copy of the *Philosophic Letters,* betrayed Voltaire, sued him, and later confessed that he had double-crossed him. Nevertheless, Voltaire forgave Jore and gave him a pension for the rest of his life. Thompson notes that Ibsen's "strong domestic yearning is suggested in an early lyric which — surprisingly enough — brings to mind that very different poet, Longfellow, and his 'Children's Hour'! Ibsen's verses are called 'A Home Study.' "

H. L. Mencken, the scourge of the middle classes and most other classes, performed sentimental, kind, and generous deeds which he was ashamed to admit. Mencken claimed to be a Nietzschean, but during World War I he gave money for milk to feed European babies; violently anti-democratic, he voted for liberal LaFollette in 1924.

Alexander Pope's "characteristic note of sentiment" is clearly apparent in the playful tenderness of "On a Young Lady's Leaving Town After the Coronation," as Dyson observed. And Joseph Warton praised Pope's great skill in handling pathos in "Eloisa" and the "Elegy"; he regretted that Pope turned from romantic to satiric poetry.

There is so much evidence of Mark Twain's sentimentality that the comment by Parsons is sufficient, emphasizing as it does a particularly quixotic characteristic. "Maddening knowledge of one sex was balanced by reassuring ignorance of the other sex. As the knightly champion of injured womankind, Clemens broke a lance 'In Defense of Harriett Shelley,' stood up for Joan of Arc. . . . Like Jonathan Swift, Clemens populated his Lilliputs chiefly with men."

According to the biography written by his son Arthur, Groucho Marx "is a sentimentalist, but he would rather be found dead than have you know it. And he's a dreamer, although he likes to pass himself off as a disillusioned realist." Groucho, his son recollects, "didn't believe in spanking. . . . He used to say that grown-ups didn't have the right to 'slug' children who were too small to defend themselves."

There are other humorists and satirists whose soft spot critics recognized, or thought they recognized. Armens tells us that "Gay's 'pose as a cynic' clothes the 'true self' — (the real Gay as sentimentalist)." Of Baudelaire, who is rarely associated with conventional sentimentality, H. W. Wells says: "Although Baudelaire has little but scorn for the upper classes, he looks with a great pity and almost a great love upon the social outcasts." Washington Irving exploited the sentimental fashion, as in "The Pride of the Village"; in E. B. White we find frequent examples of a sophisticated sentimentalism, casually and wittily phrased; Oliver Goldsmith wrote "The Deserted Village" and "The Vicar of Wakefield." Kronenberger notes that Lytton Strachey, "like so many of his fellow scoffers," such as H. L. Mencken, is "terribly likely to gush" when he is not criticizing. And Grillparzer's biographer called him "an intellectual and sentimental egoist."

Is the satirist then a frustrated sentimentalist? Is he more sentimental than other people? Many human beings are sentimentalists; the sensibility which seems startling in satirists is commonplace in most people and most writers. As a general rule, satirists are, or pretend to be, nauseated and revolted by sentimentality and spend a good deal of time ridiculing excessive sentiment. Whether the satirist's antisentimentalism is an attempt at self-protection, aroused by guilt-feelings over his own sentimentality, or a genuine indifference to sentiment, is uncertain.

There is evidence that the satirist, far from being as sentimental as the previous quotations have indicated, is actually antisentimental. Chesterton thinks that Bernard Shaw is the only idealist who is *not* also a sentimentalist; Eric Bentley remarks that Shaw is the only naturalist who is not also a sentimentalist. But A. R. Thompson names several other satirists who, he is convinced, are definitely not sentimentalists: "the great ironists . . . were men with a strong sense of the ridiculous. One can imagine the reaction of a Voltaire or an Ibsen if he had been told that he felt 'the profoundest depths of the world's great beating, laboring heart,' or that his painful amusement at the discrepancies of things made him virtuous."

Charles Rolo is convinced that Evelyn Waugh is not overly sentimental: "From the comic standpoint, Waugh's less amiable traits are actually an asset. Arrogance, snobbery, and contentiousness — when they work hand in hand with irony — are a corrosive solvent to satire. . . . The religious writer requires at least four qualities of which Waugh has displayed only one. Faith he has; but little compassion and no humility and . . . no love."

The inability of most satirists to write effective romantic scenes can be regarded as evidence either of lack of sentimentality or of suppressed sentimentality. It is true that satirists usually have difficulty making love scenes and romantic dialogue seem convincing. Jane Austen, says Mudrick, "was unwilling or unable to project tenderness; she could give [her characters] only a mechanical heart." Sinclair Lewis' inability to create convincing romantic conversations between lovers has been frequently and painfully illustrated. Samuel Johnson recognized the same inadequacy in John Dryden: "I am not certain whether it was not rather the difficulty which he found in exhibiting the genuine operations of the heart . . . that filled his plays with false magnificence. . . . He is therefore . . . not often pathetic; and had so little sensibility of the power of effusions purely natural, that he did not esteem them in others." Professor Walter Raleigh agreed; he called Dryden's love lyrics "with very few exceptions, a miracle of banality." And it is not necessarily true, as some critics have assumed, that the bitter antisentimentality and antiromanticism of Ambrose Bierce were overcompensations for his own excessive sentimentality.

Some excellent poets, such as Dante and Shakespeare, wrote satire. But a great many satirists were unsuccessful poets, or poets less successful than they wished to be. It may be that the satirist is a special kind of poet. Cannan, comparing Swift and Shakespeare, suggests that in potential ability there wasn't too much difference between them; but the satirist is likely to be a poet born "parlously out of luck." Those poets who are what Cannan calls "lucky" express themselves in a gusty or triumphant form; but, for the *unfortunate* poets, "those who for one reason or another are prevented from this *self-realization,* [the aesthetic drive] becomes a *tremendous motive force,* and possesses their souls to the exclusion of all else."

Samuel Johnson and Jonathan Swift persisted in writing poetry which their contemporaries did not value highly. When he was in his early twenties, H. L. Mencken published a book of adolescent poetry which he called "Ventures in Verse." It is said that Mencken later tried to buy up all copies of the book and destroy them. Whether true or not, the rumor is substantiated by all of Mencken's comments about poetry in his adult years: he ridiculed it. Sinclair Lewis, as a student at Yale, wrote much poetry which he later described as "milk-and-water Tennyson." Ernest Hemingway published a little-known volume of poems when he was a very young man. Lewis Carroll wrote a great deal of serious but poor poetry. Don Marquis wrote much philosophic poetry which was not nearly so well received as his *Mehitabel* verse. And Nicolai Gogol, when a young man, wrote a poem which (with a forged introduction pretending that a publisher had praised it) he used in an effort to get acceptance in the literary world.

Even Mark Twain, at the age of seventeen, may have written poetry, according to Delancy Ferguson. In the *Journal,* while his brother Orion, the editor, was out of town, Mark Twain included "a quite serious poem in the best gift-book style, entitled 'Love Concealed'. . . the verses . . . were probably his own. 'All human beings turn out such verses in their youth,' he remarked long afterward of the 'poems' of Mrs. Eddy."

The poetry which Melville, Thoreau, Hemingway, and William Faulkner wrote was largely ignored by critics and by the public. James Thurber, asked whether he had always wanted to be a writer, reminisced, "Well, I think I wanted to be a poet." Aldous Huxley published poems as late as 1931. Kronenberger says that when Shaw tries hardest to be poetic, "his rank failure is all too notorious," and suggests that Shaw may have been a "poet strangled at birth." And Cannan believes that, had Juvenal possessed a higher morality, he "would not have been a satirist but a poet."

Similar in many respects to the reaction of a frustrated poet is the reaction of a frustrated romantic. "In his youth," Thompson notes, "Ibsen's Protestant moral heroism was also colored by the Romanticism of the period. Thus the heroes of his early plays were noble-souled Vikings or Schilleresque rebels; the heroines, strong-minded Valkyries or patient Griseldas." The romanticism of Washington Irving is obvious. Cervantes wrote the pastoral romance, *Galatea,* and thirty unsuccessful plays before he created Don Quixote. And Daiches remarks, "Though Shaw was in his own way a romantic sentimentalist . . . he spent much of his energies fighting against romance. . . . Shaw considered himself a lone champion of realism against romance."

In addition to explaining the satirist as a frustrated idealist, frustrated sentimentalist, or frustrated poet, some critics have made the broader charge that the satirist is frustrated because he has proved inadequate in the ordinary competition of daily life. In his study of Anatole France, Haakon Chevalier remarks, "I shall show irony to be the product of certain radical insufficiencies of character and a mode of escape from the fundamental problems and responsibilities of life. . . . What is a loss for the man may be a gain for the artist, though the two cannot beyond a certain point be separated." And Professor Ennis concludes that Thackeray was "too large, ungainly, and unprepossessing with his broken nose to figure seriously as either athlete or charmer," and early developed a "sense of intellectual inadequacy." Trollope also felt that Thackeray "was not a man capable of feeling at any time quite assured in his position."

Thackeray has a good deal of company: Gogol, Sinclair Lewis, Dickens, Heine, and Swift also felt that they were in some socially significant way "inadequate." Dr. Pannenborg reached the conclusion that two-thirds of the satirists he analyzed were "impractical" and "poor judges of men." On the other hand, such satirists as Voltaire, Defoe, Beaumarchais, Disraeli, Quevedo, and Machiavelli proved to be extremely competent in political intrigue and financial maneuvering.

Most satirists had, when young, ambitions of becoming something other than writers of satire. But most human beings have, when young, ambitions which for one reason or another do not prove feasible. And many people settle for occupations quite different from the ones that they might have, in youth or exuberance, hoped some day to have. There are psychologists and sociologists who believe that the achievement of success in a competitive society, and socially approved aggressive behavior in general, are essentially forms of compensation.

In summary, the compensation theory assumes that the satirist is inferior or frustrated; being inferior in some way, or feeling that he is inferior in some way, makes the satirist write satire. But this does not explain why millions of other people, who are also inferior in some way, or feel that they are, do not turn to writing satire as compensation. And if it is assumed that frustration rather than inferiority motivates the satire, we face the same problem. Granted that the world proves disappointingly different from what the satirist, in his naïvete or idealism or sentimentality had expected. There are also millions of nonsatirists who suffer from a life-long disappointment because there is a prodigious difference between the ideal world and the real world. This still does not explain why, of the numerous alternatives available to millions of frustrated human beings, a few choose to become satirists.

4

Adjustment

Neither a simple explanation of the satirist's motivation — such as morality, nor a complex one — such as compensation, is wholly adequate, for there have been moral satirists and immoral, sentimental and brutal, crude and sophisticated. The satirist is a writer, but the writer is a person. That person requires Freud's sex-gratification, Adler's opportunity for aggression, Jung's continuity of race, and Karl Marx's bread. And the satirist, like everyone else, is deeply concerned with Karen Horney's "need for status" and Rollo May's existentialist "fear of non-being." In the attempt to satisfy his desires and allay his fears, the satirist, like everyone else, tries to adapt himself to society. The adaptation is socio-psychological. It consists of adjusting his particular aptitude — satiric skill — to his particular society.

What makes the satirist write satire is his unique adjustment to his society. That adjustment consists

> *A man born with a genius for juggling — whether colored balls or controversial ideas — can hardly escape the role of performer.*
> — Kronenberger

of exploiting *his special talent: a playfully critical distortion of the familiar.* The "playfulness" usually takes the form of pretense. And any or all of the motivations previously mentioned, such as morality and compensation, may play a part in determining the material he chooses to be satiric about.

Freud recognized the uniqueness of the satiric talent. "Wit seems to be a special ability," he admitted, "somewhere within the range of the old 'psychic faculties' . . . fairly independent of the other faculties such as intelligence, phantasy, memory, etc." On another occasion, Freud went even further: "It is not everyone who is capable of the humorous attitude: it is a rare and precious gift." John Dryden felt that the sense of humor was a quality with which one was born. "It must proceed from a genius, and a particular way of thinking, which is not to be taught; and therefore not to be imitated by him who has it not from nature." And Haakon Chevalier says, "A sense of humor is a gift of birth."

Comic talent seems to be similar to a young musician's aptitude for music and a young engineer's mechanical skill. Whether it is an innate capacity or one developed at an early stage is not known; social scientists disagree about the origins of such "talents." But it does not matter, for our purposes, whether this satiric ability is innate or not. What does matter is that the potential satirist, usually as a boy, begins to use his talent.

The satirist's reactions to outside stimuli constitute his "adaptation" to society. They are not the same reactions as those of a monk, or an inventor, or a boxing champion, or a research chemist, but they are quite as reasonable. The satirist may emphasize, for humorous purposes, the happiness of life, as Harold Lloyd does, or the sadness of life, as Chaplin does, or both, as Clarence Day does. It is no more necessary for a satirist to be an unpleasant individual than it is for an obstetrician to be callous toward women; both "see" more than their neighbors. The satirist is not allergic to life; he is allergic to the ludicrous elements in life. Nor need the satirist be a cynic, though he often assumes, for the purposes of accomplishing his immediate objective in satiric literature or art, that an unflattering analysis is the correct one.

Writing satire is not a "conventional" adjustment to society. Nor is writing of any kind, or painting, or composing, or acting, or dancing. Men who act usually do not write; they do not need to, for they have made a different adjustment to society. It took Mark Twain to tell about the Mississippi; as Professor Fred Lorch remarks, "The pilots were the last men in the world to write its history." And Anatole France said, "Lovers who love truly do not write down their happiness."

For the person with a satiric temperament, satiric expression becomes a method of "getting along" in or "bucking" society — a method which he has spontaneously and accidentally found he possesses. The moment of consciously recognizing his talent surprises him; like Molière's would-be gentleman, who had not realized that he already spoke in prose, the young satirist uses his skill long before he is aware of possessing it.

The use of satiric expression is interpreted, by most psychoanalysts, as a negative kind of compensation for the satirist's inadequacies in personal relations, skills, and achievements. But it is just as reasonable to accept satiric expression as a positive accomplishment, a fulfillment of a talent that the satirist possesses. It is true that the satirist becomes a critic partly because he is unable to offer satisfactory constructive alternatives — and this, in terms of conventional values, is "bad"; but he is also unable to accept without complaint the flaws that he observes in society — and this, in terms of conventional values, is "good."

Another objection to the psychiatric theory is expressed by Margaret Mead, the anthropologist. She points out that maladjustment to early conditioning is not necessarily proof of neuroticism, for among different primitive societies contrasting types of individuals prove to be maladjusted. Among some tribes, such as the Mundugumos and the Dobi, the reserved and cooperative individual is scorned and the aggressive hustler is rewarded; but among the Zuni and Samoans, it is the rugged individualist who is rejected and the passive person who is made to feel that he belongs. "It has become the fashion," says Miss Mead, "to group together all of those by whom the cultural norm is not accepted as neurotics." But such designations have no absolute value, for "gifts honored in one century are disallowed in the next. Men who would have been saints in the Middle Ages are without vocation in modern England and America." Miss Mead observed, in the primitive societies she studied, the presence of "the individual to whom the major emphases of his society seem nonsensical, unreal, untenable, or downright wrong . . . the individual for whose temperamental gifts his society has no use, nor even tolerance." Obviously there are far more such "deviants" than there are satirists; but satirists help swell the memberships of these socially disoriented groups. There is a type of unadjusted person, Miss Mead concludes, "whose failure to adjust should be attributed not to his own weakness and defeat, not to accident or to disease, but to a fundamental discrepancy between his innate disposition and his society's standards."

Before examining the adjustment to society of the satirist in particular, we ought to consider the adjustment to society of the writer in general. "Form," says Cocteau, "must be the form of the mind. Not a way of saying things but a way of thinking them." Cocteau is not implying that there is anything abnormal about this adjustment. Dr. A. A. Brill believes that the neurotic individual cannot adjust himself to the complex requirements of civilized society and becomes, in a sense, "paralyzed by his conflict"; but that the "neurotic writer," instead of behaving in a neurotic manner, solves his problem by creating literature. "My writing," says Elizabeth Bowen, "may be a substitute for something I have been born without — a so-called normal relation with society."

An elaboration on the theme of adjustment is Bolitho's suggestion that men of action sometimes lose "the power of enjoying things directly." Bolitho thinks that the need for vicarious experience is "a weakness . . . which is felt the whole length of the moral ladder, from the saint to the voyeur. It is the secret inspiration of much philanthropy and of much vice; shared by a Napoleon and by the tired cook."

Proust recognized another aspect of the writer's adjustment to society: "Great writers never create but a single work, or rather they consistently refract through different media a single beauty that they bring into the world." Dr. Rank expressed the same idea: "Great artists . . . have either a principal or a favorite work, at which they labored all their lives . . . or a favorite theme, which they never relinquished and which came to be a direct representation of themselves." [Goethe's *Faust* and Rembrandt's self-portraits are examples.]

Every human being needs, very early, some sort of ideology, Dr. Otto Rank suggests. Because he is afraid of isolation, every individual gets an ideology by identifying himself with parents, teachers, and other ideal patterns. But, about the age of puberty, the individual achieves some independence of these models — teachers and parents — and rebels also against the ideologies which they represent. The artist also, Dr. Rank continues, undergoes this liberation of the ego, and makes a switch to "the artistic ideology." His shift is not so much an aesthetic choice as a matter of vocational psychology. "The creative type nominates itself at once as an artist."

If it were true that every human being, whether he knows it or not, is modeling his life on that of some other person, then the secret of each man's personality could be found by learning who his hero actually is. William Bolitho suggests that "the riddle of a character . . . could most often be solved by the search for some book, and the hero of that book, read in youth or even childhood." For a woman, says Bolitho, that model is likely to be "some actress seen playing in a role that polarized the . . . life of her who saw and admired her. . . . Most men are the hero of an unwritten book, a sequel to one they once read. It may be a book they have forgotten even to the name; it may be a life of Alexander the Great, or Buffalo Bill . . . or Huckleberry Finn, or Frank Merriwell, or a gospel, or Jesse James . . . find that book and you will find that which is most intimate and revealing about their actions, their moods."

In *Yeats: The Man and the Mask,* Richard Ellmann discusses a large number of writers who attempted to imitate the lives of other people not only in their writings but in their behavior. Ellmann quotes Yeats's statement that every passionate man is "linked with another age, historical or imaginary, where alone he finds images that rouse his energy."

William Ewald, in *The Masks of Jonathan Swift*, elaborates on the imitation of other people as a way of life. "Clearly, the problem of imitation is not confined . . . to literary men, hypocrites, or paranoiacs! Its importance in the psychology of normal people — children and adults — would appear to be enormous." Ewald refers also to Toynbee's theory that the only way in which "the creative minority" can effectively influence the "uncreative rank and file" is "by enlisting the universal and primitive faculty of mimesis."

The enormous popularity of biographies throughout Western civilization is evidence in support of this theory. There is no question that the men Plutarch wrote about, and the imaginary men Horatio Alger wrote about, influenced millions of people. Whether similar books influence all people is of course not quite so certain.

There is evidence that this tendency to imitate can come at any stage in a man's life. Logan Pearsall Smith says, "Don't laugh at a youth for his affectations; he is only trying on one face after another to find his own." At the other extreme, the last word that composer Gustav Mahler said was "Mozart."

It is interesting, though far from conclusive, that at important stages in the lives of Voltaire, of France, and of Mark Twain, the influence of a respected skeptical older man seems to have been significant in the development of the satirist. Voltaire's godfather, early tutor, and longtime advisor was the Abbe de Chateauneuf, a sophisticated, tolerant, liberal priest who trained young Voltaire to question all authority. He even encouraged the boy to parody Bible stories, including the one about Jonah's unusual escapade. Concerning Anatole France, Chevalier says, "Without Renan, Anatole France is inconceivable. . . . The example of such a man may have intensified to a degree which we can only guess France's awareness of the complexities in his own temperament." And Mark Twain seems to have been deeply impressed by the middle-aged Scotch agnostic at the Cincinnati boardinghouse where young Sam Clemens lived during his first year away from home.

"Mark Twain was my model and I studied his method," wrote Irvin S. Cobb. "Balzac always praised [Rabelais] for having greatly influenced his writing," said Anton Bettelheim. According to Priestley, "The author upon whom Fielding modeled himself as a novelist was Cervantes." To complete this literary honor roll, among Groucho Marx's readings were Ring Lardner, Henry James, Maugham, Huxley, and Tolstoy. Groucho "was particularly delighted with the Winnie-the-Pooh stories," says his son in *Life With Groucho*. George Gobel admits having read and been influenced by Benchley and Thurber.

Sinclair Lewis has had more than one model. In his Nobel Prize Address, Lewis said that Hamlin Garland awakened his creative spirit, and that H. G. Wells inspired him. But Lewis pointed out on another occasion that at the time he read Garland and Wells he was already in the mood to appreciate someone like them rather than someone like Booth Tarkington or James Whitcomb Riley, whom he was also reading at that time.

Similarly, at the time in his early twenties when H. L. Mencken became a literary disciple of Nietzsche, he was ready to adopt someone like Nietzsche as his model. At twenty-one Mencken was already skeptical, prejudiced against "inferior" men, contemptuous of religion, and a believer in the law of natural selection. Nietzsche probably was the greatest single influence on Mencken, but Bernard Shaw and Thomas Huxley, as well as Darwin, have been paid such extravagant tribute by Mencken that all of them seem to have helped form his personality, philosophy, and expression.

In the matter of influences, James Thurber poses a problem for critic Friedrich. Friedrich quotes Thurber's remark, "I learned more about writing from White than from anyone. He taught me to write a simple declarative sentence." But, Friedrich goes on to say, "the ideal of [Henry] James' writing is implicit in most of Thurber's best fiction." Friedrich admits that "Thurber, after all, does not write like Henry James," and concludes that "Thurber's style has developed out of the conflict between these two extremes, White and James . . . assimilating and rejecting parts of each."

A slight skepticism about the value of modeling one's life on that of another person is indirectly revealed by Ben Franklin. In his *Autobiography*

Ben first wrote, "Plutarch's *Lives* there was, in which I read abundantly, and I still think that time spent to great advantage;" then he crossed out the word "great" in the original manuscript. And a warning against imitating life or art comes from Proust: "When you are in love with a work of art you would like to do something just like it. But you must sacrifice your love of the moment and think not of your taste but of a truth which never asks our preferences and forbids us to consider them."

Rank goes on to suggest that the artist or the writer becomes an artist or writer by a process of "self-appointment"; at an early stage in life, a person who has done some writing or drawing and has found satisfaction in it (either a personal sense of achievement, or the approval and encouragement of his family or friends), after a while finds himself wanting to write or paint *to the exclusion of all other major activities.* In this sense, Rank suggests, a writer becomes a writer by appointing himself one, but the reason for this appointment, the motivation for the drive, is one that the writer himself cannot explain. It lies deep in his subconscious, and he does not know why he writes.

If "adjustment" to life is the basic motivation of all writers, it is also the motivation of satiric writers. And there is a good deal of evidence to support the idea that this is true. The interrelation among the satirist himself, his technique, and the specific problems in his society, indicates that his satire is an aesthetic expression of a fundamental adjustment to life.

Speaking of writers whom he calls "great ironists," A. R. Thompson says, "these men do not merely *use* irony; they *live* ironically; and irony is as a consequence basic in their view of life." Enid Welsford contrasts tragic and comic actors: "Whereas Burbage ceased to be Hamlet when the play was over, Tarleton was Tarleton both on and off the stage; Martinelli entitled himself Arlequin even in legal documents." In his careful study of Herman Melville, Rosenberry concludes, "Irrepressible as a limp or a tic, and as distinctive, the sense of humor must always be an 'infirmity' in the sense that its ultimate springs are not art or tradition but the intimate orientation of personality."

Haakon Chevalier also supports the theory that the satiric attitude is a basic element of one's personality: "The perception of incongruity . . . may provoke a number of reactions, depending on the temperament of the individual. If he has a sense of humor, his reaction will assume some form of mockery or ridicule." Cazamian agrees: "With vigorous thinkers . . . doubt cannot be superficial and easy to bear; the universal irony with which they envelop themselves . . . disguises but ill the inward torment." And Kronenberger adds: "A man born with a genius for juggling — whether colored balls or controversial ideas — can hardly escape the role of performer."

An unusual extension of the comic technique is cited by Dr. Edmund Bergler. He tells of a patient, a young mechanical engineer, whose unusual sense of humor was revealed in his witty, sarcastic, and self-derisive attitude. The patient was involved in a feud with his father, who demanded that he take his engineering examination; the young man insisted that he was not prepared. Bergler, in his analysis, decided that the young man was subconsciously getting revenge on the father who, when the boy was three, had severely criticized him for not learning the alphabet thoroughly enough. Now, in his twenties, the son was getting revenge by pretending that he had not yet learned his engineering work thoroughly enough to satisfy the father.

Material for art is always available. The musician, the artist, the poet see it all the time; similarly the satirist, also primarily an artist, sees it and uses it all the time. Just as detective story writers Agatha Christie, Ellery Queen, and Erle Stanley Gardner get from the ordinary events of everyday life material for mystery, the humorist and satirist get from the ordinary material of everyday life material for comedy and satire. By using his special talent for distorting the familiar in a playfully critical manner, the satirist adjusts to the society he lives in.

The deathbed is a likely spot for honest comment, and "last words" have always held a certain fascination. Expressing the beliefs of men who presumably no longer have much need to conceal their honest opinions, the last remarks of satirists indicate that the satiric attitude toward life *is* permanent.

According to one account, Heinrich Heine's last

words, in reply to a friend who asked "Do you think God will forgive you?" were, "He will forgive me. That's his business." Wilde's last remark supposedly was "I am dying beyond my means." There are two accounts of Thoreau's last words. A visitor asked Thoreau what his hopes were for a future life. "One world at a time," Thoreau said. Or, in another version, asked if he had made his peace with God, Thoreau replied, "I have never quarreled with Him."

Two versions of Scarron's last words are quoted: "I could not have supposed it so easy to make a joke of death," or "Ah, my children, you cannot cry for me as much as I have made you laugh." According to Gene Fowler, "Just before W. C. Fields died . . . he opened his eyes, then winked."

Sydney Smith, having been told jokingly that he had drunk a dose of ink by mistake, said, "Then bring me all the blotting paper there is in the house!" William Wycherley, after making his young wife promise to grant him one last request, said, "My dear, it is only this, that you never marry an old man again." Joel Chandler Harris is supposed to have said: "I am about the extent of a gnat's eyebrow better." And the last remark of satirist Charles Churchill was: "What a fool I have been." *

The dying Jewish jester, Hershel Ostroplier, told friends at his bedside, "When you lift me up to put me in the coffin, be sure that you don't hold

* All quotations in this paragraph and some others in this section are from Edward LeComte's *Dictionary of Last Words.*

me under the armpits. I've always been very ticklish there."

Rabelais' last words were: "Draw the curtain. The farce is ended"; his will said: "I owe much; I have nothing; I give the rest to the poor." And H. L. Mencken, at the age of forty, wrote an epitaph to be used when he died: "If, after I depart this vale, you ever remember me and have thought to please my ghost, forgive some sinner and wink your eye at some homely girl."

For consistency of satiric attitude it would be hard to surpass the performance of Wilson Mizner, as Alva Johnston recorded it in "Legend of a Sport." Having just suffered a heart attack, Mizner was asked if he wanted a priest. "I want a priest, a rabbi, and a Protestant clergyman," he said. "I want to hedge my bet." Coming out of a coma, shortly before his death, he waved the priest away. "Why should I talk to you?" he asked. "I've just been talking to your Boss." When the priest warned him that death might come at any moment, "What?" said Mizner. "No two weeks' notice?"

Besides making characteristically wry remarks on their deathbeds, humorists and satirists reveal at other important moments in their lives a unique adjustment to society. Molière's last play, written when he was in bed dying, was a comedy which he titled *The Imaginary Invalid*. Sinclair Lewis, asked by European reporters what he would do with the

Nobel Prize money, said, "It will be used to help a deserving American writer and his family." The reporters wrote enthusiastic stories about his generosity before they learned that the writer Lewis referred to was himself. Similarly, when Lewis publicly challenged God to strike him dead, he was simply expressing an atheist's attitude toward religion.

Oscar Wilde may have been more truthful than witty when he wrote, "My great tragedy is that I put my genius into my life — and only my talent into my work." W. L. Miller said of Robert Benchley, "From his son's description of his room, his career, and his habits, [Benchley] seems to have raised the *Weltanschauung* of the *College Humor* magazine to a way of life. . . . He seems to have achieved that rare Kierkegaardian reduplication: his life and his work were one." Dr. Kanzer is convinced that "the reality-and-anxiety denying functions of Gogol's stories were created to cure his fits of melancholy." Charles Lamb taught a little girl to say the Lord's Prayer backwards. And we are told by one of his students that the great Japanese wit, Yomo-no-Akara, spent the hours in a storm-tossed boat punning about his predicament.

A. R. Thompson feels that "Irony . . . was fundamental to Euripides as it was not to the pious Aeschylus or the serene Sophocles," and suggests that the clue to understanding that puzzling play, *The Bacchae* of Euripides, "may be acceptance of his complexity as intentional"; Euripides may have been putting on the stage "the war in his own soul," and dramatizing in symbolic form similar problems on the stage. And Mudrick thinks that "As technique, as attitude, irony was peculiarly adapted to Jane Austen's temperament and genius. . . . She used her considerable wit as weapons or shields. . . . Irony was the single life-principle that her art had invoked. . . . It was Jane Austen's first choice to treat life, even in her letters, as material for comedy."

The inability of a humorist to control his behavior on occasions when it should be politely controlled is revealed by Groucho Marx's heckling the minister throughout his marriage ceremony, while brother Harpo wandered around the room camouflaged as a potted plant. At his divorce, Groucho also made facetious remarks. Groucho knows when not to be funny, his son says, but "sometimes he just can't resist his impulse to do something that will get a laugh." Most humorists have found the temptation to get a laugh irresistible. Ring Lardner, for example, chose a large party at which to pretend that he was a Pole who spoke no English. And the American comedian Jonathan Winters has frequently yielded to unconventional impulses. Once Winters turned to a friend in a crowded but quiet hotel lobby and announced in a loud, serious voice, "We shouldn't have operated in a hotel room. I admit he is alive, but you shouldn't have let that brain fall on the rug. Next time St. Vincent's."

Chevalier devotes a long book to proving his

thesis that the ironic attitude is the expression of the ironist's adaptation to society. Irony of syle, characterization, and plot "definitely point to an organic adjustment within himself that determines his relations to the outside world." Whereas for other people, and for other writers, irony may be a "transitory" phase, for the ironist it becomes a way of life. "It conditions all that he does, all that he says. . . . It is his originality, it is his virtue, his vice, his power, his insufficiency: it is the man."

Valery felt that for Anatole France the ironic tone became "a natural and almost instinctive manner of expressing himself," and that when, in brief passages, France does not write ironically, the reader feels that "France is being less himself."

Heinrich Heine, having been virtually paralyzed during the last decade of his life, was asked how he could endure his suffering. He replied that God had sent the malady only to prove that He was a better satirist than Heine himself. Shortly before he died, Heine signed a letter to a young female admirer: "Your poor friend, Nebuchadnezzar the Second. (Since I am just as crazy as the Babylonian king and eat only chopped grass, which my cook calls spinach.)" After his wife found him with another woman, Heine explained to a friend, "I am so absent-minded that once in a while I take someone else for Matilda."

With Mencken the satiric attitude was persistent, in spite of its unpopularity. During World War II he insisted that Hitler was a harmless fool and wrote such cynical articles that even the *Sun* papers, for whom he had worked most of his life, stopped publishing him. Next to that of Ambrose Bierce, Mencken's satire is the most vituperative in American literature, and one might expect the same sort of bitter personal maladjustment that is supposed to have contributed to Bierce's savage satire. Mencken himself, however, could recall no unhappy incidents from his childhood. "My early life," he wrote in *Happy Days*, "was placid, secure, uneventful and happy." Never in his childhood did he doubt his father's ability to resolve any difficulty. His parents' marriage, "which had been a love-match, was a marked and durable success. . . . We were encapsulated in affection." And there have not been many more complacent attitudes towards life than Mencken expressed in the following passage: "If I had my life to live over again. . . I'd choose the same parents, the same birthplace, the same education . . . the same trade, and the same job, the same income, the same politics, the same metaphysics, the same wife, the same friends. . . . The Gaseous Vertebrata who own, operate and afflict the universe have treated me with excessive politeness."

Sydney Smith frequently did "funny" things. He had a dramatic precedent; his father had left the newly-wed bride at the church steps after the ceremony, announcing that he had to leave for America; some years later, he returned and began married life. Sydney named his first daughter Saba, after a king in the Bible, because he felt that anyone named Smith deserved an unusual Christian name. When theater managers sent Smith tickets for free admission to their plays, Sydney sent them tickets for free admission to St. Paul's Cathedral, where he gave his sermons. Replying to a Puseyite who had dated a letter with some saint's day, Smith dated his own reply: "Washing Day." Never excessively fond of art, he announced when he visited important museums in Europe that he preferred the rooms in which there were no pictures.

Mark Twain wrote, in his last article: "To me the most important feature of my life is its literary feature." Delancey Ferguson says: "The boy who joined the Christian Sons of Temperance for the sake of their gaudy red sashes became the man who about 1870 astounded genteel Boston with a sealskin overcoat, and in his old age paraded Fifth Avenue in white clothes and wore his scarlet Oxford gown at his daughter's wedding." Ferguson describes this characteristic of Twain as "a trick Sam Clemens never outgrew, to cover awkwardness or embarrassment with whimsicality."

A similar reason for Bernard Shaw's satiric attitude is offered by Kronenberger. "The masks, the pranks, the poses were . . . of course psychologically necessary. Shaw . . . was by nature a painfully shy man; one who compensated in print for a lack of ease in ordinary conversation."

Finally, there is poignant revelation of the humorist's psychology in Logan P. Smith's anecdote: "The servant gave me my coat and hat, and in a glow of self-satisfaction I walked out into the night. 'A delightful evening,' I reflected, 'the nicest kind of people. What I said about finance and philosophy impressed them; and how they laughed when I imitated a pig squealing.' But soon after, 'God, it's awful,' I muttered, 'I wish I was dead.' "

Many satirists have used pseudonyms, and it is fair to ask whether the choice of a pseudonym is also a form of adjustment to life, whether in an evasive or detached manner this is a way of wearing a mask in public. There are, of course, good reasons for a satirist to adopt a pseudonym. If one plans to criticize people or institutions, in a society which often punishes critics, it may be sensible to conceal one's identity. Many satirists have taken pseudonyms for that reason. Others have used pseudonyms not because there was danger, but because writing comic things seemed to them, and to their society, an undignified activity.

Whatever the reason, whether the freeing of a personality from the inhibitions of his upbringing, or the desire to escape punishment and danger, pseudonyms were used by Anatole France, Voltaire, Orwell, Swift, Dickens, Molière, and many other satirists. When, during the Nazi occupation of France, Jean Bruller was writing anti-Nazi satire, not even his wife knew that he was "Vercors"; after the war Bruller continued to use the pseudonym which had established his reputation. Among the names Thackeray used were Michael Angelo Titmarsh, James Yellowplush, Major Gahagan, and George FitzBoodle. "Mark Twain" and "Saki" and "Josh Billings" are pseudonyms. So is "Lewis Carroll." But many writers other than satirists also used pseudonyms.

Much of what Eric Hoffer says about the fanatic — a personality type quite different from the satirist — is startlingly relevant. "The chief burden of the frustrated," Hoffer suggests, "is the consciousness of a blemished, ineffectual self, and their chief desire is to slough off the unwanted self and begin a new life. They try to realize this desire either by finding a new identity or by blurring and camouflaging their individual distinctness; and both these ends are reached by imitation."

F. L. Lucas' analysis is stated in a form which proponents of the adjustment theory can accept: "As the artist lives out his conflicts in creation, while the criminal turns them against society and the neurotic against himself; so the mind with a sense of humor can create from its own source of troubles a comic situation, with the momentary distance and detachment of a mere onlooker, and with the consoling satisfaction of a semi-artistic activity."

The type that Colin Wilson calls the "Outsider" adjusts to society by completely detaching himself from its values; and the type called by Hoffer "The True Believer" adjusts to society by completely identifying himself with the values of a particular group. The satirist is closer, of course, to the Outsider than he is to The True Believer. But he differs from the Outsider in always being aware that his detachment is a pose, and that he really *is* involved in his society to the extent that most people are involved in their society. Like The True Believer, who is a fanatic, the satirist distorts reality and tends to ignore pleasant truths. But, unlike the fanatic, he tries to preserve his individuality instead of seeking selfless identification.

Essentially, the adjustment theory is based on the assumption that the primary motivation of civilized man is the achievement of a desirable status among his peers. Satire is a social activity, and the satirist chooses this particular activity as his method of getting recognition and approbation.

Part Two 🦀

Personality

The Satiric Type

In his monumental study of the relationship between physiological structure and temperament,
Professor W. H. Sheldon quotes the old saying that
fat men are jolly, thin men are dour, strong men
are silent, and short men are aggressive. Neither
this saying, nor Sheldon's own theory, nor any
other formula which analyzes personality in terms
of physique has been accepted by scientists. Nevertheless, numerous efforts to find the magic pre-
scription have been made, and the temptation to
account for different personalities by dividing
men into physical types has proved irresistible to
many scientists and pseudo-scientists. The attempts
have ranged from feeling bumps on heads to measuring the space between front teeth. More recently
Kretschmer, Sheldon, Heymans, and Wiersma have
put all men into three body-type groups, and
claimed that each group possesses unique psychological characteristics. In spite of these claims,

*The temptation to account for
different personalities by
dividing men into physical
types has proved irresistible.*

satirists fail to exhibit uniform physical characteristics. They range from tiny Pope to large Johnson, from thin Shaw to fat Chesterton, from weak Erasmus to muscular Charles Churchill, from delicate Jane Austen to robust Ben Jonson.

The most detailed attempt to classify satirists by personality types was made by a Dutch scholar, Dr. W. A. Pannenborg. His *Satiric Writers: Character and Temperament* (1953) includes thirty-eight tables which profess to measure, among others, such qualities as stubbornness and credulity in satirists and nonsatirists. The statistics which Pannenborg uses were compiled by two psychologists, Heymans and Wiersma; on the basis of the Heymans-Wiersma archetypes, Pannenborg divides the twenty-seven satirists whom he analyzes into three groups.

Group One, the "Schizothymic Satirists," consists of Byron, the second Samuel Butler, Charles Churchill, Erasmus, W. S. Gilbert, Gogol, Crabbe, Grillparzer, Hebbel, Heine, Ibsen, Pope, Swift, and Strindberg. According to Dr. Pannenborg, all these satirists have certain characteristics in common. They are very egotistic. Their intense emotionalism has these results: excessive reactions, a personal emphasis in satire, a "narrowing of the mind" which makes them ignore extenuating circumstances. Extreme egotism is largely responsible for their narrow-mindedness, and the schizothymic satirists are vain, ambitious, proud, and haughty misanthropes. They like to assume positions of authority and leadership. They are thrifty and avaricious and lack "character." Although very emotional, they go through periods of apathy which are typical of this personality type. Their characteristic qualities are violence, irritability, intolerance, sombreness, fluctuation of mood, and melancholia. They are not very sociable, dislike large groups of people, and are likely to be pleasant conversationalists only within their own small circle; when they are the center of such a circle they can be very gay and entertaining, but this mood can change abruptly. As a result of their concentration upon themselves, they withdraw more and more into their own psychic and spiritual lives. They are likely to die as a result of licentious behavior — almost a third of them, says Pannenborg, died of venereal disease or alcoholism. Hypochondriacs, they constantly complain about the weather. Because they are restless, they travel much and frequently change their domicile.

Group Two, the "Sanguine Satirists" (also called Cyclothymic or Extrovert), consists of Aretino, Beaumarchais, Defoe, Holberg, Kotzebue, Mürner, Montesquieu, Machiavelli, Quevedo, Rabelais, and Voltaire. (Pannenborg points out that the French-Italian element in this group outweighs the English-Scandinavian.) Like the members of the first group, they are egotistical in character, but in their temperament a "sanguine" element replaces the nervousness of the schizothymes. They are very active, strongly aggressive personalities. Contempt for others is present but not as preponderantly as in the satirists of the first group. Uncharitableness and lack of a sustaining moral background express themselves in skepticism and cynicism, and account for the callousness they sometimes exhibit. Their "willingness to help," on other occasions, should be interpreted not as benevolence but as the result of surplus energy, which makes even a small motivation sufficient to arouse them. (Defoe, Aretino, Beaumarchais, Voltaire are examples.) The "sanguines" tend to attack groups and situations rather than individuals, and are likely to use irony in their derision.

Dr. Pannenborg discusses the similarities and differences of the two groups. The satirists in the first group are overemotional, in the second group subnormal emotionally. Egotism expresses itself in both groups in greed: the schizothymes are avaricious and frugal; the sanguines collect things and love luxury and comfort. The following characteristics are present in both groups, but in different intensity: impulsiveness, use of superlatives, immoderateness, inconsistency, jerky development, good observation, snap-judgment, good memory, concrete fantasy, imperiousness, and aversion to contemplation. Characteristics present in both groups in approximately equal (and high) intensity are amorality, conceit, ambition, avarice, unreliability, sexual licentiousness, hypocrisy, criticism, love of travel, conflict of thought and deed, and desire for freedom.

In certain respects, says Pannenborg, sanguines and schizothymes differ markedly from each other. Sanguines stay young, but schizothymes age prematurely. They are quite different in temperament: the sanguines are very active, calm extroverts; the schizothymes are subnormally active, superemotional introverts. The satirists of Group One are particularly revengeful; Group Two is less so, with the personal and violent element less evident. The satires of the latter are more businesslike, gayer, often comical and witty, but also more shameless. Other qualities are listed in the table on the next page compiled by Dr. Pannenborg.

If Dr. Pannenborg's statistics were actually scientific they would resolve many of the difficulties in analyzing satirists by classifying them in two distinct, and in some ways very different, groups. If all satirists actually did belong to either the schizothymic or sanguine category, and consistently exhibited the characteristics of each category, we would have a clear analysis of them. Unfortunately, Dr. Pannenborg himself admits, at the end of his book, that Kretschmer's theories about the contrasts between schizothymic and cyclothymic groups "are not acceptable as such." The method of Heymans and Wiersma, he feels, is an improvement and extension of Kretschmer's work, but much more information is needed about both physiological and psychological types before valid conclusions can be drawn.

Because he cannot fit Victor Hugo and Vondel into either of these groups, Pannenborg creates for them a third category, that of satirists motivated by "noble indignation."

Apart from the falsity of the Kretschmer-Hey-

Comparison of Sanguines and Schizothymes

	Sanguine per cent	Schizo- thyme per cent	Average per cent
Regularly active	82	14	56
Not regularly active	0	43	22
Persistent	64	21	39
Not persistent	9	43	17
Independent	86	50	39
Dependent	0	21	10
Decisive in opinion	73	57	33
Indecisive in opinion	9	29	9
Always alert	91	0	1
Distracted	0	36	12
Heroic	73	29	12
Cowardly	0	43	1
Optimist	64	7	43
Pessimist	0	64	22
Changing mood	9	57	28
Even-tempered	27	0	15
Timid	9	71	17
Frank	91	29	11
Like big groups	73	0	9
Aversion to big groups	0	43	17
Pleasant narrator	82	57	52
Not pleasant narrator	0	71	12
Laugh heartily	27	0	17
Not laugh heartily	0	7	3
Healthy	57	14	22
Ailing	18	68	25
Sensitive	22	86	54
Not sensitive	36	0	11
Thrifty	18	43	12
Free-spenders	60	43	32
Comfort and luxury loving	45	7	5
Indifferent to comfort and luxury	9	29	10
Collector	36	7	12
Not collector	0	21	1
Earnest	0	36	22
Light-hearted	55	21	3
Self-analytic	4	50	19
Aversion to self-analysis	22	0	5
Practical	91	7	34
Impractical	0	57	18

mans-Wiersma premises, the whole idea of measuring in percentiles such intangible qualities as sensitivity, frankness, timidity, and light-heartedness is appalling. To assume arbitrarily, as these studies assume, that only 1 per cent of the population is "cowardly," or that 64 per cent have complete "agreement of thought and deed," is to express a more optimistic opinion than satirists themselves are likely to have held.

It is true that there have been lame, stuttering, malingering, and sickly satirists. It is also true that thousands of lame, stuttering, malingering, and sickly individuals have not become satirists. And many satirists have been healthy individuals.

Voltaire was convinced that one's body has a great deal to do with his temperament. "It is not our position," he wrote, "but our disposition which renders us happy. Our disposition depends upon the functioning of our organs, over which we have no control." Ghiselin, in *The Creative Process,* suggests that the creative artist is "often a specialist, with less psychic inertia than the average man, and, sometimes, with less stability."

A large number of satirists either were ill much of their lives or persuaded themselves that they were ill much of their lives. Mencken and Sydney Smith and Mark Twain were hypochrondriacs. Maugham stuttered. Swift had several ailments. The nose broken by a schoolmate disfigured Thackeray for life; Ennis is convinced that "the misfortune . . . seriously undermined his confidence," and gives examples from Thackeray's work of recurring wishes to disfigure the noses of handsome men.

Ambrose Bierce moved from England back to San Francisco in 1876 when his health failed. Robert Burns died after a long period of suffering from "excruciating rheumatism." Thurber had only partial vision in his one eye since childhood; as he put it, he saw "one and a half." Cervantes lost a hand in the naval victory at Lepanto, long before his writing career began. Edward Lear, in addition to epilepsy, had asthma, poor eyesight, bronchitis, and a heart weakness. Anatole France was described by one biographer as having been "a boy so delicate, sensitive and timid that he did not master his stammering until he was forty." Samuel Johnson could not see very well (a condition which affected his judgment of art), hear well (which helped make him dislike music), nor walk well, and he was often ill. Clarence Day suffered from arthritis so severely that he was rarely able to leave his bed during much of his adult life; nevertheless, he attended to his duties as a stockbroker and glove merchant, and "wrote and illustrated a series of remarkable books . . . after middle age he was scarcely able to move more than a finger. Yet his writing continued serene; there was never a trace of bitterness or self-pity."

Edgar Johnson describes Alexander Pope as "this spidery dwarf who had to be laced into a canvas corset to hold himself erect and wore three

pairs of stockings to pad out his spindled shanks."
Pope was a hunchback less than five feet tall, and
had headaches most of his life. Voltaire was so sick
during the first year of his life that he was not expected to survive. Mark Twain was two months
premature and so weak that he was not expected to
live. As a child, he remained frail and sickly.
When, in his sixty-fourth year, Mark was experi-
menting with an osteopathic cure, he listed his ailments: slow pulse, "bellyache," tingling of the left
arm, rheumatic "pains," sore throat, itching piles,
constipation, "hot urine," "neckache," heartburn,
and the common cold to an unusually severe degree. Charles Lamb had a large head on a little
body, a stammer, and a tendency to collapse.

Gogol was a sickly child, "small, thin and
clumsy." He was "plagued by an unsightly nose, a
nose of such length and mobility that he could per-
form parlor tricks with it." Byron, in addition to
the lameness from which he suffered since boyhood, also had occasional convulsions. The exact
nature of his last illness is not certain: "epilepsy,
or, according to Dr. William Osler, meningitis."

Not all of the physical characteristics of satirists,
however, are of a nature indicating weakness.
Tremendous energy was possessed by Sinclair
Lewis, Chesterton, Rabelais, and Charles Churchill. In spite of the illnesses and other physical disabilities to which satirists have been subject, or
perhaps in compensation for these illnesses and
disabilities, an enormous capacity for work, an
almost excessive ability to work, was displayed by

Charles Dickens, Edward Lear, Mark Twain, Voltaire, Bernard Shaw, and Hilaire Belloc, among many others. This enormous energy may be linked with the excessive compensatory energy that Bolitho observed in dwarfs, or may be related to other psychological qualities that satirists exhibit. Whatever the reason, there is considerable evidence that satirists are extremely hard-working men.

Many satirists have also turned out to be extremely long-lived men. Having devoted a good portion of their existence to commenting on the misery of life, many of them managed to live past the biblical three score and ten. Bernard Shaw, Dean Inge, and, if legend is correct, Lucian, lived more than ninety years. Among those who passed eighty were Maugham, Voltaire, Franklin, France, and Hardy. Edward Lear, A. E. Housman, Washington Irving, Melville, Beerbohm, and Jonathan Swift were over seventy before they left the world which, judging from their comments, was not worth inhabiting at all.

Most satirists, however, died at about the same ages when most men, according to actuarial tables, die. Some, like Byron, Persius, Stephen Crane, and Robert Burns, never reached forty.

Whether satirists as a group are less attractive physically than most men is difficult to say. Byron was outstanding in his good looks, not only among satirists but among men in general. As a rule, the theory that "few handsome men are amusing; few amusing men are handsome" is true. Noel Coward is an exception who helps to prove the rule. It may be relevant that the few good-looking men who become satirists tend also to be especially cynical. Perhaps Jimmy Durante's remark is apropos: "I know dere's a million good-looking guys, but I'm a novelty."

Kenneth Burke contrasts the work of Max Nordau, who "discredited the products of genius by showing their relationship to disease," with the biographical studies of Kretschmer, who reverses Nordau's emphasis and "tends rather to show the ways in which geniuses converted their liabilities into assets." Among popular comedians Jimmy Durante, W. C. Fields, and Bob Hope made assets of unattractive noses; Ed Wynn and Andy Devine capitalized on voices not generally regarded as adequate for actors. Fred Allen described Durante's voice as "a dull rasp calling its mate." Fat Fatty Arbuckle and cross-eyed Ben Turpin made good use of their physical inadequacies.

Having gathered a number of facts about the physical characteristics of satirists — such as the pigeon-breastedness of Samuel Butler the second; the slenderness of Gilbert, Voltaire, and Kotzebue; the smallness of Gogol, Heine, Pope, Ibsen, and Voltaire; the medium size of Strindberg, Defoe, Machiavelli, and Montesquieu; and the corpulence of Rabelais and Churchill — Pannenborg concludes that the available physical data on satirists does *not* prove that the satirist belongs to a particular physiological type.

All attempts to put satirists and ironists and humorists into rigid categories on the basis of personality types have proved inadequate. But some scholars have coined special definitions to describe stereotypes, then tried to fit arbitrarily-chosen satirists into those types. Chevalier, for instance, assigns to the stereotyped "ironist" these qualities: detachment, disillusion, skepticism, universal curiosity, indulgence, aptitude for speculation, emotional sensitiveness, and mockery. He adds to these, in the person of Anatole France as the "ironist" par excellence, passivity, timidity, and vacillation. These qualities do fit France; they do not, in many respects, fit such ironists as Voltaire, Fielding, Quevedo, Waugh, and Swift. (Swift always called himself an "ironist.") Apparently recognizing that his definition is not wholly adequate, Chevalier elsewhere says that Voltaire was "a true ironist — that is, one who perceives rather than invents incongruities." Here we have quite a different emphasis— on realism. The danger of generalizing about types is further illustrated by Dr. Pannenborg, who arbitrarily concludes that five of the satirists he examines — Beaumarchais, Voltaire, Kotzebue, Defoe, and Machiavelli — are extroverts, or, as he calls them, "sanguine"; just as arbitrarily he classifies Goldsmith, Sheridan, Marivaux, and Oscar Wilde as "nervous" comic writers.

Added to the difficulty of trying to categorize people as extroverts and introverts is the fact that there is no agreement, even among psychologists, as to just what extroversion and introversion mean.

Jung, Freud, Fromm, and Horney use different terms to describe these characteristics. Dr. Ian Kent recently advanced the theory that blue-eyed individuals are extrovert doers, and brown-eyed introverted dreamers. Furthermore, introversion and extroversion are "situational." A man who would be an introvert as a salesman may be an extrovert with fellow scientists; a poet is often shy with strangers and lively with friends. It is unfair to choose at random particular kinds of social relationships as the criteria for extroversion.

Nor are such differentiations as Nietzsche's or Otto Rank's very helpful. Rank speaks of "two basic types of artists . . . called at one time Dionysian and Apollonian, and at another Classical and Romantic. . . . The one approximates to the psychopathic-impulsive type, the other to the compulsion- neurotic volitional type. The one creates more from fullness of powers and sublimation, the other more from exhaustion and compensation." That these definitions are unsatisfactory becomes clear as soon as critics try to fit specific writers into these theoretical categories; they immediately find that no two critics agree in matching writer with category.

Among satirists whom one might expect to be more extroverted than introverted (always keeping in mind the fact that the terms have only a dubious value), H. L. Mencken would seem to belong. Mencken was "vibrantly alive," with tremendous zest, vitality, and exuberance. Mark Twain was in many respects an aggressive person; he was also a very sensitive one. As an adult, Twain started or threatened to start lawsuits almost weekly; while he was writing *Tom Sawyer* his wife reported that he was in such a good humor that he "scarcely lost his temper more than four or five times a day." Whether Byron belongs with extroverts is questionable in view of his remark, "And if I laugh at any mortal thing, 'Tis that I may not weep." But Byron did not always need this particular kind of protective laughter; certainly his escapades indicate quite different moods. Nor can Bernard Shaw be regarded as a shrinking violet or timid personality, in spite of his reply, when asked what he would do if the revolution actually came: "I'd hide under the bed." Shaw was a shrewd and tough businessman, a successful self-publicizer, and an effective public debater. And if we can judge from Rabelais' works, he was another lively extrovert.

If there were conclusive evidence that all satirists possessed certain psychological characteristics, then it would be possible to create a hypothetical satirist and ascribe to him these basic characteristics. The obvious interrelationships among emotional immaturity, sentimentalism, and romanticism could be stressed. It would be easy to create a stereotype of the satirist by applying, ad absurdum, the psychoanalytic method which finds the sources of conflicting emotions in the same motivation. For example, if we assume generosity and miserliness to be simply two extreme reactions to the same stimulus, then we can group the cynical satirists with the idealistic ones, the naive ones with the sophisticated, the brutal with the gentle, and the conservative with the liberal. But, tempting though this procedure is, it oversimplifies the problems and eliminates irreconcilable differences by expediently letting them cancel each other out.

It is true that many satirists, like Gogol and Dickens and Sinclair Lewis, were emotionally immature; but some, like Molière and Horace and Max Beerbohm and Noel Coward, were quite sophisticated. Many satirists, like Fielding and Sterne and Thackeray, were sentimentalists; but many, like Rochester and Bierce and Mencken hated sentimentality, perhaps in reaction to their own repressed sentimentality. Most satirists were far kinder persons than their written work indicated, but some were vicious and churlish men. Most satirists were melancholy, but this does not conspicuously differentiate them from other writers. We will see that some scholars regard satirists as abnormally detached, but others find them deeply and sympathetically involved in their subject matter. Some satirists were timid or cowardly, but others were very brave. Satirists have shown contradictory characteristics, but dualism is a characteristic of most sensitive human beings and there is little evidence that the contradictions of the satirists are any more startling than the contradictions of most human beings. The satirist, like most writers, is more likely to be introverted than extroverted, whatever those vague and disputed terms may mean. Most satirists are gregarious with people they like and with groups that respond to their interests. The "Pagliacci concept" that the satirist is an unhappy person who conceals his misery while making others laugh, is essentially true; but so many people adopt a cheerful pose in adjusting to society that the satirist is clearly not unique in having failed to achieve perfect happiness.

Characteristics

The idea that the humorist deviates from the normal way of looking at the world is not new. In 1658 the *New World of English Words* defined "humorist" as "one that is fantastic," and Hooker quotes a 1689 definition of "humor": "the natural inclination, or temper of mind; but it rather signifies a habit of acting according to the appetite, or some irregular affection, than according to reason."

In recent studies Dickens, Strindberg, and Gogol have been called manic-depressives, Don Quixote a schizophrenic, comedian Jackie Gleason a paranoiac, and Samuel Johnson a victim of "anxiety hysteria." Nor have psychoanalysts been the only ones who thought they detected deviant characteristics in the satirist. David Worcester, in *The Art of Satire,* says "Skepticism and pessimism

There is nothing that marks the born dramatist more unmistakably than this discovery of comedy in his own misfortunes almost in proportion to the pathos with which the ordinary man announces their tragedy.
— Bernard Shaw

and melancholy are the ironist's portion, and he is content to have it so." And William Bolitho suggests a motivation which is rarely recognized as legitimate: "It might clarify our understanding of all biographies . . . if instead of assuming likely that the natural bent is only towards 'pleasure' . . . it were remembered that man is pulled to deprive himself as well as to enjoy himself; at certain ages often more strongly and irrationally; that 'pleasure' is a questionable term."

Another problem to be considered in terms of modern knowledge is the psychology of the "truth seeker." For a variety of reasons, sometimes conflicting, the satirist insists that he is seeking truth. We will see that he sometimes goes so far as to pretend that he is not a satirist at all, but a realist. Is there something abnormal about devoting one's life to a search for truth? Is it excessive in the satirist, as we feel it is excessive in a fanatic? And if we assume that the satirist's pose of constantly seeking the truth is pathological, how do we distinguish it from the "normal" searching for truth which the scientist is constantly making? When does a reformer stop being a normal member of society and become abnormal? (Dr. Pannenborg's statistics, with the reservations previously made, are interesting. Twenty-one per cent of the people studied by Heymans and Wiersma are described as "suspicious"; but 86 per cent of the satirists are "suspicious." Conversely, although 42 per cent of the population is called "credulous," no satirist is so categorized.) In some ways, Twain and Voltaire were excessively honest; in most ways, Pope and Gogol were inordinate liars.

Such characteristics as emotional immaturity, sentimentalism, generosity, insecurity, and romanticism are related. If all satirists actually revealed characteristics like these, with the consistency that Heymans and Wiersma's statistics claim, it would be possible to set up a configuration of the typical satirist. The satirist's art would then be explained in terms of his personality. For instance, the evasive technique of satire could be interpreted as an expression of the satirist's cowardice. But a rather serious objection to this interpretation is the indisputable fact that many satirists were not cowards.

Dr. Pannenborg concludes that satirists fall into two categories: schizothymia and cyclothymia. Schizothymia is "a schizoid condition or temperament remaining within the bounds of normality; — opposed to cyclothymia." Cyclothymia is "a mild manic-depressive psychosis involving recurring cycles of exhilaration and depression." Pannenborg accepts Kretschmer's classification and calls the cyclothymic satirists "sanguines." (But Dr. Sheldon, who agrees that the manic-depressive psychosis is the motivation of the sanguine type, believes that Kretschmer was wrong in attributing that psychosis to the "pycnic" type. It should have been the "athletic-asthenic" type. So there you are.)

Two-thirds of the satirists Dr. Pannenborg studied were restless and loved to travel. But paradoxically (or, as the psychoanalysts see it, consistently) the same satirists who were always moving about insisted on a machinelike regularity in their daily schedules. Sinclair Lewis worked by the clock and felt so strongly about the importance of punctuality that he published an article on the subject. Ibsen "regulated his schedule like a watch." Samuel Butler "imposed a pattern on the life within him." W. S. Gilbert carried out many routines "like a machine." When he was living in Italy, Byron "rode daily on the same road, at the same pace, and ate at the same inn at the same time." Grillparzer followed a rigid daily schedule of working hours, restaurants, and relaxations.

A few other statistics gathered by Dr. Pannenborg may be relevant here:

	Satirists per cent	Humorists per cent	Average per cent
Sharp observer	64	80	33
Good memory	36	80	30
Objective opinion	0	—	28
Subjective opinion	79	—	12
Not methodical	71	45	20
Good in mathematics	7	10	14
Poor in mathematics	36	50	11
Good in languages	50	35	13
Poor in languages	14	20	18
Musical	43	10	20
Not musical	14	50	15

Tables and charts may be interesting, but they do not explain why the introspection of the satirist results in literature which is concerned only with the external aspects of life, whereas the introspection of other serious writers results in literature which often concentrates on internal qualities. Statistics do not account for the relationship between banter and lack of profundity, nor suggest that the banter may be an attempt to camouflage the lack of profundity. No one seems to be certain of the relationship between intelligence and the creative imagination, Osbert Sitwell for example suggesting that great intellect is likely to interfere with the creative process. Even Freud was unsure enough about wit to say that it "seems to be a special ability somewhere within the range of the old 'psychic faculties,' " and to distinguish it from such qualities as intellect, memory, and fantasy. And Herbert Muller remarks that "Character is primarily a matter of sentiment and will, not of intelligence." Nor do statistics reveal whether the ability to parody, which all great satirists have, is evidence of an admirable flexibility or of an unsavory flaccidity.

Immaturity

The satirist has often been described as immature. One of the difficulties in examining this aspect of his personality lies in defining immaturity as a social rather than biological condition. Involved in the definition are such disparate qualities as self-sufficiency, economic status, impulsive behavior, and many other elements. By some standards, a saint would be regarded as immature in modern society. By other standards, the academic scholar who neglects using his intelligence to accumulate more money than his contemporaries is regarded as "immature." The fundamentalist can be called immature; the extreme individualist; the iconoclast; the theorist; the miser and the spendthrift; the man who refuses to change his foreign name in his new country; the member of a religious minority who refuses to join the majority in his community; the man who tries to practice, literally, his religious beliefs in everyday life. By the standards of some religious sects, everyone is immature who devotes his efforts to any aim other than eternal salvation. And, as defined by a currently popular psychologist, maturity consists simply of accepting one's obligations to other people.

A definition of maturity must also consider ethics and expediency. Is the man who openly expresses political disagreement with his boss being immature? From a practical point of view, he is; from a democratic society's point of view, he is not. Is the person who gives a large part of his energy, time, and money to philanthropic and humanitarian causes being immature? In neglecting his own material advantages, he is; in accepting obligations that he believes transcend personal desires, he is not. In one sense, maturity in the professional and business world consists of attaining that level of personal development where one is unconcerned with any problems but his own. This may be called sophisticated maturity; it may also be called jungle morality.

Another test of maturity is the ability to distinguish between appearance and reality. The mature individual is expected to reject the former and adjust to the latter. By that test, young thieves mature most quickly, whereas people who keep longest the illusions of honesty, kindness, and generosity remain immature longest.

By any of these tests, the overwhelming majority of adults in our civilization could be classified as immature in one respect or another. One might question the maturity of the successful politician who finds aesthetic pleasure only in western stories, the millionaire who constantly bets on horses, the professor who doesn't understand the members of his own family, and the famous Russian musician who referees soccer games. One might say that the satirist is immature in attacking people who have done him, personally, no harm, and in defending people who cannot pay him. If maturity is defined as adjustment to the *status quo* (whatever that *status quo* may be), in such a way as to get a large share of those rewards which his society regards as most desirable, the satirist is likely to be immature.

Another definition of maturity is the ability to see the general rather than the particular: to recognize principles which underlie specific acts. In this respect, the immaturity of the satirist can be compared to the "simplicity" of both the child and the wise old man. The satirist has a propensity for observing "useless" oddities; while a shrewd businessman or a skillful politician is detecting those contrasts between theory and practice which can be useful to him in a material way, the satirist is, instead, detecting contrasts which may be harm-

ful to society but are of no value to him. The
satirist is likely to be "impractical" in this sense, in
the same way that Cassandra could make no practical use of the prophetic gift she had been granted.
Like the character in *Three Men on a Horse* who
could pick winners in horseraces only so long as
he did not bet on them, the satirist seems to have
an allergy to incongruity which is most sensitive
when he is not making personal, "practical" use
of it.

Ironically, when the satirist becomes mature he
is likely to be a less successful satirist. He needs to
be unfair, or angry, or immature, in order to be
effective, for satire is, in its concept and technique
and very nature, an unfair and distorted treatment
of material. When the satirist becomes fair and
reasonable, he stops being a satirist. Distortion is
immature.

According to Freudian theory, a person in whom
the Oedipus complex has not been satisfactorily
resolved at an early age is likely to retain a number
of immature traits. In those particular traits he
reveals an arrested emotional development, and in
times of emotional stress he tends to revert to the
childish level at which those traits had become
fixed. Margaret Mead observes that in every society
— primitive and civilized — the "neurotic" individual (that is, the individual who deviates from the
values of his particular society) "is regarded as
immature; he has not grown up sufficiently to
understand the obviously realistic and commend-
able motivations of his own society." Nor is im-

maturity limited to satirists, or to artists. Emotional immaturity sometimes nullifies cooperation among military services, complicates relationships among statesmen, intensifies rivalries among professors, and affects the behavior of businessmen.

Mark Twain exhibited what people call immaturity by sometimes dressing in ludicrous clothes on dignified occasions, by exploding vituperatively in public, by threatening to sue everyone who argued with him. Alexander Jones believes that Twain "never outgrew his clinging dependence" on his mother and centered all his affection on her; that he later transferred the feeling to other older women, such as "Mother" Fairbanks; and that when he eventually married Olivia, he still wanted to be mothered. Twain's nickname in the family was "Youth."

Priestley says of Charles Dickens, "This return to the child-like imagination is the secret of both the great absurd Dickens characters and his little marionettes." Dyson called Pope "a spoiled child." Ambrose Bierce was abnormally sensitive to criticism. Goethe said, "Lord Byron is only great as a poet; as soon as he reflects he is a child." Clifton Fadiman wonders whether Lewis Carroll was "a Peter Pan, refusing to grow up," and says of G. K. Chesterton: "It is hard to think of him as a crusader, except as one of the Children's Crusade, for a certain childlike innocence clung to him all his life." Mencken was called an "overgrown boy." Dr. Greenacre feels that Swift's "continual infantile longing was apparent through the years in his 'little language' to Stella," and Aldous Huxley called Swift an "emotional adolescent." Huxley accused Swift of being childish in his refusal to accept reality, but Huxley himself was described by Bald as a novelist who "has never completely grown up." And there is a kind of permanent childishness about Edward Lear.

Delmore Schwartz found at the heart of Ring Lardner's writing "an innocent purity of heart and mind which was continually shocked by the frustrations of life." But satirist Wilde was certainly not chiding satirist Beerbohm for immaturity when he said, "The gods have bestowed on Max the gift of eternal old age."

Discussing Aristophanes' ability to handle material which might seem in other writers obscene and obnoxious, Thompson says, "he has in this respect a small boy's or primitive man's undivided attitude." In a psychoanalytic article on Gogol, Dr. Kanzer says, "His life was molded from the beginning by a solicitous and possessive mother, only fifteen years older than himself. . . . She made him self-centered and kept him in an infantile and dependent state." S. P. Mais writes of Saki: "Munro's understanding of children can only be explained by the fact that he was in many ways a child himself; his sketches betray a harshness, a love of practical jokes, a craze for animals of the most exotic breeds, a lack of mellow geniality, that hint very strongly at the child in the man. Manhood has but placed in his hands a perfect sense of irony and withheld all other adult traits."

After punching Theodore Dreiser, whom he had unjustly accused of plagiarizing from Dorothy Thompson's articles on Russia, Sinclair Lewis said: "I'm just a country hick living on a farm; every time I leave it I get into trouble." Ludwig Lewisohn wrote: "Sinclair Lewis lives intellectually from hand to mouth." Howard Mumford Jones said of Lewis: "Except for his latest novel [*Dodsworth*], his books are those of an immense and clever adolescence." DeVoto said of *Main Street* and *Babbitt*: "Maturity of mind, maturity of emotion . . . these are not discoverable in these books." Walter Lippmann called Lewis a halfbaked, naive, adolescent rebel, without a single mature, reflective character in all his books. And Benjamin Stolberg saw Lewis as an "irreverent adolescent." When *Dodsworth* was published, Frances Russell wrote, "Sinclair Lewis seems at last to have shed his literary adolescence," and H. S. Canby said, "*Dodsworth* . . . is a *Main Street* sophisticated and matured." What these critics failed to realize was that *Dodsworth* was also the end of Lewis as a significant satirist.

Emile Hovelaque, a friend of Anatole France, described him as "that grown child." Another friend wrote, "This Epicurean, smiling, skeptical, and indulgent, was very timid in love." France managed to have with him, all of his long life, a woman who functioned primarily as mother, and sometimes also as mistress or wife. Mother, wives, mistresses, and housekeepers took care of him. Chevalier notes: "The charm that pervades the

work of Anatole France is the charm of immaturity
. . . but it is charm of a kind that one looks for
only in a child." And: "That which France expressed — often with profound sophistication —
was the naive, the fresh, the immature approach to
experience, the first contact with life, the budding
emotions, the tentative intellectual discoveries that
each youth must make anew. Life remained for
him always clothed with mystery and enchantment,
fraught with danger. It is an ecstatic youth's vision
of life, even when his reactions are those of a
disabused old man."

In the autobiographical novel, *Le Livre de mon
Ami,* France has a character say: "There are times
when everything surprises me, times when the
simplest things give me a mysterious thrill," and
"I have been inclined at all times to take life as
a spectacle. . . . I shall preserve . . . all my life, the
ingenuousness of the idlers of the big city whom
everything amuses and who preserve into the age of
ambition the disinterested curiosity of little children."

The adult who has retained "the disinterested
curiosity of little children" is not necessarily immature. Dr. Jung accepts the Freudian theory that
all artists are narcissistic — that is, "undeveloped
persons with infantile and autoerotic traits." But
this condition "is only valid . . . for the artist
as a person, and has nothing to do with the man as
an artist." His art may be mature and detached,
even if he is personally emotional and introspective. And the satirist who is immature, in terms of

conventional social judgments, may still have a mature and realistic perspective of society. It is that perspective which gives his satire its special quality.

Again, before condemning the satirist for being immature, one might scrutinize objectively the behavior of his friends, acquaintances, and neighbors and see how many of them can be honestly described as mature individuals. It is significant that not only great satires such as *Gulliver's Travels, Alice in Wonderland,* and *Don Quixote,* but also such works as *Moby Dick* and *Huckleberry Finn* are popularly regarded as children's books.

Melancholy

One day a gaunt, sad-faced man walked into the office of a doctor.

"I'm depressed," the man said. "Nothing gives me any pleasure. I have nothing to live for. If you can't help me, I will kill myself."

"I can help you," the doctor said. "You must get outside of yourself, expose yourself to genuine laughter and happiness."

"What shall I do?"

"Go to see Grimaldi the clown. He is the funniest man in the world. He will cure you."

"Doctor," said the sad-faced man, "I am Grimaldi."

Grimaldi's biographers have not been able to authenticate this anecdote, but the belief that humorists are melancholy people is widespread.

Whatever the reason for the belief, whether wish-ful thinking or accurate observation of humorists, the concept that the funny man is not a happy man goes back much further than the Pagliacci aria. And humorists apparently are not alone in their gloom. Twenty-four hundred years ago Aristotle wrote, "Famous artists and poets and statesmen suffer from melancholia and madness, as did Ajax, and in recent times Socrates, and Empedocles, Plato, and many others, especially poets."

Before examining what the attitude of humorists is, it seems reasonable to ask what the correct attitude toward life ought to be. What *is* the proper view? Is Pollyannaish cheerfulness the proper attitude? Cynical indifference? Romantic escapism? Selective sentimentalism? Callous brutality? Isolation? Weeping? Laughter? Montaigne decided that if he had to choose between the philosophy of Heraclitus, who constantly wept, and Democritus, who constantly laughed, he would certainly choose the latter's attitude. Both had reason for weeping as they looked at the world around them, but Montaigne thought that scoffing at fate was healthier than crying about it.

Montaigne assumed that the cause of laughter is external rather than subjective, that it is the world which is out of joint rather than the humorist. From this point of view, the world, to anyone but an idiot or a brute, may indeed appear to be a sad place. The idea that suffering is inevitable is deeply imbedded in Western philosophy and literature. It permeates the Bible, folk literature, epics, and expositions ranging from the books of philosophers to the remarks of barflies. Schiller once said, "What would live in song immortally must in life first perish." Because the satirist is extremely sensitive to incongruities he is more than most men constantly aware of the wide chasm between the ideal and the actual. He is acutely conscious of discrepancies, many of which deal with unfulfilled expectations and are, consequently, tinged with sadness.

The satirist usually *is* a melancholy individual. When Don Herold says that a humorist is "a man who feels bad but who feels good about it," he is not necessarily implying that masochism is at work, although most psychoanalysts do draw that inference. E. B. White shifts the emphasis from the humorist's sadness to everyone's sadness: "One of the things commonly said about humorists is that they are really very sad people — clowns with a breaking heart. There is some truth in it, but it is badly stated. It would be more accurate . . . to say that there is a deep vein of melancholy running through everyone's life and that a humorist, perhaps more sensible of it than others, compensates for it actively and positively."

Bernard Shaw said of this phenomenon, "There is nothing that marks the born dramatist more unmistakably than this discovery of comedy in his own misfortunes almost in proportion to the pathos with which the ordinary man announces their tragedy." E. B. White puts it another way: "Humorists fatten on trouble. They have always made trouble pay." Another explanation is Sydney Harris': "Humorists have been sad men in their personal life because they became aware quite early in their careers that there was little market for their honesty, but an insatiable demand for their humor." And the public, because it sees only one side of the humorist, assumes that this side is the whole man.

Chevalier offers another explanation. Only two possible ways of achieving happiness are available to man, and both depend on "integration." The usual way is "the subordination of all the functions to a dominant desire or illusion." But the ironist chooses another, a rarer way, "which lies in the renunciation of all desires. . . . The former is a philosophy of action, the latter one of inaction. The former is dependent on the supremacy of an emotional need; the latter upon the absolute control of the intellect upon the emotions."

A psychoanalytic explanation is provided by Dr. Martin Grotjahn, and he applies it to the likable "humorist," not to the nasty "wit." "The grief over the loss of the good mother shows occasionally in the sadness of the humorist, who always seems to smile through tears." But since humorists are not the only people who regret "the loss of the good mother," they are hardly unique in their sadness.

The satirist's reactions are frequently more intense, in joy and in sorrow, than a mature adult's reactions are supposed to be. If one's temperament is definitely set by the end of the first year, as the Freudians once believed, or by six, as many psychiatrists still believe, or even by adolescence, sub-sequent events make the melancholy humorist "comfortably melancholy" or "uncomfortably mel-ancholy." But he remains "melancholy" because his permanent personality pattern has been ir-revocably determined. And some psychoanalysts suggest that this melancholy pattern is due to a masochistic desire on the part of the satirist him-self to suffer, or to be punished, and that he sub-consciously wills the misfortunes to which he be-comes exposed.

Many psychiatrists believe that the humorist is a person suffering from a neurotic maladjustment to society, a man who uses humor as his defense against, or aggression towards, a menacing world. Dr. Jacob Levine, for instance, says, "It is no ac-cident that comedians are often basically sad, de-pressed persons. For them, humor serves as a de-fense against anxieties arising from their relations with people. The wish to make people laugh be-comes a pervasive and consuming drive; they must have laughter and applause as an expression of love." When they are alone, they are likely to be "withdrawn, melancholy, preoccupied."

Dr. Edmund Bergler also assumes that all writers are unhappy except when the device of writing gives them "temporary escape." According to Berg-ler, clinical evidence supports the popular view that humorists and satirists are melancholy people. "They are on the border-line of psychotic depres-sion with a saving grace of occasional manic-de-fense." Attempting to explain why there are so few great writers of satiric comedy, Bergler says: "It is exactly that 'temporary health in the shadow of psychosis' which explains that the necessary psychic ingredients are so seldom met with, ingredients indispensable for the writer of satiric comedy." The satirist, according to Bergler, is really afraid to criticize society, and when he does so is indulging in "pseudo-aggression," a brief and artificial act. "The writer of satiric comedy is handicapped in his productivity by the constant duality of deep masochistically tinged depression and the tendency to direct unproductive irony against himself. Only in exceptional cases does he . . . muster enough aggression to 'hit back.' That rarely-encountered half-miracle makes him a writer of satiric comedy."

Dr. Annie Reich is convinced that the humorist is a neurotic who transmutes his anxiety into external objects. The mechanism of the humorous process, she says, consists of transforming the anxiety and self-accusation and insecurity of the humorist into an attack upon the object of hatred or fear, in an indirect manner. The approval of his audience serves to assure the humorist that he has achieved this transformation, and that he has shifted the need for fear from himself to someone else. But when he fails to achieve such applause, and in the periods between successful achievements, the humorist (because he is insecure and anxiety-ridden) is likely to be melancholy, depressed, and peevish. In other words, according to Dr. Reich, the humorist is unhappy most of the time, and especially depressed when his effort at escape — his humorous activity — has failed.

This attitude of some psychoanalysts would be more convincing if it were not for the contradictory statements by other psychoanalysts, such as Dr. Alfred Winterstein: "Humorists as character types," he tells us, "are either optimistic, primarily narcissistic, and reconciled, or pessimistic, melancholic, and distracted." Since most human beings are either more optimistic or more pessimistic than the hypothetical norm, it is difficult to see what particular distinction there is in being a humorist. Most psychoanalysts do not agree with Dr. Winterstein.

Whatever its appeal — perverseness, sadism, or irony — the "laugh, clown, laugh" theme has always struck the fancy of the audience. For Charlie Chaplin the role has been a personal one as well as a theatrical one: "I've known humiliation. And humiliation is a thing you never forget. Poverty — the degradation and helplessness of it! I can't feel myself any different, at heart, from the unhappy and defeated men, the failures."

A popular American comedian, Orson Bean (pseudonym for Dallas Burrows), is convinced that all humorists are sick people in need of psychoanalysis. They "are driven to being comics out of their unhappiness," he says. "Comedians have a great need for acceptance." Having undergone psychoanalytic treatment which he feels has helped him, he admits that his art suffered. "I was funnier with my problems."

Samuel Johnson had a deep-seated melancholy; grief and instability were persistent characteristics of Jonathan Swift; Washington Irving recorded in his notebook the recurrent melancholia from which he suffered. Edward Lear wrote in his diary: "Woke to impatience, blindness, and misery, incapable of deciding whether life can be cured or cursed." Because Sydney Smith was subject to "acute attacks of depression . . . he hated solitude and silence." Charles Lamb wrote, "My waking life has much of the confusion, the trouble and obscure perplexity of an ill dream." Bernard Shaw said of Charles Dickens: "When he was not infectiously laughing he was a melancholy fellow." Ibsen wrote, "I received the gift of suffering, and so I became a poet." Damon Runyon was an unhappy man who looked sad even when joking. Groucho Marx's son says that his father never expected his good fortune to last long and always worried. And James Thurber confessed, in the Preface to *My Life and Hard Times*: "To call such persons humorists . . . is to miss the nature of their dilemma and the dilemma of their nature. The little wheels of their invention are set in motion by the damp hand of melancholy."

Gogol said, "I became prey to fits of melancholy," and Herman Melville wrote: "I once, like other spoonies, cherished a loose sort of notion that I did not care to live very long. But I will frankly own that I have now no serious, no insuperable objections to a respectable longevity." There is evidence that Byron already suffered from melancholy at the age of six, and his adolescent poems refer to death often. Robert Burns certainly included himself among the thousands when he wrote: "Man's inhumanity to man makes countless thousands mourn"; he had had a series of unfortunate experiences, including the loss of his father's farm, the failure of his own, a love affair which he called "a most melancholy affair which I cannot yet bear to reflect upon," and the depression which made him unable to resist alcohol.

"I brought this misery with me into the world," wrote Henrich Heine. "It lay in my cradle with me, and when my mother rocked me she rocked it, too. . . . When I grew bigger, the misery grew too, and finally became quite big. . . . We are all playing a comedy with ourselves, to the last moment. We even disguise our distress; dying of a wound in the breast, we complain of a toothache. . . . But I had the toothache in my heart. That is one of the worst ailments, but it is cured very well with a filling of cold lead and Guy Fawke's tooth powder."

The idea that no one is really happy fascinates many satirists, either as a form of wishful thinking or as a recognition of fact. Thoreau wrote, "The mass of men lead lives of quiet desperation." Like Thoreau, Anatole France was interested in the legend of the king who could cure himself only by putting on the shirt of a happy man, and whose emissaries found that the only happy man in the world had no shirt. "Do what we may, we are ever alone," said France repeatedly. His mother said,

"His character has become uneven, bizarre, he passes brusquely and without cause from joy to sadness." A character in France's *Le Livre de Mon Ami* says: "I acquired as a mere child a profound sense of the evanescence of things and of the nothingness of all. I divined that things were but changing images in the universal illusion. I have been since then inclined to sadness, to gentleness, and to pity."

Deaths are liberally sprinkled in the works of Evelyn Waugh, and in Twain's *Huckleberry Finn* one reader counted 200 references to death. In his notebook Twain wrote, "Everyone is a moon and has a dark side which he never shows to anybody." Paine called Twain "high-strung and neurotic," and DeVoto remarked that "the fear of death and the threat of death colored his phantasy from childhood on."

At a time when his work was most successful, Ring Lardner thought of committing suicide. Desperately unhappy, unable to sleep, he tried alchol and morphine but could not relieve his anxiety. Maurois notes, in his life of Disraeli, "the profound melancholy hidden beneath the Disraelian irony." Thackeray said, "I was so unhappy myself as a child that I don't think I have said a rough word to one twice in my life," and Ennis comments on "the nearly incessant melancholy of [Thackeray's] later years." Many other satirists, Pope, Bierce, and Butler among them, were unhappy individuals, some with more apparent external cause than others.

While people tend to accept confessions of unhappiness, they are more suspicious of professions of joy. But some satirists have claimed that they were happy. In his biography of Mencken, Isaac Goldberg described the satirist as a happy, exuberant man, successful, healthy, hard-working, hard-headed, with a strong liking for beer, women, music, and argument. Mencken himself wrote: "I hold that life upon the earth is a very agreeable thing, and that men should concentrate their greatest efforts upon making it more agreeable."

Thompson believes that Bernard Shaw was, "unlike Molière, a man whose temper is one of unquenchable gaiety and optimism." Rabelais is regarded, on the basis of his writing, as a happy man, and some scholars have described Henry Fielding as a genial personality. Among popular comedians, Harold Lloyd is exceptional in being a happy person. The movie character whom Lloyd created was, in Samuel Grafton's words, a man who "believed firmly that this was the best of all possible worlds and that success in life depended entirely on his own almost eerily ingenious efforts." It is significant that Harold Lloyd's happy character achieves his comic effects by emphasizing fear rather than pathos.

"Immature" and "melancholy" persons exhibit some of the characteristics of the manic-depressive type. There is a relationship between the manic-depressive temperament and the use of exaggeration and understatement, which are the basic technical devices of the satirist. The connection between personality and technique (here, and in the use of indirection by timid persons) applies to the satirist. The essence of humor is distortion, and distortion usually uses indirection, which it achieves either by exaggerating or understating actual conditions. The manic-depressive state is an alternation of exaggerated and understated personal temperamental conditions.

Dualism

When E. B. White said that all men are schizos he meant it. Dualism, or ambivalence, or conflict between contradictory desires is the lot of most civilized human beings. There are many obvious causes for this conflict in personality. What used to be called the struggle between the animal in man and the divine in man, even when restated in modern terms as the conflict between individual desires and social ideals, remains a conflict. It has at times been called the conflict between reason and emotion; Freudians labeled it a war between the id and the super-ego, and neo-Freudians added a struggle between the ego and the super-ego. Conflict also stems from recognizing the difference between the real and the apparent, the truth about men and the illusions about men, the facts of society and the myths of society.

This dualism is of course not limited to satirists or to abnormal personalities. Every sensitive human being, every honest self-analyst, every intelligent adult recognizes the presence of these conflicts. But most human beings learn to accept these conflicts as an inevitable condition of life. Instead of being excessively disturbed by these contradictions, the normal man concentrates instead on activities more useful to him socially and profitable to him economically. The satirist, on the other hand, concentrates on recognizing different aspects of this contrast between the apparent and the real, and evolves an artistic version (sometimes realistic, sometimes symbolic) of the dualism that he has observed. Because of his temperament, the satirist chooses to adjust to life by emphasizing this dualism and dallying with it, instead of minimizing it as most nonsatirists choose to do. An adjustment of this kind involves economy in psychic expenditure; people who use their energy for making a living and getting ahead can't afford to waste much of that energy on unprofitable and irrelevant speculations concerning the contradictions in man and in society. But the satirist can afford to use his energy for that purpose because he is making a career out of commenting on contradictions. For the satirist it is not a useless obsession to be observing incongruities and hypocrisies in society; it is a logical search for artistic material which is suitable for his particular kind of art.

E. B. White himself is an excellent example of dualism in the satirist. He sometimes sounds like a conservative moralist, sometimes like a sophisticated cosmopolitan, sometimes like an ingenuous nature lover. In his work sentiment is usually restrained but often present, and sentiment and sophistication are not usually regarded as compatible in Anglo-American culture. And White, like Thurber, writes charming books for children. A delightful example of the attempt to live in two worlds simultaneously is Thurber's *The Secret Life of Walter Mitty*. In his stories and cartoons Thurber shows society as a perpetual war, sometimes between men and women, sometimes between institutions. Thurber also handles the eccentric and the insane with a great deal of sympathy, implying that abnormality is not an unreasonable way of adjusting to modern civilization. It is not surprising, then, as Friedrich points out, that Thurber fills the gap between the extremes of total war and madness with a "never-never land, a land of children, poets and harmless cranks, where Thurber's heroes find as much safety and peace as can be found." And even sophisticated Noel Coward turns out sentimental and chauvinistic work on occasion.

Cazamian observes that "Duality of thought is the master condition of humor." It is also the master condition of the humorist. Rosenberry believes that Herman Melville "was in uneasy possession" of this secret. Edgar Johnson suggests that in both Aldous Huxley and Sinclair Lewis the failure to solve an "inward division" resulted in a confusion of motives which hurt the work of both men. "Intellectually," Sinclair Lewis admitted, "I know that America is no better than any other country; emotionally I know that she is better than every other country." In Don Marquis, Norris

Yates has shown, the revolt against his home town and the affection for it are exhibited throughout his work. Ring Lardner posed as a "low-brow" and specialized in illiterate characters; but he had been brought up in a well-to-do family which liked literature and music and provided him with a tutor and a dancing master. Steve Allen says that Phil Silvers is a greater contrast to his brash stage personality than any other comedian — a withdrawn, sad individual.

Thompson finds a remarkable likeness between Ibsen and Euripides. "It is so in no feature more than . . . their division of soul or spiritual irony." Because Euripides was "a soul divided against itself," irony was for him a device and also "the expression of his view of the universe." As for Ibsen, "The idealist in Ibsen continued to strive with the satirist." The fruitless search was for a religion "that could satisfy modern man both emotionally and intellectually." As Thompson sees it, the "two antagonistic persons . . . in his soul" were the domestic man and the egotist.

Chevalier suggests that in Anatole France, as in most exceptionally endowed individuals, "the emotions of the mind tend to grow disproportionately." France's intellectual development, says Chevalier, was remarkable, "but his emotions were tender and clung fondly to visions and dreams that were lovely; they wanted beauty; his mind wanted knowledge. . . . They wanted to believe; his mind did not. His emotions were credulous; his mind was skeptical."

Edmund Wilson concludes that Charles Dickens was a painfully divided personality: one part of him wanted to be a Victorian gentleman, the other felt that he was an outcast from society and expressed his guilt, among other ways, by an obsessive interest in criminals and crime. There is also in Dickens the dualism of the writer about Victorian domestic morality who himself is keeping a mistress in Victorian society.

In Mark Twain the popular humorist is counterbalanced by the bitter and moody pessimist. There is fun and playfulness in much of Twain's work, certainly in his popular work; but the undercurrent of pessimism in *Huckleberry Finn* and in *The Mysterious Stranger* is clear evidence of the divided personality of Sam Clemens. DeLancey Ferguson says, "Behind his fierce intensity, his wild pleasure in shocking people with ribaldries and profanities, Clemens' central and final personality Howells discerned as something exquisite." Ferguson also suggests that the crude character "Brown" (who appeared in Twain's writing from 1865 until the end of the *Innocents Abroad* trip) served for Twain the same purpose as young John in Holmes' *Autocrat of the Breakfast Table* and Sancho Panza in *Don Quixote*. "The more vulgar utterances about smells, sea sickness and insects . . . all attributed to Brown instead of being spoken by Mark himself. Brown became a projection and dramatization of the coarser side of Mark's nature." Another writer, quite unlike Twain, who used different aspects of his own personality as characters in fiction was Jean Giradoux. In story after story, Giradoux created individual spokesmen out of the contrasting elements in his own temperament.

Charles Dodgson's headmaster observed that the boy insisted on absolute accuracy in solving mathematical problems but playfully distorted the language. An early biographer spoke of this "irreconcilable dualism" of Lewis Carroll, the "incongruous blend of extravagant frolic with self-conscious puritan repression." As he grew older, Dodgson insisted more and more on the separate identities of himself and Lewis Carroll, returning to the dead-letter office letters addressed to Carroll at Oxford, and marking them "Not known."

Kronenberger notes that although Mencken has been exacting about accuracy in language, he has been far less concerned with the correctness of his facts about society. Similarly, Swift was meticulous about avoiding obscene language in the spoken word, and used it flagrantly in his writing. And Ennis concludes that "the most important of Thackeray's 'ambivalences' . . . is the opposition within him of cynicism and sentimentality."

Dualism is not limited to Western writers. The most militant, brutal, and unfair satire in modern Ceylon was written by a man who considered himself a gentle follower of Gurdjieff's mysticism. And Professor Blyth finds in Sei-Shonagon, the woman who wrote Japan's classic *Pillow-Book,* such contradictory characteristics as "piety and irreligiousness, warm-and-cold heartedness, irritability and

philosophicality, self-criticism and self-compla-
cency." Juppensha Ikku, the author of "the funniest book in the Japanese language," was a reserved and stern person "but his book is lively and
Rabelaisian."

There is a good deal of evidence to support
Cazamian's belief that "without the divided mind
there is no humor." Speaking of Heine, Ernest
Dowden discusses the problem of being "born with
diverse souls." The result is "that life is to be no
steady progress, directed by some guiding light,
but a wavering advance through a countless series
of attractions and repulsions, and of repulsions
transformed into attractiveness." Heinrich Heine
was a sentimentalist and a skeptic, light-hearted
and morbid, a romantic and a cynic.

The fact that opposites attract has been observed
by Greek philosophers, Manichean priests, and
modern psychoanalysts. "Only deeper investigation," says Dr. Greenacre, "shows the intrinsic
likeness which exists in all opposites."

Inconsistency

Satirists, like most men, are sometimes inconsistent. In everyday life there is often conflict between an individual's desire and society's law or
custom. In everyday life men first react, emotionally and spontaneously, to different stimuli — then
try to find logical reasons to justify those reactions.
Because civilized society imposes a constant restraint on certain physical desires and violent

emotions, most men live under a pressure which produces discord within them. This discord is least likely to be apparent in two extreme types: the saintly person who represses forbidden impulses, and the hypocritical person who conceals his enjoyment of those impulses. This discord is apparent in the lives of most men, and an accurate recording of a full day's activities and thoughts would show a number of inconsistencies and contradictions. Men fail to practice what they preach because emotions as well as reason motivate many of their actions, because men are subjected to social pressures of changing intensity, and because a man's loyalties sometimes come into conflict with one another.

One reason why the satirist appears to be even more inconsistent than most people is the fact that he is likely to be continuously making fun of things. When one ridicules everything, he finds that some of the things he is ridiculing are directly opposed to one another, such as capitalism and communism, and his criticism seems to be inconsistent. The satirist has no trouble finding in both capitalism and communism material for criticism; neither institution is perfect. And whether he writes some of his satire in order to comply with the artificial pose a satirist is expected to maintain or writes most of his satire to satisfy his spontaneous adjustment to society, every satirist keeps observing incongruities and contradictions in individuals and institutions.

Bernard Shaw and Sinclair Lewis offer a different explanation for the apparent inconsistency of the satirist. The satirist, they insist, is actually a realist, who gives society an unexpectedly honest picture of society's contradictions. It is the world that is inconsistent, not the satirist. That world may appear consistent through the rose-colored glasses of the sentimentalist, or the dark glasses of the unobservant, or the distorted goggles of the fanatic, but it seems clearly inconsistent to the satirist with his 20/20 vision.

Still another analysis of the satirist's contradictory character comes from Haakon Chevalier in *Anatole France: The Ironic Temper*. Chevalier sees "the lack of integration between mind and emotion" as the central clue to an ironist's character. "It explains the many contradictions, the willful and conscious oppositions of character. . . . He emphatically asserts the supreme claims of the emotions. He is a penetrating . . . critic in quest of truth and fact; yet he clings to fantasy and fiction. His skepticism is so constant as to be a reflex; yet he wants, he needs to believe." Chevalier goes on to develop the idea that men of action, and nonspectators in general, have to seek in the world "some principle of organization . . . a certain minimum of order and harmony. The ironist is not subject to this compulsion . . . it is not necessary for him to evaluate the world according to a single code or system. . . . The ironist accepts the chaos. He has no preconceived hierarchy of values to guide him in selection and rejection. All things are of equal value."

Anatole France confessed, "It is in human nature to think wisely and to act in an absurd fashion." Renan once remarked that men ought to change their opinions from time to time, to increase their chances of being right at least once. France was sympathetic to this point of view, saying that Renan "occasionally contradicted himself: let this not weigh too heavily against him. It is the right of men who like him are capable of examining questions from different points of view." France certainly shared this attitude, having himself said, "One must suffer each one of us to possess at the same time two or three philosophies."

Because W. H. Auden's formal expressions of philosophic belief have changed several times, Randall Jarrell accuses him of rationalizing. But Professor Spears defends Auden, on the ground that the formula of consistency could be applied critically to everyone "from Augustine to Cardinal Newman." This point of view is supported by Dr. Otto Rank: "The individual, it seems, cannot permanently endure one sort of condition — even if it be happiness — because he immediately loses a part of the full humanity which is needed for his real personality." Frances Russell suggests that the romantic satirist needs certain more or less inconsistent traits: inventive wit of romance, plus the shrewd logic of satire; a degree of exaggeration, without overstraining our credulity; the need to concentrate highlights as life does not yet preserve dullness and vapid inanity to simulate reality.

According to Rosenberry, in Herman Melville

"is the suggestion that the true marriage of bright and dark, of the comic and the tragic views, is brought about not by chance but by a continuous, creative act of will. Indeed, the lesson for the artist is that it *is* a marriage, not a manic-depressive alternation of warring personalities."

Trying to account for the contradictions of Alexander Pope, Dyson said, "The easy good breeding of the world in which he lived did not make for deeply held convictions." Even Dr. Pannenborg's "statistics" indicate that the satirist is more contradictory than other people. Whereas the figure he postulates for the average man's "agreement of thought and deed" is 64 per cent, for the satirist it is only 7 per cent. As for "disagreement of thought and deed," the figures are 13 per cent for the average, 50 per cent for satirists.

The popular view is that the satirist is an unstable personality; unstable personalities are likely to be inconsistent; and inconsistency results in contradiction. But some satirists, we have seen, reverse the argument and insist that it is society itself which is unstable, inconsistent, and contradictory, and that the satirist, both in his personal adjustment and in the content of his work, is merely reflecting a schizoid and artificial society. A conclusion based on this "everybody is out of step except me" reasoning has never proved very popular. But the satirist feels that to a large extent it is true nevertheless.

The satirist has to be keenly aware of and close to the problems of his day; at the same time, he has to be detached enough to retain a more accurate perspective than most contemporary judgments are likely to express. He has to be sensitive enough to observe the weaknesses of men and institutions; at the same time, he has to be insensitive enough to disregard (for purposes of satiric representation) whatever extenuating qualities may be present. For, if he analyzes completely, he may have to sympathize with his victim. Tout comprendre est tout pardonner. But the satirist can't afford objectivity to this extent; a genuinely fair satirist is likely to be a poor satirist.

Nonsatirists are also guilty of inconsistency and contradiction. The epitaph which Catherine the Great composed for herself read: "She forgave easily and hated no one. Tolerant, undemanding, of a gay disposition, she had a republican spirit and a kind heart. She made good friends." Francis Bacon had written, "Judges ought to be more learned than witty. . . . Above all things, integrity is their portion and proper virtue." Later, having been, as a judge, found guilty, Bacon addressed the court with these words: "I do plainly and ingenuously confess that I am guilty of corruption, and do renounce all defense. I beseech your lordships to be merciful to a broken reed."

Ben Franklin once said, "Strange! that a man who has enough wit to write a satire should have folly enough to publish it." But Franklin himself indulged in the folly by publishing a number of

first-rate satires. Ambrose Bierce attacked socialism and at the same time defended the worker's
right to work; Mark Twain attacked trusts and
newspaper publishers who attacked the trusts;
Byron attacked both friends and foes in his
"English Bards and Scotch Reviewers." Juvenal
admired liberty but was furious because the freed-
men of Rome had been given more freedom.
E. B. White, the most prominent writer on that
most sophisticated magazine, *The New Yorker*,
lives in the country. In his numerous novels, Booth
Tarkington "raced back and forth between sheer
escapism and frank realism," says Untermeyer.
"Tarkington remained a middle-Westerner, alter-
nately sentimental and cynical, accurate, forth-
right, and conservatively idealistic." Having
analyzed Anatole France's political beliefs, DeGoff
concludes: "He has sufficiently contradicted himself to leave us in uncertainty as to his real political
opinion." Groucho Marx read every section of the
newspaper except the comics; vacillated between a
"you-can't-take-it-with-you" philosophy and miserliness; and, after purchasing numerous annuities as
the result of his "pathological concern about the
future," was earning more money near the end of
his career than he ever had before.

If Bergson were correct in his theory that
sentimentality and wit are incompatible, it would
be difficult to account for the mixture of sentiment and wit in Heine, Byron, Burns, Sinclair
Lewis, and Dickens. A writer of fairy tales, Heine
was also a genuine realist. And although Heine's

affairs with women were notorious, he boasted on his deathbed that he had never seduced a virgin or another man's wife.

Heywood Broun had been a Socialist and an agnostic, and died a Roman Catholic. "Renan," says Chevalier, "never lost his native religious fervor and his love of religion, of things ecclesiastic, though he lost his faith." In a period of great industrial expansion, Lewis Carroll invented dozens of gadgets but failed to commercialize on any of them. And, as Fadiman points out, Carroll objected to the "unpleasant" characters in *Wuthering Heights,* yet created the kitchen scene in *Alice in Wonderland,* the duchess, the red queen and the white.

Having made nothing but comedies up to that time, Charlie Chaplin in 1923 produced and directed a tragedy, "A Woman of Paris"; it received critical acclaim but was not financially successful. W. S. Gilbert disliked music and hated grand opera; he said that all he knew was two tunes — one was "God Save the King" and the other wasn't. The Italian satirist Guareschi, creator of Don Camillo, having spent years attacking Communism, was sent to prison for attacking a conservative premier. George Ade, having written a successful play which satirized the mercenary elements of college football, donated a large sum of money to help build the Ross-Ade football stadium. John Dryden, who had himself shifted political and religious affiliations in suspiciously coincidental relationship to changes in Restoration England, criticized Horace for being change-able: "He . . . is sometimes an Epicurean, some-times a Stoic, sometimes an Eclectic, as his present humor leads him."

Many satirists reveal inconsistencies in their philosophic positions. Sinclair Lewis and Samuel Johnson and Jonathan Swift express a distrust of reason, and a simultaneous distrust of intuition. Norris Yates points out the conflict in Don Mar-quis between his belief in naturalism and social Darwinism on the one hand, and his interest in mysticism, intuition, reincarnation, and social re-form on the other. And Melville's definition of a comic situation was: "Half melancholy, half far-cical — like all the rest of the world."

The major contradictions of Thackeray have been summarized by Professor Ennis: "He waged war on cant and false emotion, yet he could be as sentimental as a schoolgirl. He was famous for waging war against snobbery, yet was not free of the imputation of snobbery. . . . Secretly in love with the lax moral code of the eighteenth century man of fashion, he was also a staunch defender of Victorian morality. . . . He had enormous com-passion for the suffering, yet in him was a savage streak."

Professor A. R. Thompson lists the contra-dictions he finds in Ibsen: "shy, yet assertive . . . timid and even . . . cowardly, yet as a dramatist undaunted by the sharpest criticism; thin-skinned yet satirical; idealistic and poetic yet keenly observant . . . self-critical yet vain; stiff and reclusive towards society, yet hungry for love and affection; without a faith, yet deeply religious."

Analyzing George Orwell, Voorhees compiles a catalogue of contradictions: "An intellectual, he continually damned intellectuals; he hated politics, but was a first rate political writer; he was contemptuous of Socialism yet felt that it was the only way to save England; he deplored violence, but was almost mortally wounded while fighting for the Loyalists in the Spanish Civil War; after graduating from Eton, he worked as a dishwasher; after serving in the Indian Imperial Police, he lived as a tramp; having written unsuccessful novels and essays for thirteen years, he wrote two best sellers within three years; and when he became rich and famous he retired to a harsh and uncomfortable Scotch highland and soon died."

Sinclair Lewis attacked the American middle class and the critics of the American middle class. He rejected the Pulitzer Prize but accepted the Nobel Prize; he satirized honorary degrees in *Ann Vickers,* then accepted an LL.D. from Yale; he ridiculed the National Academy of Arts and Letters, and quietly became a member when invited to join. In 1929, having covered a North Carolina mill strike, Lewis published "Cheap and Contented Labor," an angry, factual defense of the workers and attack on the owners; but in *Prodigal Parents,* ten years later, Lewis denied in fiction every point that he had made on behalf of labor in the earlier pamphlet. For many readers Lewis' reputation is based on his criticism of business in *Babbitt*, but Lewis had a genuine interest in and a romantic respect for business all his life. To complete the Lewis contradictions, there is wide disagreement among critics as to whether he is a realist or satirist, morbid or idealistic, a creator of characters or a producer of types, a dated anachronism or an up-to-date commentator.

Having had incestuous relations with his half-sister, and having publicly expressed his indifference to propriety, Byron insisted on putting the natural daughter of himself and Claire Clairmont in a convent. He rejected Claire's protests, never examined the convent, and said that he wished the child to be brought up a Catholic. The girl died a year later.

It is not really fair to say, as Armens does in his study of John Gay: "A strange irony is that Gay, who seems to know a phantom when he sees others pursuing it, himself pursued various ones such as money the greater part of his own life." In this particular irony, Gay has a great deal of company. And although Gay wrote the "Shepherd's Week" with the intention of ridiculing the manners and speech of rustics, he unintentionally revealed in the parody his own affection for the spontaneity and innocence of rural life. His characters are absurd, as he intended them to be, but they are also appealing and refreshing, as he had apparently not at all intended.

Like Sinclair Lewis and Ambrose Bierce, H. L. Mencken despised Christianity and, like them, admired Christ. The vehemence of his attack on religion led Edmund Wilson to suspect that Mencken protested too much; he called Mencken a "thorough Puritan." Mencken was well liked by people who knew him, his colleagues as well as his subordinates. He called himself a Nietzschean, his writing was caustic and brutal and cynical, but in his actions and personal relationships with people he was often generous, helpful, and charitable. A contradiction in Mencken's Nietzschean philosophy is his condoning the "righteous exploitation" of the weak by the strong, but attacking Judge Gary and Theodore Roosevelt for "exploiting." If, as Mencken says, no act is immoral but only profitable or unprofitable, he had no reason to condemn those who successfully practiced his precepts. One explanation for Mencken's inconsistency is the fact that he is not interested in the *solutions* of problems; he is only interested in *problems*. He indiscriminately criticizes some people for not trying at all, some for not trying hard enough, and some for trying too hard. Because he was so individualistic and impulsive, Mencken could not be consistently Nietzschean or humanitarian. His was a frank selfishness, and he admittedly defended for others those liberties which he himself did not want to lose.

More evidence of Mencken's inconsistency appears in the following quotation from his Preface to *Happy Days*. Mencken had changed the word "bourgeoisie" to "booboisie" in his own writings of the 1920's, yet this is what he wrote in 1940: "I was a larva of the comfortable and complacent bourgeoisie. . . . To belong to that great order of mankind is vaguely discreditable today, but I still maintain my dues paying membership in it, and continue to believe that it was and is authentically human."

Alexander Pope is loaded with inconsistencies, one of the most amusing appearing in the Preface to his first book of poems. The man who would one day write *The Dunciad,* a devastating and vituperative criticism of poets, said in the preface to his own poems: "I think a good deal may be said to extenuate the fault of bad poets. . . . And if he happens to write ill (which is certainly no sin in itself) he is immediately an object of ridicule. I wish we had the humanity to reflect that even the worst authors might endeavor to please us." As things turned out, no writer in English showed less humanity to poets he regarded as "bad." Pope preached morality and honesty and decency, and was himself called the most untrustworthy man of his century.

G. K. Chesterton paid tribute to Sydney Smith's inconsistency in defending Catholics: "In one aspect it is all the more to the credit of Sydney Smith that he fought so hard for the rights of a religion that he did not in the least understand." And Hesketh Pearson says of Smith: "We find him attacking Catholics, Dissenters, Whigs, Tories, the Evangelical and Puseyites of his own Church — every section of the community, in fact, which held an extreme view of anything — and then defending all of them against their opponents."

Smith's "Noodle's Oration" satirized both the Whigs and the Tories, and each party quoted it against the other.

William Empson accounts for the apparent contradiction of a clergyman's writing the *Tale of a Tub* and other attacks on Christianity by suggesting that Jonathan Swift's literary power made his satire too strong. Swift was sincerely devoted to the Anglican Church and did not intend to undermine it; but his comments on the contradictions and shortcomings of religion in general were so cogent that the Church itself suffered. The Dean of St. Patrick put baby-talk in the *Journal to Stella,* wrote the savage *Modest Proposal* and many lighthearted bagatelles, left his money to a mental hospital and then died insane. The greatest English satirist reveals the same kinds of contradictions that we find in second-rate writers. Swift generously helped casual acquaintances, but preferred not to see his sister; he was pure in speech and filthy in verse. And, as Dr. Greenacre points out, he suppressed his sexuality but not his appetite for food, drink, and society.

In spite of his skill in making paradoxes, Bernard Shaw is probably more consistent in his philosophy (or perhaps more skillful in making his philosophy seem consistent) than most satirists have been. If one accepts Shaw's major premises, then his conclusions follow logically from those premises. Shaw's search was for a way to make men achieve Utopia on Earth; in seeking that Utopia he sometimes took devious paths, but they all led in the same direction, and many of his ideas, once regarded as shocking and paradoxical, are now commonplace. Krutch suggests that Shaw's inconsistency stems from his attempt to reconcile a materialistic determinism with a mystical creed; and Kronenberger thinks that Shaw's contradictions are not nearly so important as his showmanship: "rather to exhilarate than to enlighten the audience." Kronenberger adds to the list of Shaw's contradictions: Shaw was a poseur and a puritan; he was simultaneously a bourgeois and an antibourgeois writer, working for Hearst and for posterity; his didacticism is entertaining and his pranks are purposeful; he supports socialism and is tempted by fascists.

Of the numerous contradictions in Mark Twain, the mixture of sentiment and sadism is regarded by psychoanalysts as not paradoxical but typical. Although Twain proclaimed that the human race was not worth bothering with, he often took part in public or social action the results of which were intended to help the human race. "What Twain thought . . . depended . . . rather upon h i s momentary mood than upon any deep and subtle conviction. . . . Consistency was never Mark's strong point," wrote Ferguson. Alexander Jones suggests that Twain managed to be "simultaneously Victorian and Elizabethan," by repressing his desire to write about "sexual" matters but circulating among friends unpublished "pornography." Jones' analysis of Twain, if it is correct, is an explanation of contradictions in other satirists as well: "in an individual like Twain the cycle is complete: masochistic self-abasement gives way to sadistic behavior, which in turn produces sadistic guilt."

There is no lack of contradictions in Voltaire. At the time he was waging his war against the Church, he began building a church on his Ferney estate. A scathing critic of hypocritical flattery, Voltaire, in his letters and in his relations with the wealthy and aristocratic, used nauseating flattery. Sometimes guilty of petty dishonesty in his personal relationships, he fought for abstract justice with a passion, a sincerity, and an expenditure of money that were almost pathological. On his death bed, he asked for Catholic absolution and burial. He was one of the causes of the French Revolution, but he himself believed in monarchy and distrusted mob action. Lytton Strachey called him a "revolutionary in intellect . . . and a high Tory in taste."

In Euripides critics have observed contradictions similar to those we found in Sinclair Lewis. Each has been called a satirist and a realist, moral and immoral, reverent and skeptical, a cynic and an idealist, a creator of great characters and a creator of types. Each was an innovator and a conservative, a sentimentalist and a rationalist. Each was inconsistent. A. R. Thompson offers a blunt explanation of the apparent contradiction in Euripides' work: "But suppose the ambiguities and incoherences are intentional? That they are part, at least, of what Euripides wanted to say? . . . Perhaps we are justified in assuming that such moral contradictions existed first in his mind, and that he meant to express them."

Some of the contradictions in Anatole France are similar to those in Lewis and Euripides. France was a poet and a realistic novelist, a cynic and a reformer, an anticleric and a mystic dreamer, a dilettante and a man who spent twenty years working on the life of Joan of Arc. Like Lewis, who had ridiculed the National Academy of Art and then joined it, Anatole France had ridiculed the French Academy and then became a member. He attended few meetings and did not take the Academy seriously, but the title pages of his books bore the phrase "Member of the French Academy"; Lewis' publisher advertised Lewis as the man who had refused the Pulitzer Prize. Like Lewis, old man France was passé before he died. And critics disagreed not only in evaluating his stature but in analyzing the elements of his work. France and Euripides both reacted to the great wars of their generations at first with patriotic fervor, then with disillusioned cynicism.

Commenting on the irony of France's life, Chevalier observes that in his habits and desire for quiet and peace, France was essentially a middle-class nonentity; but destiny, a strong-willed woman, and an ambitious literary group made him a world figure and socially prominent. France's indolence and irresponsibility made it possible for him to live by an "as-if" philosophy, and to regard the world with a detachment that was impossible for most men. On definite issues France took sides (the Dreyfus affair, the separation of Church and State), "but in all cases . . . taking sides was only a momentary attitude of his mobile mind. It engaged him to no sense of responsibility." France had the same impulsive and emotional and transient reactions that we have seen in Sinclair Lewis and H. L. Mencken and Sydney Smith, and that a number of critics observed in other satirists whom they analyzed.

Ikkyu Zenji, one of the best known Japanese humorists, exhibits many of the contradictions that we find in Western satirists. Although he was the son of an Emperor, he lived through most of the fifteenth century as an impoverished Zen Buddhist priest. Wielding a good deal of political power, he rarely accepted high office himself. And although he is considered, in Professor Blyth's words, *"the funny man of Japan,"* much of his writing is gloomy, pessimistic, and preoccupied with the tragedy of life.

Since a satirist's contradictions are impulsive emotional reactions at different times, rather than carefully reasoned philosophical conclusions, it is not safe to assume that because the satirist criticizes one thing he approves of its opposite. He is just as likely to criticize that opposite position at another time, again responding to an impulse of the moment. Nor is it safe to assume that the satirist dislikes the things he is criticizing. France said of Rabelais, "It is one of the characteristics of that great mocker to cherish what he makes fun of." France himself cherished many of the things that he made fun of. John P. Marquand cherishes the New England tradition, Sinclair Lewis liked the middle class that he ridiculed, and George Orwell believed in the socialism whose excesses he so devastatingly satirized in his two most popular books.

The satirist tends to criticize all the incongruities he sees, even when such criticism weakens the consistency of his own position. If people and institutions were all "good," or all "bad," he would be more consistent. But the dualism of man's nature, the need for pretense in civilized society, and the relativity of good and evil make consistency difficult for fallible human beings. And the satirist has never been accused of infallibility. The propensity for making fun of vulnerable objects spurs him into ridiculing everything that is vulnerable, including his own position. Unlike an intellectual conclusion which has been attained through logic, the satiric impulse is a spontaneous one. It is not limited by dialectical rules. And it often leads to contradictions and inconsistencies.

Detachment

Some critics believe that detachment is an indispensable quality for the satirist, that he must be objective to achieve the satiric effect. (We will see later that other critics maintain the opposite theory: the satirist must be sympathetic.) Henri Bergson rejects sympathy; he insists that laughter is dependent entirely on the intellect, and requires "an anaesthesia of the heart"; any appeal to emotions or to sympathy is harmful to the creation of laughter.

Detachment is not, of course, limited to the satirist. The expert in every profession has a detachment which permits him to recognize errors made by inexperienced workers. There is a detachment which age gives, permitting ordinary old people to forecast accurately, on the basis of years of previous observation of similar phenomena, the likely results of certain marriages and arguments and relationships and law-suits. There is a detachment which permits the mortally ill to see the actions of other human beings from a fresh perspective. But always there is the implication that to achieve complete detachment the observer should not be personally involved in the action he is observing, that he be an "outsider." Whether it is necessary for the satirist to be always the "outsider," and whether satirists have as a result of their temperament become outsiders, is the problem to be considered here.

If the artistic process consists not of a journalistic recording of experience but of imposing a pattern on the disorganized material of life, then detachment is a necessary quality for the artist. And for he satirist, who is primarily a social critic, art requires not only detachment from his own experience but detached observation of the experience of others. Yet the danger of detachment is recognized by Toynbee: "It is the disciples of

Gautama that have had the courage to pursue detachment all the way to its logical goal of self-annihilation. As an intellectual achievement this is imposing; as a moral achievement it is overwhelming; but it has a disconcerting moral corollary; for perfect detachment casts out pity, and therefore also love, as inexorably as it purges away all the evil passions."

The detachment that Toynbee is analyzing here is that of the Buddhist. Another Oriental philosophy, Taoism, may have a more light-hearted effect. "Being resigned to nature," Geoge Kao suggests, "the Taoist can see man in his limitation; being the perennial outsider, he can afford to relax and laugh." Speaking of the Western ironist, David Worcester says, "Men and women, in his view, tend to become puppets, jerked about by their passions." And A. R. Thompson feels that the comic dramatist, more than any other writer, has to treat life objectively and record external manifestations rather than internal speculations. "The supreme comedists," says Thompson, "Aristophanes, Shakespeare, Molière — were notably objective."

The detachment of the ironist means that he is describing objects and people without any concern for their possible relation to himself as an individual. Of Maurice Brilliant's remark about Anatole France, "It is fine to play the detached . . . while detaching oneself from nothing (except from what annoys one)," Chevalier says: "That is precisely the position — peculiar but possible — of the ironist. He knows the world's vanity, yet he does not abandon the world."

Detachment, or the pose of detachment, exposes the satirist to the charge of callous indifference. Chekhov defended himself against that charge in a letter to a critic: "You abuse me for objectivity, calling it indifference to good and evil, lack of ideals, and so on. You would have me, when I describe horse-stealers, say 'Stealing horses is an evil.' But that has been known for ages." The satirist uses objectivity as a technique, a method of contrasting unpleasant or shocking material with calm, restrained, dispassionate expression. It does not prove that he does not care about the events he is describing; it simply means that he has chosen a particular artistic form to describe those events. Unless one accepts the notion that the man who cries loudest is necessarily the one who suffers most deeply, there is no real reason to assume that the quiet writer, the detached commentator, is unmoved by the events that he is describing or indifferent to them.

It is never fair to ascribe to an author the remarks of his characters, but when the same character appears in a number of stories and consistently expresses attitudes similar to those of the author, there is some justification for thinking that his statements reflect the author's opinions. The character Ashenden, like Maugham, did secret-service work for the English government during World War I. In a short story called "The Trader," Maugham writes, "Ashenden admired goodness, but was not outraged by wickedness. People sometimes thought him heartless because he was more interested in others than attached to them, and even in the few to whom he was attached his eyes saw with equal clearness the merits and the defects." Such clearness Maugham the ironist also possessed.

Voorhees recognizes a similar detachment in George Orwell, about whom he says, "When he writes about himself, there is an objectivity like that in the writings of doctors who, for the sake of science, have reported their own symptoms in the impersonal terms of the medical dictionary." In his autobiography, C. S. Lewis shortens his accounts of World War I because, he says, the experiences he had undergone seemed to him at the time of writing "as though they happened to somebody else." And Edgar Johnson notes "the insuperable detachment of a Martian observer" in the writing of Thorstein Veblen; the aloofness of Wycherley; and the attitude of Lucian which he describes as "not so much supercilious as sympathetic, an understanding without hate, an amusement without malice."

Mudrick suggests that Jane Austen invariably used one of two attitudes towards life and literature: irony and social convention. "Distance — from her subject and from her reader — was Jane Austen's first condition for writing. . . . To events, literary or actual, she allowed herself no public response except the socially conventional or the ironic; for neither of these endangered her reserve." Like Anatole France, who once described people as "unreal toys," Jane Austen saw the world in terms of "men and women, it appears,

[who] are not persons about whom one feels, but figures in a comedy, whose audience may laugh at every exhibited incongruity of social behavior without becoming involved or responsible." The men and women Mudrick is talking about here are not characters in novels, but the actual human beings whom Jane Austen described in letters to her sister.

Detachment can be carried to extremes, and Evelyn Waugh is quite willing to oblige. In her analysis of Waugh's *The Loved One,* Joan Griffiths says, "On the last page of that novel he is to know 'that he was singularly privileged.' . . . His vision is no longer that of the suffering participant. . . . He has gained his apotheosis; he is dehumanized. And to us this seems the crux of all Waugh's work." And George Mikes concludes that "Waugh's point of observation is not a pedestal but an elevated stool."

That Mark Twain regarded detachment as a necessary quality for writing satire is indicated in this excerpt from a letter: "I wish I could give you those sharp satires on European life which you mention, but of course a man can't write successful satire except he be in a calm, judicial good humor, whereas I *hate* travel, I *hate* hotels, I *hate* the opera, and I *hate* the old masters. In truth, I don't ever seem to be in a good enough humor with anything to satirize." It is the persistence of this attitude in Mark Twain that has led some critics to decide that he is not really a satirist. If detachment were regarded as an indispensable quality for satire, Mark Twain might not qualify. But it is not an indispensable quality.

Bernard Shaw said that although his parents had never mistreated him they had shown so little affection for him that he learned early in life to be self-sufficient and immune to emotion, or as immune to emotion as a human being can reasonably become. One biographer suggests that, having left Ireland when he was twenty, Shaw remained "a man without a country," and could easily regard all of western civilization with critical disapproval; since he was detached emotionally, he could be amused by it.

Like Shaw, Anatole France attained an extraordinary degree of detachment which permitted him to observe society with amused objectivity. Madame de Caillavet once said to France, "Friends? You have no friends. You have only habits." Shanks agrees. "Compared to ideas," he says, "people had for this skeptic only an external reality. . . . All his life he found more amusement in ideas." France himself tried to differentiate between two ways of looking at life: "I have never been a real observer, for the observer must have a system to guide him, and I have no system at all. The observer directs his vision; the spectator lets himself be led by his eyes."

Detachment and the pretense of detachment provide the satirist with an inexhaustible source of suitable material. From a Martian's perspective, many American activities may seem absurd. To a detached observer, the excitement of millions of adults over the World Series, television programs, horse races, psychological obsolescence, and movie-actresses' weddings may seem ludicrous. So may the indifference of the same millions to armament races, crowded schools, hypocrisy, and mental illness.

Genuine detachment is an "abnormal" quality. Man wants to believe what is pleasant rather than what is painfully true; most of his institutions are dedicated to the perpetration of that illusion. To be detached about society is to be truthful about society in a manner permitted only saints and clowns. The detachment of the satirist is likely to be amoral; it leads to apparent contradictions; and it is a helpful but, as we will see in the next section, not an indispensable quality for the satirist.

Sympathy

The New Yorker's device of listing contra-dictory items under a "What Paper Do You Read?" heading would be an appropriate way of introducing the critics who reject the detachment theory. Far from agreeing that the satirist needs detachment, Gilbert Cannan insists that the satirist "must love his material before he can begin to work on it." He is convinced that "Satire . . . cannot thrive where no love is. Its energy is the energy of love repressed and denied its sustenance, and it cries havoc upon all love's enemies." Humbert Wolfe is another strong advocate of the "sympathy" theory: "The satirist must have love in his heart for all that is threatened by the objects of his satire."

Max Beerbohm has a character in *Seven Men* say, "One can't really understand what one doesn't love, and one can't make good fun without real understanding." And Bernard Shaw gives the bishop in *Getting Married* the following lines: "Since we are both funny people, let us not forget that humor is a divine attribute." The word "divine" is not characteristically Shavian, but Shaw was serious about the need for empathy in humor. In an early review, he wrote, "Unless comedy touches me as well as amuses me, it leaves me with a sense of having wasted my evening. I go to the theatre to be moved to laughter, not to be tickled or bustled into it."

E. B. White also feels that sympathy for one's characters is a necessary quality for the humorist. He praises Finley Peter Dunne because he "had the sympathetic feeling for his character which is indispensable." White believes that "this same sympathy is discernible in Jewish humor — in the work of Gross, Kober, and Ross. It is sympathy, not contempt or derision, that makes their characters live." And although most critics call Lardner a caustic writer, White says, "Lardner's ballplayer was born because the author had a warm feeling for ballplayers, however boyish or goofy."

"In order to be a humorist," says Priestley, "you must have a needle eye for the incongruities, the pretensions, the inconsistencies, all the idiocies and antics of this life, but you must also have — strange and contradictory as it may seem — an unusual quickness and warmth of feeling, an instant affection for all that is lovable."

Sinclair Lewis wrote in 1928, "I am frequently credited with being the worst crab, next to Father Mencken and Father Nathan, in our beloved States. . . Actually, I like the Babbitts, the Doctor Pickerbaughs, the Will Kennicotts, and even the Elmer Gantrys rather better than I like anyone else on earth." John P. Marquand's ironic commentary on New England Brahmins is clearly tempered by his admiration for them. And sympathy for their characters is obvious in the work of Fielding, Sterne, Dickens, and Chaucer.

In the effort to avoid the obvious contradiction between the writer's need for detachment and his need for sympathy, some critics have tried to distinguish between wit and humor. John Erskine, a good satirist himself, unexpectedly expresses a preference for humor: "Humor is allied to sympathy, to a soulful feeling for the unfortunate and unhappy, to the animal pathos of life. . . . The true sense of humor keeps the mind too occupied and the heart too alert to laugh. For the same reason it is at its best when divorced from wit." Thomas Carlyle also distinguished between humor and satire: "True humor springs not more from the head than from the heart; it is not contempt, its essence is love; it issues not in laughter, but in still smiles, which lie far deeper." Carlyle announced that he would no longer write satire, for satire was an expression of devilish cruelty rather than the gentle magnanimity of soul which Carlyle apparently thought he possessed, and which his wife and friends must have been amazed to learn he venerated.

Thackeray is still another satirist who differentiated between humor and satire, as in his attack on Jonathan Swift: "The humorous writer professes to awaken and direct your love, your pity, your kindness — your scorn for untruth, pretension, imposture — your tenderness for the weak, the poor, the oppressed, the unhappy. . . . He takes upon himself to be the weekday preacher, so to speak."

This view of course directly contradicts Bergson's theory. "Laughter," Bergson insisted, "is above all a corrective, intended to humiliate. . . . By laughter, society avenges itself for the liberties taken with it. It would fail in its object if it bore the stamp of sympathy or kindness." It is difficult to find much evidence of love or sympathy in the satire of Juvenal, Pope, Swift, W. S. Gilbert, Bierce, and Saki. Strindberg was a misogynist, Aretino was cruel, both Samuel Butlers exhibited more venom than warmth, Grillparzer's biographer called him a brutal misanthrope, and Charles Churchill specialized in vitriolic contempt. Gogol himself mentioned "the aridity of his heart" and was described by one critic as "hard, insensitive, indifferent." And Dr. Pannenborg maintains that, although three out of four men are "compassionate," not a single satirist whom he studied is.

Franklin P. Adams felt that there are disadvantages to being humorous: "When he [H. S. Can-by] says, 'A sense of humor is worth gold to any writer,' I disagree with him vehemently. For the writers who have amassed the greatest gold have, it seems to me, no sense of humor; and I think also that if they had it, it would be a terrible thing for them, for it would paralyze them so that they would not write at all. For in writing, emotion is more to be treasured than any sense of humor, and the two are often in conflict."

The theory that the humorist must be sympathetic to his subject contradicts the theory that the humorist must be detached from his subject — unless we assume that it is "detachment of method" only, and not personal disinterestedness, that is involved.

Generosity

Now that the Freudians have explained that what people call generosity is really a subconscious attempt by the selfish to buy affection, and by the insecure to buy status, one hesitates to call generosity a virtue. Fortunately, Dr. Theodor Reik admits that psychoanalysis brings out not only hidden vices but also unsuspected virtues from the subconscious. With that encouragement, if may be safe to confess that the satirist's bark is usually worse than his bite. Many satirists have been generous men; and regardless of whether that generosity was due to frustrated sentimentality, or guilt feelings, or genuine munificence, on the whole they behave better than the men they criticize in their satires.

From his school days to the end of his life, Thackeray passed out gifts lavishly. He gave to children, to beggars, to needy artists. When he was editor of *The Cornhill Magazine* he sometimes attached his personal check to rejected manuscripts that were returned to destitute authors. During the financial panic of 1858 he became, as Ennis puts it, "a one-man alms bureau." But Ennis concludes: "Noble and admirable as such practices were, they can — nevertheless — be traced back psychologically to the schoolboy's need of winning his fellows' regard."

Sydney Smith contributed to impoverished clergymen's families. Oliver Goldsmith was poor and generous all of his life. In *Walden* Thoreau made a strong case against charity and philanthropy; but in his personal journal he recorded financial contributions to a number of poor families. Mark Twain's life-long generosity and his honesty, especially after bankruptcy, are well documented. Bernard Shaw never publicized the fact, but he supported several philanthropic projects; Thompson observes that "no matter how bitterly a former friend might revile him (as did Henry Arthur Jones), Shaw never returned evil for evil, but always retained his admirable magnanimity." Sinclair Lewis helped younger writers with his personal advice, with his influence among publishers, and with extravagantly laudatory reviews. In his Nobel Prize Address, Lewis paid tribute to Dreiser and other American writers who, he claimed, were more deserving of the honor than he was. John Gay had a reputation for practical benevolence, and the friends of John Arbuthnot were unanimous in describing him as a kind, tolerant, and generous man.

Persius was described as being "of a pleasing personality . . . the most gentle manners . . . pure and temperate in his life, and exemplary in his domestic relations." Having known H. L. Mencken for many years, Gerald W. Johnson wrote: "I have yet to encounter man, woman, or child who knew Henry Mencken and hated him. He was too expansive, too free of envy." Vondel was a generous and warm-hearted man. Of John Dryden William Congreve wrote: "Mr. Dryden . . . was of a nature exceedingly humane and compassionate; easily forgiving injuries, and capable of a prompt and sincere reconciliation with them who had offended him. . . . I have been told of strong and generous instances . . . by the persons themselves who received them, though his hereditary income was little more than a bare competency." And comedian Phil Silvers, well known in show business for his generosity, sends encouraging letters to young comedians.

In order that his friend Hodgson could get married, Byron gave him a gift of fifteen hundred pounds; twenty years later he gave Hunt five hundred pounds and nine cantos of *Don Juan;* asked to lend his prestige to the efforts for Greek independence, he subsidized a guard of soldiers; in a letter to Augusta Leigh, he wrote: "I have been obtaining the relief of about nine and twenty Turkish prisoners — men, women, and children — and I have sent them at my own expense home to their friends."

Examining Jonathan Swift's charitable activities, Professor Landa traces the record back to the account books of 1702: "his benefactions grew in proportion to his income." All of Swift's biographers agree that he was "a charitable person," and it is probably true that "Swift divided his income into three parts — one for living expenses, one to be disposed in present charities, one to be saved for posthumous charities."

Although, as Steevens wrote, "He studiously concealed the many acts of humanity he performed in private," Samuel Johnson's charity to the poor "was uniform and expensive. . . . He not only disposed liberally out of his own purse but . . . would beg from others, when he had proper objects in view." Boswell tells of returning to London and finding that the room previously assigned to him was "now appropriated to a charitable purpose; Mrs. Desmoulins, and I think her daughter, and Miss Carmichael, being all lodged in it. . . . He allowed her half a guinea a week. Let it be remembered that this was about a twelfth part of his pension." The Seraglio which Johnson accommodated under his roof made him, as Boswell remarked, uncomfortable by their constant bickering. Concerning these charity cases who lived with him, Johnson wrote in a letter to Mrs. Thrale: "Mrs. Williams hates everybody; Lovett hates Mrs. Desmoulins, and does not love Mrs. Williams; Mrs. Desmoulins hates them both; Tal (Miss Carmichael) loves none of them." Boswell also tells us that Johnson once found a poor woman lying in the street, took her home on his back, and nursed her back to health and away from her previous occupation as a prostitute. To avoid inconveniencing his servant, the Great Cham used to go out himself to buy oysters for his cat.

It is possible of course that by working off their aggressions on paper satirists find it easier to be pleasant in their relations with real people. Still, it is not really to their discredit that they often behave generously in their private lives.

Unfairness

The fact that satire often is, or appears to be, unfair seems to contradict the theory that satirists are detached and objective. The satirist offers a defense. He feels that the object of his criticism deserves to be criticized; to that extent the satirist is being fair. He does exaggerate the iniquity of his adversaries and does minimize the faults of his colleagues; but this he insists is only an unfairness of technique, an excess of vehemence in demonstrating the truth. Whether that truth is expressed softly in terms of understatement, or loudly in terms of exaggeration, is not especially important.

The satirist concedes, however, that when he says something essentially untrue, he is guilty of unfairness.

The truth that he is trying to show, the satirist assumes, justifies the unfair means that he uses to show it. In Brobdingnag Swift exaggerates, which is technically unfair, and in Lilliput he understates, which is technically unfair, but what he is saying about society is essentially true. And if it is true, he is being fair in the important thing. Furthermore, to be "fair" in the conventional sense is impossible for a satirist. A complete investigation of any human action, taking into account all of the elements that motivate it and justify it (from the point of view of those involved), would eventually lead to some measure of vindication for everybody. The satirist cannot afford to make that kind of tolerant, judicial examination of all possible mitigating circumstances. Once having decided what he is for and what he is against, in view of his aesthetic purpose, he tends to paint his adversaries black and his friends white. He has to distort. All of the basic techniques of satire — exaggeration, understatement, inversion of values, pretense, misrepresentation, vehemence, and indirection — are unfair. But these unfair techniques constitute the satiric method. Without unfairness there can be no satire.

When a satirist does try to be fair, his satire suffers and its significance diminishes. When the satirist tries to present fair or logical alternatives, he becomes platitudinous or fantastic. When he tries to show society realistically, he usually presents a dull picture of it. If satire were restricted to the accurate statement of ideas, its appeal would be as limited as is the appeal of formal philosophy. The satirist feels that it is no more unfair for other writers to make their material interesting by injecting melodrama, adventure, romance, or suspense, than it is for him to inject distortion.

Kronenberger says of Henry Fielding: "It is the 'serious' side of Fielding that is the weak side, the comic side that is truly expressive. . . . The earnestness does honor to the man, but it does damage to the novelist. For it remains creatively unabsorbed; it comes off a little preachy." Aristophanes was unfair to Euripides and Socrates, Voltaire was unfair to the Catholic church, Swift was unfair to Dissenters, Mencken was unfair to democracy, and Sinclair Lewis was unfair to many individual members of the professions which he satirized. The defense of these satirists, and of all other satirists, would be that the hypocrisy they expose should be exposed and the incongruity they reveal should be revealed.

The satirist is sometimes vehement in his unfairness, but it is not necessarily a personal hostility that motivates his vehemence. His technique requires controlled vehemence. The golfer need not hate the ball he drives, nor does the boxer have to hate the opponent he punches. Their techniques too require controlled vehemence.

Nor is the satirist's vehemence necessarily moral. He is more interested in inadequacy than achievement, injustice than justice, illusion than truth. Because man prefers to believe in the pleasant rather than the true, and because man's institutions help him in that pretense, the satirist often has to be vehement and loud because he feels that he is outnumbered and outshouted.

Intelligence

It is not necessary for a writer to be an intellectual giant. Proust even goes so far as to suggest that it is better for the writer to be close to the intellectual level of ordinary people, so that he can share their attitudes and ideas. Leslie Fieldler believes that "intelligence and style alike are optional for the writer." But with the satirist we face a special problem; if satire appeals primarily to the intellect, then presumably the mind of the satirist should be superior to that of the average man. Whether it actually is superior is not certain. Satirists are clever men, but few of them are brilliant men. They are agile in using logic, and they are skillful in manipulating and distorting what seems to be evidence, but this agility and skill do not necessarily denote an intellectual capacity of the highest order. In general, satirists tend to use logic which supports their own position, and to ignore logic which refutes that position.

This anti-intellectualism has appeared in the work of many great satirists. Jonathan Swift felt that he was very logical and rational, but in the *Voyage to Laputa* he ridicules people who depend excessively upon reason. Samuel Johnson thought that he annihilated Berkeleyan idealism by kicking a table and saying, "There, sir, that is how I disprove it." Anatole France and Aldous Huxley ridiculed the efforts of scientists to extend their activities to social fields. Sinclair Lewis objected to the attempts of others to put people in categories (although in his own writing he insisted on categorizing people).

In trying to determine whether the greatest satirists are those with the most powerful intellects, we run into semantic problems. Without having the IQ's of the great satirists available, it is difficult to decide who had great intelligence. Voltaire was a brilliant student, but Anatole France was at the bottom of his class. Jonathan Swift wrote powerful satire, but he expressed no original ideas in reference to society, politics, economics, or religion. And it took special dispensation to award Swift his bachelor's degree.

It may be that different kinds of satire require different intellectual qualities. David Worcester thinks that "Of all the types of satire . . . burlesque offers the greatest freedom to the artist and exacts the most from him in terms of creative inventiveness." But Frances Russell disagrees; she feels that burlesque is the easiest type of satire to write. Is the ability to write parody indication of a weak personality, or of a flexible one? In originality of technique both Swift and Lewis Carroll are great satirists, yet we hesitate to group the two closely in terms of achievement. If the discussion of originality is limited to content, we must admit that few satirists have anything new to say; what they do is to popularize and present, in interesting and stimulating form, opinions which have already been held by other men for some time. Two qualities of the satirist make him, at first glance, *seem* original: first, an unexpected honesty which is startling because it is unusual and, secondly, inversion of the conventional view. But honesty is not limited to intellectuals, and inversion and paradox are simply satiric devices.

"In literature, irony is the shoe-horn of new ideas," says David Worcester. But it is especially ironic that new ideas are precisely the ones which satirists have been least able to communicate successfully in their satire. It is not the "creative evolution" theory of Samuel Butler and Bernard Shaw that has been effective in their satire. Only rarely is the original idea successful in satire. What is successful is the unusual *manner of presenting ideas* for which the ground had already been broken, ideas which people, at least at the more educated levels of society, had been prepared to accept. Oscar Wilde's manner is startling, but little that he said is a genuinely original contribution to knowledge. The *methods* of *Don Quixote* and *Brave New World* and *The Modest Proposal* and *Penguin Island* were original; the *ideas* expressed in them had long been familiar to educated readers.

"The matter of Dryden's work is not original," says Cazamian. Nichol Smith tells us that all

Dryden did "was to lead the taste of the time in the direction in which it already was going." Chevalier says of Anatole France, "It is generally accepted that he was not a great originator of ideas, any more than he was an inventor of plots." Herbert Davis admits, "It is sometimes said that Swift was not a great intelligence, that he was no profound scholar, no outstanding political thinker, and no really original genius." Of H. G. Wells, Edgar Johnson writes: "The merit of his satire lies much more in the vigor and vividness of what he sees than in any profound intellectual grasp. . . . He is not a thinker." And Mikes says of Thurber: "his observation is superb, his imagination is poor."

William Irvine says: "Shaw and Chesterton came more and more to admire each other as writers and to discount each other as thinkers. Chesterton had probably learned most of what he could learn from Shaw before they met. Shaw was too old and too proud to learn at all." Cazamian feels that the first Samuel Butler repeatedly struck at dead enemies, Puritanism and scholasticism, without being able to turn towards a future." P. G. Wodehouse, thinks George Mikes, "is an able and ingenious comic writer; but he is not an intelligent man." Daiches admits that if we consider only the "philosophy" of Shaw, we find little that is original. Williams observes that Washington Irving's "intellectual weight has been . . . often challenged." And Samuel Johnson disposed of the problem of free will with the remark: "All theory is against it and all experience is for it."

Stephen Leacock contributed little original work to political economy. In his professional work mathematics, Lewis Carroll was "generally conservative rather than imaginatively explorative.' Dr. Greenacre remarks that Carroll was "chiefly concerned with defending Euclid from any sacrilegious attempt to question him or modernize him.'

The anti-intellectualism of satirists is sometimes expressed in criticism of reason, as in Swift and Sinclair Lewis, sometimes in reliance on nonrational elements, as in Bernard Shaw's reverence for the "life force" and in Huxley's mysticism. It is an anti-intellectualism probably based on the satirist's conviction that in the final analysis and in most situations men are motivated more by their emotions than by reason.

Courage

The satirist is a person who attacks, ridicules, criticizes, or unmasks, usually with the aid of humor. Attack implies courage; but whether the satirist is courageous or not depends on whether his attack is regarded as a positive act of valor or as the kind of whining that any malcontent can afford to indulge in. Also, we must agree on some definition of courage, choosing among varieties of physical, moral, social, and intellectual boldness. And we must distinguish between persistent courage and "one-time" acts of daring which spring from hysteria or desperation.

We must consider also the relationship of the

satirist's temperament to his technique — that technique utilizing distortion and indirection. Is the satirist, because the satiric technique often involves indirection, the possessor of a devious personality? Does he speak around a subject because he is afraid to speak of it directly? Is his usual choice of superficial subjects to criticize, and his lack of daring in suggesting alternatives evidence of this timidity?

Few satirists have dared attack the fundamental organization of their society. They have shown more freedom in democratic societies, of course, than in totalitarian ones. But even in democratic societies, where public opinion rather than official censorship is the deterrent, few satirists have dared suggest radical innovations. Their inversion of the *status quo (Erewhon, Gulliver's Travels)* should not be interpreted as a serious alternative; it is merely a satiric device.

Is the degree of a satirist's personal courage related to the directness of his satiric technique? Many satirists who openly criticized society were personally brave men. There is nothing indirect about the satire of Samuel Johnson, Victor Hugo, H. L. Mencken, W. C. Brann, and Ambrose Bierce, and there was no lack of personal courage in any of these men; they deliberately and sometimes pugnaciously went out to face possible critics and potential attackers. On the other hand, indirect and subtle satirists have also shown considerable personal courage, as Voltaire did when he challenged de Rohan to a duel, and Evelyn

Waugh did when he fought with the commandos.

In defense of the satirist we might say that indirection is a "civilized" rather than a "cowardly" form of communication. And the satirist's failure to attack the basic problems in his society may be defended on the grounds that *important* things provide less suitable subject matter for laughter than does insignificant material. Since humor deals primarily with the social and superficial qualities of life, it is not likely to be successful with deep passions or profoundly held beliefs.

Contradictory evaluations of the satirist's courage have been expressed. In an essay published in 1744, Corbyn Morris wrote that only the satirist "has the courage to cry out, unmoved by personal resentment: he flourishes only in a land of freedom, and when that ceases he dies too, last and noblest weed of the soil of liberty." But modern psychoanalysts see the satirist from a very different perspective. Dr. Kanzer, for example, believes that the satirist sometimes "pushes aggression to provocative limits that result in a counterattack . . . which gratifies his need for persecution and suffering," and suggests that the satire of Gogol was motivated by an unconscious desire to be punished. Nor does Dr. Edmund Bergler have much respect for courage of satirists. According to him, the satirist's "aggression against authority is very tame. He uses indirect and not very transparent ridicule of it. . . . A rebel who is always looking in the direction of the authority he is supposed to have overcome is *no* rebel at all."

Satirists have from the earliest times divided themselves into two groups, one insisting that the evil action rather than the evildoer should be satirized; Juvenal so proclaimed. The other group asserts that the individual evildoer should be satirized, and Voltaire, Bierce, Mencken, Hugo, and Frenau have been especially effective in that kind of satire.

When World War II broke out Evelyn Waugh joined the Royal Marines; later, as a commando, he gained a reputation for extraordinary bravery by participating in a series of dangerous martial exploits. (A psychoanalyst may object, as some of them have objected, that this type of behavior is not courage but an expression of the "death-wish." To this kind of reasoning there can be no reply; it is a case of "Heads I win, tails you lose." If the psychoanalyst accepts cowardly acts on the part of the satirist as cowardice, but rejects the satirist's brave acts as a "death-wish," it becomes impossible to defend the satirist.)

Ambrose Bierce went into the Civil War a drummer-boy and came out a brevet-major; throughout his life he openly attacked, by name, people whom he disliked or whom he accused of improper behavior. At the time he was making these attacks on the West Coast, beatings and shootings were the customary methods of reprisal. Bierce never stopped making these attacks. And W. C. Brann continued to ridicule Texans, in spite of being kidnapped, beaten, caned, and horse-whipped, until he was shot in the back.

H. L. Mencken vigorously criticized World War I during World War I and World War II during World War II, attended the Scopes Trial, and went to Boston to sell *The American Mercury* so that he could get arrested and test the censorship law. Although Cleon was the most powerful man in Athens, Aristophanes called him "a public robber." There is a legend that, when several actors refused to play the part of Cleon in *The Knights*, Aristophanes played the part himself, defying the demagogue in public. In other plays he demanded the death of specific citizens and called certain high military officials "pigs" and "liars." Sydney Smith, although he disliked Catholicism, persistently wrote and spoke on behalf of Catholic rights during the Reform movement, and probably lost a bishopric as a result. When Macpherson threatened Samuel Johnson, the latter got himself a cudgel and invited Macpherson to come whenever he was ready. Lucilius, the first of the great Roman satirists, during the days of the republic attacked his enemies by name in the satires he published. Fred Allen showed considerable courage in defying the conventions of modern radio. And Vondel courageously fought political and religious intolerance.

Jefferey Hudson was a midget court-fool at King Charles' court. When, in France, a man laughed at him, Hudson challenged the man to a duel; the man appeared armed only with a squirt and Hudson shot him dead.

Voltaire and Twain (neither of whom had been

expected to survive his first year) both challenged enemies to duels. When Voltaire challenged de Rohan, the latter's family obtained a *lettre de cachet* and had Voltaire put in the Bastille. For half a century Voltaire carried on, sometimes single-handed, a war against the church. He managed to free several men who had been unjustly convicted, and to have others who had been unjustly executed declared innocent; he faced continuous harassment by his enemies. It is hard to accept Bolitho's remark that Voltaire was, "like all rationalists, squeamish at heart."

Under special conditions, courage is expressed in special ways. In a totalitarian society it may require more courage to publish anonymously than to attack openly in a democracy. It is difficult, consequently, to judge just how brave Juvenal was in his vitriolic attacks on the moral sins of Roman society. In his first Satire he said that his examples referred to the dead, not the living, and that the cause of Roman decay was the infectious influence of Greeks and other foreigners. He did not name any of his contemporaries in the satires and he did not attack the institution of monarchy. He was a moral critic, not a political critic. It is usually safer to remain a moral critic.

Although Ennis calls Thackeray a courageous man, he admits that religion "was hardly the stuff from which a writer like Thackeray could weave fiction. He was too cautious of his public." Rice was not impressed by Byron's attack on the late King George in *Vision of Judgment,* saying, "In fact, Byron here only reverberates wide-spread sentiment. It took no courage to do so." Russell Kirk commends James Russell Lowell because, "often displaying remarkable courage," he attacked the city bosses and the spoils-system after the Civil War. And Aretino was a bully to the weak, abject and apologetic to the strong.

Carl Van Doren thought that Sinclair Lewis had "more mental and moral courage" than Mark Twain, but this is difficult to determine. Twain and Lewis both concentrated on social criticism, and both accepted the economic organization of their society. They criticized what many intelligent and educated contemporaries were also criticizing.

Concerning Mark Twain's courage there are conflicting opinions. Bixby, who was Twain's instructor, once said that Mark was a good pilot; but fifty years later he told Albert B. Paine, "Sam Clemens knew the river, but being a coward, he was a failure as a pilot." Ferguson notes that Bixby was not likely to have chosen Mark as his partner if he had thought he was a coward, and suggests that Twain probably did have the kind of fertile imagination which would make the life of a pilot nerve-racking. There are many examples of Mark Twain's physical courage; when pilot Brown hit Sam's younger brother Henry, "Sam went into action with a fury. . . . Brown was the bigger man, but Sam knocked him flat with a stool and then pounded him with his fists." Twain attacked General Funston at a time when the general was being idolized. When Twain's older brother, Orion, got into trouble with Governor Nye of Nevada, "Sam defended his brother in a fiery interview with the governor, with the result that Orion remained in his post."

But Van Wyck Brooks feels that Twain lacked courage. He cites Twain's refusal to publish his most pessimistic works until after his death, and insists that Twain attacked only the insignificant problems of materialistic America. Twain's vituperative invectives against Theodore Roosevelt and the trusts were posthumously published. He was afraid, says Brooks, to challenge the public on serious issues, but concentrated on such popular objects of attack as monarchy, tradition, and European art.

As to Mark Twain's failure to enlist during the Civil War, there seems little likelihood of anyone's proving definitively why Mark did what he did. Ferguson believes that having tried in a childish escapade imitation-guerilla warfare, the members of Mark Twain's company found the procedure uncomfortable, dull, and restrictive — and disbanded.

Ibsen was "physically timorous" and Gogol became so terrified of public disapproval and the possibility of eternal damnation that he almost died of fright. Martial wrote extravagant praise of the vile Domitian when the latter ruled Rome; Domitian rewarded Martial handsomely, and was repaid by a vicious attack immediately after his death. Leacock admitted, "I had no real 'nerve,' no real 'gall.'"

> Satire's my weapon, but I'm too discreet
> To run amuck, and tilt at all I meet.

That's what Pope wrote, and that's what Pope meant.

C. F. Calverton criticized Dickens and Thackeray for satirizing the superficial aspects of Victorian society but accepting its fundamental values. No great courage is necessary to write the kind of social satire that John P. Marquand writes, or the kind that P. G. Wodehouse writes. Horace, according to Dryden, "complied with the interests of his master (Augustus) and avoiding the lashing of greater crimes, confined himself to the ridiculing of petty vices and common follies." Persius satirized the poetry of his day but never complained about the loss of political freedom.

In her history of the fool, Enid Welsford refers to "the traditional connection between buffoonery and cowardice," but does name a few fools who were brave. Though the court fool Gringoire wrote a vehement attack on the Pope, "this apparently bold satire is not really a very daring incursion into politics," Miss Welsford says, "for Gringoire was a good courtier and it took little courage to attack the papacy at that particular moment in French history."

Chevalier concludes that Anatole France is "without courage. . . . There is no bold defiance of evil, no challenge to the incomplete and imperfect order of things. There is pity and tenderness; there is acquiescence." A character in one of France's novels says, "I had audacity of spirit as I had timidity in manner. . . . I was violent and revolutionary when I was alone." When World War I began, France wrote a letter to the newspapers, urging moderation. Violently attacked by hundreds of letter-writers, he immediately changed his attitude and volunteered to fight for France; having failed the physical examination, he turned to propaganda work, writing patriotic pamphlets and anti-German material. On the Dreyfus issue, however, France remained consistently courageous.

Priestley's remarks about an English humor magazine in some ways apply to satirists. "Mr. Punch has always taken most things — our etiquette, our social and moral code, our class distinction, and the rest — for granted, and has been content to find his fun in the more superficial of our pretensions."

Inasmuch as courage varies in quality, in duration, and in the circumstances under which it appears, it would be very difficult to prove that the fortitude of satirists is markedly different from that of other men.

Psychoanalysis

Before we can evaluate objectively the contribution of psychoanalysis to our understanding of the satirist, we must admit the existence of several special problems. To begin with, there is the problem of communication. Orthodox Freudians use a jargon which non-Freudian psychologists reject and neo-Freudian psychoanalysts modify, qualify, and change. Non-Freudian psychiatrists call psychoanalytic terminology "intuitive"; Freudians insist that it is "clinical" and submit as evidence the results of psychoanalytic treatment. They believe that cures achieved by psychoanalysis prove the correctness of psychoanalytic premises; they deny that cures achieved by faith healing prove the correctness of religious premises.

In general, psychoanalysts agree that the satirist is a maladjusted individual who expresses his maladjustment by writing satire. But this indictment is not especially severe, for most psychoanalysts

> *The writer does not produce his works, as naive people think, because he has something important to convey to his eager listeners, but solely to solve an inner conflict.*
> — Edmund Bergler

begin with the assumption that almost every person is to a varying degree "maladjusted" and laden with a guilt-complex, and that many people try to compensate for this feeling of guilt by attacking. To that extent, millions of people are potential satirists, limited only by the amount of satiric technique that they develop.

Furthermore, most of the examples of "humor" that psychoanalysts like Lucille Dooley, Annie Reich, and Ernst Krist offer are based on case studies of psychotic patients. It is not at all certain that these situations are any more typical of the normal humorous experience than hysterical laughter is of "normal" laughter.

Another problem is the implied assumption of such psychoanalysts as Reik and Bergler that criticizing society is, *ipso facto,* neurotic. According to Dr. Bergler, creative writing is simply a pseudo-aggressive alibi on the part of the writer; it takes the form of chronic attack on institutions and individuals. Bergler's implication is that everyone who criticizes anything is "abnormal," or neurotic, or prompted by some motive other than justifiable criticism of a faulty condition. If this reasoning were sound, everyone ought to meekly accept whatever *status quo* exists in whatever society he inhabits, because if he did not accept it he would be guilty of "maladjusted" behavior. There could not be any "healthy" criticism of evil, error, hypocrisy, or viciousness; consequently, no one ought to complain in a Communist or Fascist or any other kind of society.

In actual practice, of course, psychoanalysts

themselves believe no such thing and spend a good deal of time criticizing individuals, institutions, and other psychoanalysts who disagree with them. To a naive layman it might appear that there is no difference between a "criticism" by Dr. Edmund Bergler, who continually attacks writers, critics, and other psychiatrists, and a "criticism" by a realistic satirist like H. L. Mencken. In one of his books Dr. Bergler explains that men who think they are writing for some innocent reason are actually motivated by the "peeping" instinct of a boy wanting to see forbidden aspects of sex; he cites as proof of this theory a man whose subconscious reason for becoming a professor of dairy industry was the fact that in this socially acceptable position he could write about cows' teats without being accused of peeping. Dr. Bergler sees no connection between this professor and an eminent New York psychoanalyst who has published a large number of socially accepted books and articles about sex.

Some psychoanalysts, such as Dr. Annie Reich, insist that the reason a humorist needs an audience is to relieve him of his guilt feeling and anxiety. But why do dogs show off? Porpoises? Why do cats bring in dead birds to exhibit before their owners? It is true that the humorist needs an audience; it does not necessarily follow that because he needs an audience, he needs it to dispose of a guilt feeling or a feeling of anxiety.

Many of the comments about humor and satire suffer from the psychoanalyst's assumption that inasmuch as many obvious causes are not the real causes, *all* obvious causes are not real causes. It is an assumption easy enough to refute, by changing Samuel Johnson's illustration slightly and hitting a psychoanalyst over the head with a bat to demonstrate that sometimes the obvious cause of a reaction is the real cause of it. The psychoanalyst and the satirist are similar in that both seek "real" motivations which often prove to be unsavory.

Finally, although psychoanalysts agree that the satirist is a neurotic, they don't agree on the type of neurotic he is supposed to be. If satire is an "aggressive neurosis," as some psychoanalysts have suggested, what is the relation of the satirist to the writer of tragedy? Is the latter a "normal" type, or a neurotic type different from the satirist, or the same type choosing a different approach? And what of writers like Shakespeare and Melville and Congreve and O'Neill who wrote both tragedy and comedy? The psychoanalyst tells us that human beings have seemingly paradoxical impulses which are really compensations for each other. But perceptive writers have known this for centuries, and psychoanalytic terminology has simply complicated the problem without solving it.

Psychoanalysis has given us fascinating new approaches for speculating about subconscious motivation and understanding symbol and myth. But it is an inescapable fact that on many issues psychoanalysts not only disagree with other psychiatrists but directly contradict one another. Contradiction does not, of course, necessarily mean that both sides are completely wrong (or even that one is right); but it does make it difficult to choose among disputing experts. For instance, psychoanalysts disagree on whether sex, or the Oedipus complex, or the death-wish, or something else is the writer's motivation; whether the satirist is a sadist or a masochist, or primarily masculine or feminine, or has a stern or mild super-ego; how a child develops the temperament of a clown; and to what degree satirists are neurotic.

Even on the initial question of whether the creative process can be explained, psychoanalysts disagree. Freud once said that it is impossible to analyze aesthetic activity. But a number of Freudians point out, reasonably enough, that Freud himself made many subsequent efforts to analyze the creative process. And Dr. Bergler offers the ingenious suggestion that because Freud had emotional difficulties in "clarifying the dichotomy of mothers," he made an unconscious "intra-psychic" shift to deny the possibility of understanding artistic creativity.

Freud postulated that the basis for the creative impulse is sexual, and one of his followers, Dr. Winterstein, went so far as to suggest that humor has its origin in the sucking stage. But Dr. Rank tells us, "This creative-impulse is not sexuality, as Freud assumed, but expresses the antisexual tendency in human beings."

It used to be dogma among Freudians that the Oedipus complex was the motivation of the writer; but Dr. Bergler and Dr. Grotjahn now insist that the Oedipus complex has nothing to do with the writer's motivation. Dr. Fromm accepts the evidence of recent anthropological investigations that the Oedipus complex is not universal, that the rivalry between father and son may not occur in societies where strong patriarchal authority is missing, and that the tie to the mother may be not a sexual one but the result of conflict between an authoritarian father and a freedom-seeking son. According to Dr. Adler, pampering by the mother is likely to develop the Oedipus complex. Jung considers it a "possession-complex." To Rank, the Oedipus complex seems an unsuccessful attempt to compensate for the birth trauma. Karen Horney accounts for the Oedipus complex mainly on the basis of family relationship, including sexual stimulation by the parents, and anxiety aroused by the conflict between dependence and hostile impulses toward the parents. Dr. Sullivan's interpretation is based on familiarity and strangeness between parent and child.

Satire is an art form which expresses aggression, and Freud suggested that an innate "death-wish" accounts for man's aggressive urges. But Dr. Fenichel rejects this explanation; he insists that aggression is a response to frustration. Dr. Grotjahn tells us that man's tragedy, and consequent violence, comes from the loss of the womb-shelter and early love when he is exposed to the conflicts of reality. But Karen Horney and Harry Sullivan find the source of aggressive action in interpersonal difficulties of human beings torn by conflicting social demands.

It is masochists who create humor, says Dr. Lucille Dooley. No, say Winterstein and Tarachow, sadists also create humor. Excuse me, says in effect Dr. Dooley: it is "wits" who are sadistic, "humorists" who are masochistic. Dr. Bergler agrees with Dr. Dooley, and then ingeniously resolves the dispute: "Sadism in *adults* is but an inner defense against more deeply rooted masochism." This amounts to saying that sadism may be the other side of the coin from masochism, and that the two actions are interrelated. But if that is all that the psychoanalysts are saying, they are not contributing anything new.

Tarachow and Bergler tell us that the humorist is likely to have a strong element of femininity in his personality; but Winterstein insists, "Humor is a male characteristic." If the psychoanalyst is saying that every human being has both male and female characteristics, he is again reducing the issue to a platitude which has long been recognized. As for Dr. Franz Alexander's drawing of a parallel between humor and "the Spartan attitude," Bergler disagrees once more, saying, "Their mental content is as opposite as the poles."

Another contradiction among psychoanalysts appears in their description of the super-ego's role during the humorous act. Dr. Robert Walder suggests that "humor may not develop in those whose childhood conflicts were too severe — with too strict a super-ego formed." But Dr. Lucille Dooley reports that two of her patients, one with a puritanical upbringing and the other with a very kind and unrestricted one, showed exactly the same humorous symptoms. So Walder's theory — a strict upbringing results in a humorless individual — is contradicted.

Dr. Bergler also rejects Walder's theory that the super-ego of the humorist must be mild in order to permit humor to occur. This problem of whether the super-ego is for some special reason benign during the humorous process, graciously permitting the ego a moment of pleasure, is one about which several psychoanalysts, including Freud and Winterstein, have expressed differing opinions. Especially provocative is Freud's suggestion that the super-ego plays the part not just of the stern "father" but of the "parent"; this permits the super-ego sometimes to be the genial "mother," and it is in that role that it relaxes its supervisory and censoring duties, and permits the ego to enjoy a humorous experience. Dr. Winterstein accepts this assumption about the motherly gentleness of the humorist's super-ego. But Bergler insists that it is punishment rather than mercy that the super-ego provides in the humorous process. And Dr. Theodor Reik, who defines humor as "an act of mercy of the super-ego," adds a startling admission for a psychoanalyst: "We know too little as yet about the nature of the super-ego."

Dr. Annie Reich's study of humor in children has led some psychiatrists to accept her theory that humorous behavior on the part of children is a sign of insecurity. The child, in this view, is attempting to overcome insecurity and fear of a parent by burlesque mimicry of his action, a mimicry which is always followed by guilt feelings and fears of retaliation. Both Dr. Reich and Dr. Bergler give examples of children who developed into humorists as the result of attempts to achieve status in the family group. Bergler's example is a boy who was intellectually inferior to his older brother and acted as a clown in order to get attention; he remained a clown, in social relationships, all his life. Dr. Reich cites the middle one of three sisters, who acted as a clown in the family to compete for the father's love, and who also retained the clown's personality in her social relationships later in life.

Psychoanalysts seem to agree that the satirist is an abnormal type, but they do not agree in identifying either the degree of abnormality or the type. Part of the confusion is due, of course, to the differences of opinion over larger issues than the nature of the humorist. Among the "orthodox" Freudians are Fenichel, Anna Freud, Melanie Klein, and Phyllis Greenacre. Jung, Adler, and Rank broke away early. Franz Alexander is hard to classify, and Karen Horney, Harry Stack Sullivan, and Erich Fromm are usually called "neo-Freudians." Freud emphasized sexual motivation, Bergler gives equal importance to the aggressive and sexual drives, and some neo-Freudians reject "instinct" altogether. Even on such a basic issue as self-love there is disagreement, Freud having assumed that narcissism was an unhealthy tendency, but Erich Fromm disagrees, on the grounds that "a person capable of genuinely loving himself is actually more capable of loving others."

Another difference of opinion is revealed in the evaluation of humor. Dooley, Reich, Brill, and Tarachow clearly regard the humorist as a neurotic personality. All writers, Dr. Brill assumes, are neurotic by the very choice of writing as an occupation. We have seen that Dooley and Reich have interpreted comic behavior as evidence of maladjustment. And Dr. Tarachow observed that some of his patients, "mostly men with strong, unresolved sado-masochistic tendencies and femininity, fear failure in genital aggressions and substitute for it comic aggressions and a debased clowning type of exhibitionism."

But Dr. Bergler's position is not as clear, since he makes a sharp distinction between the writer and his writing. Bergler, who identifies the writer as a neurotic from the same group in which alcoholics and homosexuals originate, denies that "writing" is neurotic. Readers have misunderstood him, Bergler explains, because they have confused "the neuroticism of writers in their private lives and writing as a neurotic expression." Such confusion, Bergler insists, is unjustified, for "writing is sublimation and therefore a healthy, though temporary, defense against reproaches of the inner conscience."

Other psychoanalysts give the humorist more credit. Theodor Reik, for example, respects many writers and regards literature as a valid approach to experience. Otto Rank distinguishes the writer, as a desirable productive type, from the neurotic, who does not create. "The capacity to laugh," says Dr. Jacob Levine, "is a measure of one's adjustment to his environment." And Dr. Ernst Kris, discussing the limitations of the comic spirit, suggests that though the comic "cannot bring permanent relief . . . in a particular form the comic relief is permanent," for it may result in "a permanent transformation of the ego." And after paying tribute to the humorist's achievement, Dr. Kris concludes: "The precious gift of humor makes men wise; they are sublime and safe, remote from all conflict."

The psychoanalytic assumption that the humorist is neurotic stems, presumably, from Freud. But the master himself was cautious. "Owing to insufficient data," Freud wrote, "we certainly cannot maintain that such a psychoneurotic constitution is a regular or necessary subjective condition for wit-making."

According to Sigmund Freud, the humorist adopts towards the listener the attitude of an adult (or parent) towards a child, minimizing and laughing away the child's (and the listener's) problems. By pretending that the disturbing problems are actually unimportant, the humorist provides comfort and reassurance to the listener. But the "original and more important" situation, says Freud, is that in which "a man adopts a humorous attitude towards himself in order to ward off possible suffering." The apparent paradox — treating oneself like a child and simultaneously playing the part of a superior adult — Freud explains in these terms: the super-ego treats the ego as a parent treats a young child. In other respects the super-ego is a stern master, but in the comic activity it kindly provides pleasure to the ego by comparing the problems of the world to child's play. In giving this comfort to the ego, the super-ego plays the part of a sympathetic mother rather than its usual role of a stern father. The humorous attitude, then, consists of removing the burden from one's ego and transferring it to one's super-ego.

This holds true for the "humorous" situation. When, however, wit is used to express "sexual or hostile tendencies," when it becomes aggressive, then a different situation exists and "the psychic process is consummated between the first person — the ego, and the third person — the stranger, and not, as in the comic, between the ego and the object-person." It is this aggressive humor, which Freud calls "tendency-wit," that corresponds most closely to satire. What happens here is an attempt to avoid what Freud calls the Censor. The Censor is the repressive force of society which forbids, in a civilized community, the expression of certain basic instincts and desires. The most powerful instinct, Freud tells us, is the sexual drive, and the Censor puts a rigid limit on what a person is permitted to do or say in relation to sex. Wit permits a person to evade the Censor's restrictions by referring to sex indirectly — and for that reason "dirty" jokes are universal. Another strong instinct is the aggressive drive — and, as a result, an enormous amount of humor is at the expense of somebody or something. And since the Censor protects the dignity of institutions — the State, Religion, Authority, etc. — the wit provides the pleasure of ridiculing these institutions without being legally liable. Avoiding the Censor, then, becomes the major contribution of the man who creates "tendency-wit."

Dr. Lucille Dooley, accepting Freud's suggestion that in the humorous situation an individual treats the person involved (whether himself or another) as a child, develops the theory that humor is an escape from suffering. Humor, she thinks, resembles neurosis in being a renunciation of reality, but it differs from neurosis in that the escape through humor is achieved without cost to mental health. Humor is a triumph of narcissism, developing after the birth of the super-ego. Unlike wit, humor is never sadistic. Dr. Dooley believes that the relationship between humor and masochism corresponds to the relationship between wit and sadism.

According to Dr. Dooley, the person who makes himself the subject of the humorous attitude reduces his ego to the level of a child. By displacing psychic energy from the ego to the super-ego, the humorous person is living "more as super-ego than as ego." To this enlarged super-ego the ego now seems absurdly small, and its problems laughably unimportant. Humor is similar to neurosis and intoxication in that it permits fantasy to replace reality, but it is different from these other two forms of escape in that the humorous defense achieves pleasant escape without any loss of mental health and without "withdrawal of the actual painful content from consciousness." The ego, having temporarily gotten rid of "threatening instinctual drives of a sadistic or masochistic tendency" by shifting them to the super-ego, can enjoy the pleasure of laughter undisturbed by sexual or aggressive impulses. The humorous attitude, Dr. Dooley feels, invariably has two characteristics which preserve narcissism: (1) it emphasizes littleness, "the little thing being really the ego," which is shielded from suffering by this diminution, and gets narcissistic satisfaction by seeing the world in pygmy proportions; and (2) it provides fantasy, which is also a childish activity, and coats with a comforting playfulness the unpleasant real world. Dr. Dooley concludes that only a small number of people possess a genuine gift of humor and admits, "I have no answer to give to the question of why one develops it while another does not."

Dr. Annie Reich has formulated a theory of humor based primarily on her analysis of a young woman patient who had an outstanding talent for "grotesque-comic acting." The girl, who was "by far the most intelligent, talented, and charming" member of her family, began playing the comic role in her family when she was six years old. The butts of her clowning were always her mother and sisters, never her father. Because she had had a violent sexual experience with a little boy when she was five years old, and because she felt that her nose was too small, she suffered the feeling of a secret deficiency all her life. In the effort to get rid of this guilt-feeling, she became even as a child "a fanatic for truth," and developed a remarkable capacity for perceiving "all the deficiencies, insincerities, and ridiculous aspects of her environment." She proved to have "a peculiar faculty" for understanding the deep-seated motivations of human beings she knew, to spot "all secret vices, weaknesses, and hypocrisies, and . . . to portray them with a casual word or gesture."

Unlike Freud and Dooley, who think that the super-ego is a sympathetic helper in the humorous act, Dr. Reich is convinced that the ego achieves its pleasure only by "an active, spiteful conquering of the cruel super-ego." The victory gives the humorist great elation, a joy comparable to the bliss of mania. But such victories are rare, and when the attempt to overcome the super-ego fails, the humorist suffers terribly. For his super-ego is an especially cruel one, and when the ego's "criminal attempt at rebellion has failed" the super-ego punishes it ruthlessly. Then the humorist experiences intense melancholy, and since the struggle with the super-ego never ends but is continually repeated, the humorist exhibits many of the characteristics of the manic-depressive.

Another psychoanalyst who sees a relationship

between the satirist and the neurotic is Dr. Mark Kanzer. "Wit and paranoia," he says, "offer related and alternative forms of discharge for certain repressed drives as well as social tendencies." Dr. Kanzer traces the relationship between the paranoiac Gogol and the discontented social classes of Russia in the nineteenth century, and suggests that Gogol served (as at other times Cervantes and Voltaire had served) to express the growing protest against the *status quo*. A persecuted society, Dr. Kanzer thinks, can identify itself with a paranoiac individual, and find in his work not only a release for its own inhibitions but also a prophecy of forthcoming social change.

Accepting Freud's distinction between the comic and the witty (in *Wit and the Unconscious*), Kanzer suggests that the "comic" process, with its simple two-person relationship and its economy of thought, is especially attractive to the manic-depressive temperament. But wit, "with its distorted three-person interplay, its subtle intellectual mockery, and its sensitivity to the social scene," is much more suitable for the paranoiac personality. Wit resembles paranoia, Dr. Kanzer suggests, in attacking common sense and trying to establish a logic of its own; like the paranoiac, the witty person uses sublimation "to make an uneasy peace with the world he detests," and like the paranoiac he is likely to be overprovocative in his attack, so that "the resultant counter-attack gratifies his need for persecution and suffering."

In recent years a number of psychoanalytic

"studies" of satirists have appeared. Jonathan Swift has been a particularly popular subject, and many attempts to analyze him have been made. In one, "A Freudian View of Jonathan Swift," Donald Roberts concludes that the key to Swift's personality lies in the oversevere toilet training he was subjected to between the ages of one and four. During that period he was under the care of a nurse who had abducted him and trained him. Swift eventually sublimated this excessive concern with personal cleanliness into "a passionate thirst for truth and justice, and it caused him to cleanse and purge his prose style until it became a miracle of force and concision."

Swift's psychosexual development, Roberts tells us, was arrested at the anal-erotic level, and he never became capable of enjoying mature sexual love. But he compensated for this personal deficiency by sublimating his neuroticism into artistic creation and by creating excellent satires which applied devastating moral criteria to the weaknesses of society.

Finally, a leading Freudian analyst, Dr. Phyllis Greenacre, has published a psychoanalytic study of Swift and Lewis Carroll. She explains that she began the study after observing the sensations of patients who suffered from fetishism. It occurred to her that these were precisely the sensations which Gulliver and Alice experienced in *Gulliver's Travels* and *Alice in Wonderland*. Intrigued by this phenomenon, Dr. Greenacre made a careful study of Swift and Carroll. It is somewhat anti-

climactic to report that, although she found orthodox Freudian concepts operating in the development of the neurotic, and quite different, personalities of Jonathan Swift and Lewis Carroll, she
reached the conclusion that neither was a fetichist.

The most prolific and belligerent writer on the
nature of the humorist is Dr. Edmund Bergler.
What the layman regards as obvious, Dr. Bergler
assumes is untrue; what other psychoanalysts accept as true, Dr. Bergler attempts to modify, as
when he suggests that the creative urge is not a defense against a guilt-feeling, but a *defense against
a defense*. All writers, says Dr. Bergler, are masochists, and "the writer does not produce his works,
as naive people think, because he has something
important to convey to his eager listeners, but
solely to *solve an inner conflict*." Bergler differs
from Freud in assigning to aggression an equal
role with that of sex, and in recognizing to a much
greater degree the importance of social "ideals."
His theory is too complex to be adequately summarized here, but essentially it is this: every man
is the product of the "drama of the nursery," the
period when the infant begins to resent the growing failure of the world to cater to his every wish.
Since the world is symbolized for him by Mother,
the Emperor of the Nursery develops an irritation
with Mother whenever she fails to provide in-
stantaneous food, physical comfort, and consolation. The infant destined to become a "normal"

adult expresses his irritation by yelling, biting, or hitting — natural outlets all. But some infants take refuge in imaginary revenge instead — and eventually wish that Mother was dead. Out of this crime develops an overwhelming feeling of guilt, which the criminal tries to overcome by pretending that Mother never existed — and since she never existed, she could not have been murdered, even in thought. By a complicated series of symbolic interpretations, Dr. Bergler tries to prove that some members of this group substitute another liquid for Mother's milk, and become alcoholics. Others prove Mother's nonexistence by substituting males — and become homosexuals. And still others — writers — substitute words and create a more satisfactory world than the one in which they committed the Crime of the Nursery.

In Dr. Bergler's view, *humor always presupposes an unhappy situation,* humiliating to the ego. Humor is the result of the ego's involvement in a situation where the super-ego has to relieve some of the tension. The super-ego allows the ego some pleasure by showing that the situation is child's play. And every man who laughs, at any time, is laughing to relieve this neurotic need for an artificial aggression against society. "Whether a writer strikes out at institutions, mores, prejudices, or injustices, the basic common denominator is identical; attack." It is basic in Dr. Bergler's theory that every writer is fighting his own masochism, to which he offers a fake aggression as a substitute.

According to Bergler, the purpose of creating

satire and comedy is to permit the writer "to deny inner dependence on the upbringers in childhood, later projected upon the 'great' and not-so-great." The child is weak, and "irony, wit, satire, are the weapons of the weak." The ridicule against an authoritative person in a comedy "is not real but compensatory *pseudo-aggression,* covering deeper repressed psychic masochism."

This, says Dr. Bergler, is the humorous process: Act 1. The humorist's super-ego has *aggressively* brought a desperate situation for the ego. Act 2. Turning to the super-ego for help, the masochistic ego begs for assistance at the price of punishment. Act 3. The super-ego pretends to comfort the ego, but actually scorns it. Act 4. The ego, disappointed and desperate, now "undertakes aggression against itself . . . relapses into primary narcissism," and enjoys a few moments of "a sort of intoxication" by deceiving itself as to what reality is.

The satirist, says Dr. Bergler, is, like many other neurotics, afraid. He needs constantly to prove that everyone has "feet of clay," in an "unconscious attempt to demonstrate that the alleged adversary is too weak to be dangerous." Bergler is convinced that the effort of certain neurotics to find weak spots is a compulsive necessity, and that "under the disguise of making fun," the neurotic is really trying to control his own anxiety. Furthermore, says Bergler, the complaints of his own patients are so petty and malicious that their very insignificance is proof that the complaining is motivated by guilt-feelings. Bergler chooses to ignore the work of such satirists as Swift, Voltaire, France, Huxley, and Orwell who, some readers think, have made significant observations about genuine problems in society.

The reason there are few great satiric comedies, says Bergler, is explained by "the specific psychic make-up of the writer of satiric comedy," who is equipped with "a stronger defensive aggression than the typical literary man has at his disposal." Every writer, according to Bergler, vacillates between the fear that his inner conscience will reject the subconscious alibi ("Mother does not exist.") and the artificial alibi which the writer has concocted to console himself ("I don't want to be refused; I refuse."). The writer of comedy somehow manages to avoid both extremes; but because that avoidance is rarely attainable, few satiric masterpieces have been written.

The satirist's criticism, Dr. Bergler insists, is not normal aggression, but pseudo-aggression. In support of his argument, Bergler lists nine differences between the two: Normal aggression, he says, is used only in self-defense; neurotic or pseudo-aggression is used indiscriminately. In normal aggression, the object of aggression is a real enemy; in pseudo-aggression, the object is a "fantasied" or artificially created enemy. In normal aggression there is no accompanying unconscious feeling of guilt; in pseudo-aggression the slightest provocation may result in great aggression. Normal aggression is always used to harm the enemy; pseudo-aggression is often used to provoke masochistic pleasure expected from the enemy's retaliation, or to refute the accusation of masochistic passivity on the part of the inner conscience. Normal aggression includes the ability to wait until the enemy is vulnerable; pseudo-aggression cannot wait, since it is used as a defense mechanism against the inner reproach of psychic masochism. Normal aggression is not easily provoked; pseudo-aggression is. In normal aggression, the element of infantile play is absent, the feeling being that a necessary though disagreeable job has to be done; in pseudo-aggression, the element of infantile play is present. And, finally, in normal aggression success is expected; in pseudo-aggression defeat is unconsciously expected.

The position of Dr. Martin Grotjahn is in many respects similar to that of Dr. Bergler. Grotjahn, however, makes a clear-cut distinction between the personality of the wit and the personality of the humorist, and is more sympathetic in his interpretation of the latter than Bergler is. He accepts Bergler's concept that artistic creativity is a reaction to the infantile experience of wishing "to kill the bad mother who has thrust it out of paradise into this world of reality." The artist atones for this crime by recreating the destroyed object and putting it on the stage, and finds relief only when the audience, by applauding his work, "absolves him from his crime of having trespassed the taboo."

The special quality of the comic writer, says Grotjahn, is that he has developed free access to his unconscious. Although the artist, like the neurotic, may feel anxiety, he overcomes that fear and achieves such control over his "repressible energy" that he is able to transform his unconscious and repressed tendencies into witticisms and works of art.

"The wit," says Grotjahn, "is witty not by choice but by destiny." He makes witty remarks compulsively, in response to inner necessity. Wit-making is his way of releasing hostility. "The wit . . . is hostile, often with a skillful, artful, highly developed, sophisticated meanness and viciousness." An angry man constantly in search of a victim, he is really afraid of people, and attacks them in an indirect way so that he can keep them away. Beneath this façade of aggressiveness, the wit is likely to be "lonely, often unloving and unloved . . . near to tears and suffering." Because he plays with "incompletely controlled hostility," Grotjahn believes, the wit gets burned himself. As a person, the wit "is closely related to the sadist."

But the humorist, according to Grotjahn, is a quite different personality type. He is "related to the masochist and to the melancholic." Like the depressive, he accepts resignedly the departure of Mother from the childhood paradise. But unlike the depressive, who simply broods, the humorist tries to take over the good mother's role and play it himself. He is kind and sympathetic to himself, and tries to be kind and tolerantly humorous to others. Instead of denying the existence of misery, he pretends to be victorious over it. And although

his victory is only temporary and partial, he provides pleasure by "illustrating the victory of infantile narcissism over all experience." But he
never completely forgets the Tragedy of the Nursery, and the occasional sadness of the humorist is
proof of his recurring "grief over the loss of the
good mother."

Much of what psychoanalysts say about satirists
has been said, in nontechnical language, by other
writers, especially by proponents of compensation
theories. Whether the original contributions of
psychoanalysis are valid cannot really be determined by laymen who do not fully accept the
premises on which psychoanalysis is based. Certainly those contributions are ingenious, provocative, inconclusive, and contradictory.

Development

In the life of many a satirist there occurs an early disturbance — a severe disappointment or a tragic event. Because of this some scholars have assumed that the disturbance created the satirist. But far more important is the fact that, in every case, the potential satirist had *before the disturbance* already revealed a satiric attitude and was ready, temperamentally, to become a satirist. The particular unpleasant event is not the cause of the satiric attitude; it merely intensifies an attitude which was already present. For many satirists, the following is the pattern of development: early evidence of satiric temperament; a relatively happy period during which mild and restrained satire is written; a disturbance; a return, with a vengeance, to the earlier caustic tone. In the lives of Dickens and Pope, Johnson and Swift, Melville and Cervantes, we find a sequence of events illustrating this pattern.

A difficult early life seems to be an essential requirement for admission to the ranks of the eminent clowns.
— Steve Allen

The young satirist often shows affection for only one person, or only a very few people, and exhibits merely detached interest in others; because of this disproportionate and concentrated affection (often for people older than himself) he is likely to be deeply hurt when that affection is rejected or ignored, or when the object of his affection departs.

Although it may surprise most people to learn that the harmony or jerkiness of their development can be measured mathematically, psychologists Heymans and Wiersma did not think that the assignment was difficult. They have published statistics which purport to measure those phenomena. According to these statistics, 11 per cent of the population has a jerky development, compared to a figure of 29 per cent for satirists; only 7 per cent of the satirists have a harmonious development, compared to 25 per cent of the nonsatirists.

Most satirists display a facetious attitude in their teens or earlier. Their reminiscences repeatedly mention sarcastic or humorous remarks they made when they were boys which aroused marked reactions, either of approval or irritation. Sometimes the irritation of victims proved a stronger stimulus to satiric development than the approval of friends. The satirist's adjustment to society, we have seen, consists of using the special critical talents that he discovered he possesses. Whether the motivation is self-defense, exhibitionism, sadism, or status-seeking, the satirist quickly learns that a special way of looking at things — a playfully critical distortion of the familiar — results in what society chooses to call a humorous commentary on life; and that it elicits from others a reaction that pleases the satirist.

The young satirist gets a grudging recognition from his companions, sometimes because they are afraid of becoming the objects of his jibes, sometimes because they are ashamed of having respected something which one of their peers despises. The length of the satirist's conditioning period depends on the response he gets — encouragement, indifference, or opposition — and his opportunities for making satiric remarks depend on the amount of hypocrisy observable in his immediate environment. Teachers, athletic heroes, historical characters prove to have flaws, and the satiric spirit feeds on disappointments and evidences of pretense and dishonesty.

This disillusionment first appears on an elementary level. Mark Twain decided that the bad are not always punished when he learned that a boy expelled from Mark's Sunday School had obtained a very desirable job on a Mississippi river boat. Sydney Smith said, when he was still a young man, "I never heard a story well proved on one side without being equally well proved on the other." H. L. Mencken was a young skeptic; at the high school he attended, he says, "All but a few of the boys regarded the Bible-reading as an affront to their dignity." Anatole France makes it clear in his autobiography that he was early aware of the contradictions in life; in another book he makes a character say, "I found the philosophy which I had been taught so stupid, so inept, so silly, that I believed nothing of the truths which it established." And Benjamin Franklin says that what drove him away from orthodox Christianity was a stupid book written in its defense.

Spontaneously the young satirist learns that the easiest way to find satiric material is to look for discrepancies between what people say and what they do. This skeptical attitude gives the satirist satisfaction and self-esteem. At a later and conceivably higher level of disillusionment he may discover support for himself in sociological theory, such as the concept that activities like art, religion, revolution, and regression may really be manifestations of an unconscious search for stability in a world of constant change.

Tracing the usual stages of a young writer's development, Malcolm Cowley lists three periods: first, voracious reading from an early age; second, maladjustment to one's own group, loneliness (actual or imagined), "isolation" for physical or social or racial reasons; third, approval of his writing by others. Cowley knows that psychoanalysts call the third stage "exhibitionism," and he admits that the "young writer exposes his mind, sometimes indecently."

It is generally assumed that personality, for writers and nonwriters, is determined relatively early in life. The precise length of the formative period is still disputed: some psychoanalysts say that the first few months set the permanent pattern; some child-development experts think that by the age of six one's temperament has been pretty well developed. Willa Cather believed that a serious writer experiences by the age of fifteen most of the material that he will use. Calverton was convinced that all of Sinclair Lewis' major characters originated in Sauk Center. And Ferguson says of Mark Twain that "every character he ever wrote about, including Joan of Arc, was either drawn from the intensive experience of his first thirty years or conceived in its spirit."

Sinclair Lewis insists that he was a happy child, but most critics refuse to believe him. Dickens insists that he spent a miserable childhood, and every critic believes him.

After his graduation from Harvard, Henry Thoreau and his elder brother opened a school in Concord. The school was successful and Henry seemed happy; but his brother died suddenly and painfully of tetanus, and Thoreau gave up teaching forever. The tragedy did not make Thoreau a satirist; he had already shown his irony, his independence, and his capacity for corrosive phrasing. The death of his brother merely intensified the satire he subsequently wrote.

When he was twenty years old, Voltaire entered a competition for poetry. In an unpopular decision the judges gave the prize to an old priest. Voltaire was very bitter and wrote satiric attacks upon the winner. A few years later his first play was hailed as a critical and financial success, and Voltaire seemed to be at the threshold of a brilliant career. But he was then sent to prison for eleven months, on the false charge that he had written a slanderous poem about the king. When the real author confessed Voltaire was freed. On a later occasion Voltaire was again unjustly accused of libel and exiled from Paris until the culprit confessed. But these incidents did not make a satirist out of Voltaire; they merely made a more intense and bitter satirist out of the boy who had already written witty parodies of the Bible in grade school.

Jonathan Swift was still a student at Trinity when he attracted attention for writing abusive, insolent, and merciless criticism. Later Swift is said to have deeply resented the remark of "Cousin" John Dryden that Swift would never become a poet. William Ewald speculates: "Could the decade of the 1690's have seen a relatively secure young man turn into another sort? . . . During the 1690's he had things to be proud of; King William taught him to cut asparagus in the Dutch way, and Oxford gave him an M.A." But when Swift left Temple "in anger . . . it was no doubt humiliating to have to request a letter of recommendation."

Mark Twain had enough misfortune and tragedy in his life to make anyone unhappy, but there is evidence that *long before* he had such external stimuli to melancholy, he was already an unhappy boy. His mother says that he had always been a moody and nervous boy who walked in his sleep and got into more scrapes than all the other

Clemens children. By the time Sam was eighteen, his older brother had often commented on his unhappiness and restlessness. And Twain was only thirty-one when he was so depressed that he thought of putting a pistol to his head. He was predisposed to misery long before the misery came. Henry Clemens' tragic death after the steamboat explosion was, Ferguson thinks, "in one sense . . . the end of his brother's youth." Years later, when Twain was getting along very well as a journalist, an unfortunate series of events interrupted his career. He chose a particularly inappropriate moment to challenge the editor of a rival newspaper to a duel, a moment when Nevada was trying to obtain statehood and was enforcing its antidueling law. Twain was ordered to get out of the state, and did. (To a Freudian, Twain's action may appear to be wishful rather than unfortunate.) In his autobiography Twain records the shocking effect of a boyhood incident: as a result of skating on the river without permission and then swimming ashore, his friend Tom Nash became ill and remained for the rest of his life deaf and impaired in speech. Twain refers to this disproportionate punishment for a small sin in *The Mysterious Stranger* and seems to have brooded about it; according to his autobiography, he blamed himself when he was a little boy for a number of contemporary calamities.

Ring Lardner blamed his alcoholism on the financial requirements of his large family. But he had begun drinking heavily long before he had children, and he suffered most at a time when his income and popularity were at their highest point.

Bernard Shaw's recollection of his childhood is revealing. "Though I was not ill-treated — my parents being quite incapable of any kind of inhumanity — the fact that nobody cared for me particularly gave me a frightful self-sufficiency . . . that leaves me to this hour a treacherous brute in matters of pure affection." His father's drunkenness had lowered the family's prestige, and his mother escaped to music in her own room. Long before he left Ireland, Shaw had lost all belief in orthodox religion, and before he had written his first play, at the age of thirty-six, he was, as one biographer put it, ready "to view the whole of Western civilization with critical disapproval."

Thackeray impressed his schoolmates with his talent for scoffing while he was still at Charterhouse. Later, at Cambridge, he published a burlesque on the same subject which Tennyson chose for his prize-winning poem, and after leaving school Thackeray spent his time with young wits and professional journalists who were caustically contemptuous of their society.

When Ibsen's well-to-do family lost its money he had to leave home at fifteen and work as a druggist's apprentice. Heine was shocked by the refusal of his wealthy cousin to marry him. Groucho Marx wanted to be a doctor but had to leave school at fourteen. John P. Marquand's long-established New England family lost its money when he was a boy. And Kronenberger feels that for Alexander

Pope "Life, all in all, had perhaps not grown sunnier as it grew more distinguished . . . the hump . . . loomed larger and larger in Pope's mind . . . he had never been allowed to forget his appearance."

E. B. White's reminiscences reveal an early disposition for humor — detachment, shyness, wry comment, eye for incongruity, distortion of anecdotes — which had long preceded the following incident: "My life as a humorist," he says, "began in a Childs' restaurant when a waitress spilled buttermilk down my neck. That great smear of white wet coming down over a blue serge suit, and her words, 'Jesus Christ,' were the turning point in my career."

The popular entertainer who has made a study of other popular entertainers, Steve Allen, accepts the premise that "a difficult early life seems to be an essential requirement for admission to the ranks of the eminent clowns." He lists a number of popular comedians who had unhappy childhoods, and recollects that as a boy he had attempted certain forms of humor which his family and acquaintances did not find funny. He desisted; later he saw precisely the same devices being used by professional comedians and realized that he had been a humorist for a long time.

Lewis Carroll was a stammerer from childhood. "He was a good child," says psychoanalyst Greenacre, "whose angers were controlled by an early and very strong conscience."

Anatole France was sardonic in his teens, happy

during the early years of marriage and pleased with the favorable reception of *Sylvestre Bonnard,* then bored with his wife and his social position. A sense of humor is apparent in his schoolboy letters and his diary. He had what Chevalier calls "a constant alertness to fun; a natural playfulness, and a fertile inclination to mockery, principally at the expense of school, teachers, and schoolmates." France called his nonage "those years of youth whose taste was so bitter to me," and Chevalier is convinced that France lost both his illusions and his happiness when quite young. His favorite writers, in his teens, were Renan, Montaigne, and Rabelais.

Few satirists were good students. And even those who, like Voltaire, were recognized for academic achievement, resented their schoolmates or hated their schools. Sydney Smith was "lonely and unhappy" at Oxford. Anatole France's schoolmates were wealthier and more sophisticated than he was, and the recognition of that fact made France dissatisfied not only with school but with his home and prospects. His teacher ranked him "twenty-sixth out of twenty-six. It is a shame. He can do well."

At Harrow, Byron was "not a good scholar but a wide reader." In spite of his lameness he swam, boxed, and played cricket against Eton by arranging to have another boy run for him. Marquand was reportedly unhappy at high school and at Harvard. Voltaire was the most brilliant student in his class and won the top prizes, but he wrote later, "I learned little but Latin and nonsense." There were two classes of students at the college: sons of noblemen, who had separate rooms, valets, and special privileges; and a large group of humbler boys like Voltaire. A frail youngster, Voltaire avoided sports and games. Lewis Carroll also won prizes, high grades, and recommendations at Harrow, but he wrote later that he would never want to relive those years.

C. S. Lewis had a fantastic education, first at a boarding school run by an insane headmaster who beat the pupils, underfed them, and taught only geometry. Next he attended a great English public school where he developed a hatred for social distinctions, unusual sex practices, and intellectual snobbery. Pope's education, because of his illnesses, was haphazardly provided by priests, schools, and tutors. Swift was classified as a poor student at the secondary and college levels, and always felt disgraced by the fact that his Bachelor's degree from Trinity was awarded only by special dispensation.

Thackeray frequently said that the most miserable years of his life were his early school days. Thoreau's individualism led to disputes with, and sometimes failing grades from, Harvard professors. Sinclair Lewis resented the social discrimination at Yale. Mencken refused to go to college, having been disillusioned by high school educators. Ibsen had to leave school early for financial reasons. And such satiric writers as Dickens, Franklin, Bierce, and Twain never did go to college.

Men usually grow more conservative as they grow older. There are biological, social, and economic reasons for this, and most satirists, like most other writers and most other people, follow this pattern. Like most men, Dryden, Swift, Sinclair Lewis, and Sydney Smith progressed from an early liberalism to a late conservatism; and, like a few men, Anatole France and C. E. S. Wood progressed from an early conservatism to a late liberalism. Those satirists who became successful were exposed to the same indirect pressures toward conformity which most reasonably successful men are exposed to. A satirist whose work is selling well becomes to a certain extent a businessman, and he shares the problems of a businessman regarding conditions most favorable for continued or increased prosperity. A middle-aged satirist is likely to consider his own future prospects at a time when strength may fail and money be scarce. These are social pressures to which all men adjust in one way or another.

Shaw once said that man becomes like his work. A man's temperament, once congealed, rarely changes. The religious conversions of Evelyn Waugh, Roy Campbell, T. S. Eliot, and Graham Greene did not result in a shift toward the positive affirmation of the good, true, and beautiful in their writing; it simply changed the objects of their attacks. They remained as vehemently critical as ever.

That financial success does not automatically lead to political conservatism is shown by Sinclair

Lewis' career. Lewis became financially independent with *Main Street* in 1920; but he wrote his best and most liberal satire in the decade that followed. Oddly enough, in that decade Lewis the literary nonconformist became absurdly sensitive about correct dress in England and on the continent, and tried to keep abreast of the latest sartorial fashions. In the 1930's Lewis did become more conservative politically; but his political conversion, like the religious conversions of Waugh and Eliot, resulted only in a change of content, not of method; he became a critic of the critics of the *status quo,* not a defender of the *status quo* itself.

Anatole France became a "well-tailored boulevardier . . . in his fat and sleek middle years." Having sympathized with the royalists before the Dreyfus case, France became an ardent liberal, active on behalf of the socialists. At first sympathetic to the Russian revolution, he soon became disillusioned and melancholy during his last years.

Greig suggests that two of Thackeray's characters reveal stages of the novelist's own development. "Harry Warrington resembles the improvident and gullible Thackeray of the thirties; George Warrington, the Thackeray of the forties, when misfortunes have sobered and aged him." Ennis tries to identify "protective shells" that Thackeray assumed: "During his earlier career as professional author he sought a reputation as a daring young writer of slashing articles. In his later years, conversely, he loved to think of himself as the kindly old worldling preaching 'lay sermons.' " Toward the end of his life Thackeray showed "an ever-increasing nostalgia, the form of sentimentality most natural to the aged." And after attacking hypocrisy all his life, Thackeray wrote in *The Virginians,* "Oh, let us be thankful, not only for faces, but for masks! Not only for honest welcome, but for hypocrisy, which hides unwelcome things from us!"

W. S. Gilbert became in his last years an exceptionally cantankerous magistrate. W. C. Fields also turned into a "terrible old man." Having been independent enough as a boy to run away from home and set up housekeeping in a boiler on an empty lot, Fields became paranoiac in his old age, suspected all of his servants, and excoriated the government for its plot to pauperize him. Dickens was almost pathologically gloomy during the last years of his life. Gogol was terrified of mob ridicule. H. L. Mencken expressed no new ideas during the last thirty years of his life, gradually intensifying his cynicism and curtailing his humanitarianism. And Charlie Chaplin turned to tragic satire near the end of his career.

Lincoln Steffens tells of an interesting glimpse of Ibsen. Told that the old gentleman sitting alone in a European restaurant was the famous playwright, Steffens walked quietly behind Ibsen to get a look at him. He was startled to find that Ibsen, in a mirror concealed under his hat, was observing the commotion over his presence and primping. By this time Ibsen had presumably reached the final stage described by Thompson:

"At first, as he was maturing, he sought a substitute for the faith he could not accept. Failing, he grew disillusioned and bitter, and at length desperate."

Aldous Huxley progressed, or degenerated, from sophomoric cynicism through "D. H. Lawrence-sensualism" to "scientific mysticism." And Sydney Smith, having spent most of his life fighting for liberal causes, wrote, "I love liberty, but hope that it can be managed that I shall have soft beds, fine linen, etc., for the rest of my life. I am too old to fight or to suffer."

Satirists have had their troubles, but there is no evidence that they had more trouble than other people, or other writers. The Tories did not reward the Reverend Jonathan Swift adequately with religious preferment for his labors in their behalf, and the Whigs did not reward the Reverend Sydney Smith adequately with religious preferment for his activity in their behalf. Robert Burns suffered from poverty, frustration, alcoholism, and illness most of his short life. Dickens never got over the misery of his early months in the blacking factory; nor did he forget the visits to his imprisoned father. Butler hated the entire orthodox family into which he had been born. Cervantes lost a hand in battle, and was a slave in Algiers and a prisoner in Spain.

At one time or another, Cervantes, Voltaire, Hugo, Chaucer, Wilde, Villon, and Molière were in prison. Young Heine was forced to study law instead of literature and during his last years was almost completely paralyzed. Edward Lear spent a frustrated, sickly, lonely, long life.

Ambrose Bierce prospected for gold but did not find it. Dryden, having become a Roman Catholic while James was king, lost the poet laureateship when William took the throne. "We continually get the impression," says Nichol Smith, that Dryden "thought of himself as fighting the battle singlehanded, or with too few allies . . . the sense of disappointment is unmistakable." Damon Runyon's son tells us that Runyon was a hated tyrant who drove his wife and son to drink, and his daughter to a mental institution.

According to Sydney Smith's will, his son Wyndham was to be paid a certain sum each quarter, on condition "that he live apart from his mother." Mark Twain was exposed under particularly painful circumstances to deaths of people he loved. Anatole France was so bitter toward his daughter that even at her death he could not forgive her. Groucho Marx lost all his savings in the 1929 crash, was divorced more than once, and on several occasions thought that his career had ended. Thurber was blinded in one eye at the age of six. Thackeray lost his entire inheritance as a result of gambling and the Indian bank failure. Leacock's father deserted the family, and they had to give up the farm they had bought in Canada. Charles Lamb took care of his recurrently insane sister all his life, but it is not fair to assume that this responsibility was the cause of his alcoholism or of his particular kind of humor. Similar responsibilities caused many other men to become sober and humorless.

Like other human beings, the satirist has often experienced personal disappointments in his relationships with other people. As Freudians see it, any man's chances of leading a happy domestic life are not too good; the likelihood of a writer's doing so is even more remote. And many a satirist had his troubles with women. Sinclair Lewis was divorced by both of the women whom he had, in proper legal sequence, married. John P. Marquand was divorced three times. Charles Dickens and Ambrose Bierce made their wives extremely unhappy before separating from them. Thackeray's wife was committed to a mental institution early in their marriage. Ring Lardner's wife became an alcoholic. When Alexander Pope told Lady Montagu that he loved her, she burst out laughing. Heine never got over the refusal of his cousin to marry him. Charlie Chaplin's early marriages proved unsatisfactory. Swift never married but was uncomfortably intimate with two women; Voltaire never married and was comfortably intimate with many women; and, to the extent that our information is trustworthy, Socrates' relations with Xantippe were not completely satisfactory. In his study of Middle Eastern humor during the first centuries of Islam, Franz Rosenthal observes that "the usually unfriendly and coarse dealings of fools with their mothers constituted part of the repertory of Muslim jesters." And Dr. Pannenborg's statistics convince him that only 7 per cent of the satirists were "happily married."

However, many nonsatirists have also had problems with women, with domesticity, and with promiscuity. Also many writers, satirists and nonsatirists, have been happily married and devotedly attached to their wives for long periods of time. Shaw, Twain, and Mencken were "good" husbands.

Arnold Toynbee's theory — that great men and great artists undergo a period of "exile" from their society — does not help us much with satirists. Some satirists experienced exile, but most didn't — unless one is willing to accept spiritual isolation from society as a form of exile. Ibsen felt so stifled in Norway that he left it and did most of his writing abroad. Shaw left Ireland for England, happily; Swift left England for Ireland, unhappily. Voltaire was officially exiled, sometimes from Paris and sometimes from France, a number of times. Byron and Cervantes and Washington Irving also underwent "exile" of a sort. Dante was driven out of Florence and Heine out of Germany. Butler left England for New Zealand, and Thoreau exiled himself when he went to Walden.

Satirists have had their troubles. But many other writers have had troubles without becoming satirists, and many more people have had troubles without becoming writers. It is not enough to say that a satirist became a satirist because he had problems. In almost every case, the satirist showed satiric tendencies and temperament *before* misfortunes befell him. If, as some psychoanalysts believe, a desire for punishment may become a source of punishment, then these satirists had trouble because deep down in their Freudian hearts they really wanted trouble. But even this would not distinguish the satirists from the rest of society. The same theory would hold true for all people who have been exceptionally unfortunate.

Part Three

Influence

Beliefs

Very few writers have been able to support themselves by writing satire. The great variety of jobs which satirists have held indicates that, whatever their preferences, they accepted whatever work they were able to find.

Jung believes that the artist's occupation and personal life are not especially relevant to his art. "He may go the way of a philistine, a good citizen, a neurotic, a fool, or a criminal. His personal career may be inevitable and interesting, but it does not explain the poet." A. R. Thompson suggests that ironists and humorists are unlikely to take active part in affairs of the community and society because, as he puts it, "They relieve their feelings by their mockery." Many satirists have tended to let their writing substitute for actual physical participation. Goethe said that poets and politics don't mix, although he himself was a poet who had proved extremely successful at politics. But Christie points out that "almost all the leading

Cynic: A blackguard whose
faulty vision sees things as they
are, not as they ought to be.
— Ambrose Bierce

Greek poets were men of action as well as men of letters," and that in the Orient, "literary and official classes tended to become identical." Dante, Voltaire, Machiavelli, Quevedo, and, among English satirists, Milton, Chaucer, Fielding, Canning, Defoe, Addison, Steele, A. P. Herbert, and Swift were active in politics.

If it is true that the satirist becomes a satirist by adjusting to society, having found that his particular skill as a humorous commentator rewards him with prestige or money, then it is not surprising that his choice of profession is fortuitous. In this respect he is similar to nonsatiric writers, many of whom begin either with a quite unliterary ambition or by writing literature quite different from the form in which they find eventual success. The element of chance, of sardonic fate, was recognized by Keats:

> Fame, like a wayward Girl will still be coy
> To those who woo her with too slavish knees,
> But makes surrender to some thoughtless boy.

Having published two unsuccessful books for adults, Hans Christian Anderson wrote in a letter to a friend: "Now I am going to begin some fairy tales for children. I will try to win the future generation, you know." Don Marquis' ambition was to write a great, serious poem; but his poetic drama of the crucifixion, "The Dark Hours," failed, whereas "Archy and Mehitabel," a series of verses about a cat and a cockroach, became very popular. Marquis was conscious of the irony; he said, "It would be one on me if I should be re-membered longest for creating a cockroach charac-ter."

Writers, of course, are not the only ones whom fate thrusts into positions and occupations they may not want. Arthur Sullivan was contemptuous of the popular music he wrote for Gilbert, and dis-appointed over the failure of his "serious" music. U. S. Grant had never wanted to be a soldier; but he hated the prospect of working in his father's tannery even more, so he went to West Point. Eli Whitney, a Yale graduate, had gone to Georgia to look for a teaching job; while waiting on the plantation of a friend he invented the cotton gin.

Art as a vocation, or an avocation, shows up in the careers of many satirists. For some it proved to be a frustrated ambition; for others, a life-long hobby; for a few, the major way of earning a liv-ing. But in this respect, too, the satirist does not differ from the writer in general. Albert Schweitzer regards a number of writers primarily as painters: "Many other authors," he says, speaking of Goethe, "have passed from painting to verbal description and remained pictorial in essence." Schweitzer mentions Taine and Gottfried Keller, discusses Michelangelo as a poet, and concludes, "We call Heine our greatest lyricist. Should we not call him . . . the most inspired painter among lyric poets?"

Emmett Kelly, the famous American clown, says in his autobiography: "My ambition as a kid and as a young man and, even now, has been to be an artist." Bernard Shaw, when he was complimented on a self-portrait he had drawn, replied that it had been his ambition at one time to be "a second Michelangelo, not another Shaw." Having shown some aptitude for art, Lucian was apprenticed to his uncle, a sculptor; fortunately for satire, he ran away after being flogged for breaking a piece of marble. And the eleventh-century Japanese monk, Toba Sojo, was a famous artist as well as a great humorist.

Thackeray studied art (as well as law) before he settled for journalism and fiction. In 1857, when he was independently wealthy and could indulge in whatever activity he chose, he deliberated between returning to art and getting into parliament. Washington Irving was skillful with brush and pencil. Lewis Carroll included, among his hobbies, expert photography. And Anatole France, at the age of fourteen, won a school prize for drawing.

Among satirists who earned a living as artists are Guareschi, the author of the Father Camillo stories; Vercors, who gained a reputation as a satiric painter before he became a satiric writer; and James Thurber, whose cartoons are as well known as his writing. Edward Lear was in his time one of the world's best painters of natural history, his paintings of parrots and turtles being famous for their realism and accuracy.

When young Ibsen was working as a druggist's apprentice, he got into trouble for drawing a local citizen — drunk, embracing his horse, and kissing it fondly. In Ibsen's *When We Dead Awaken,* the sculptor Rubek says, "At bottom they are all re-

spectable, pompous horsefaces, and self-opinion-
ated donkey muzzles, and lop-eared, low-browed
dog skulls, and fatted swine-snouts — and sometimes dull, brutal bull-fronts as well." The artist's
eye, or at least the caricaturist's eye, is at work.

"I did not set out to be a writer," says Evelyn
Waugh. "My first ambition was to paint." He attended art school, but quit when he decided that
he did not have enough talent to make a first-rate
artist.

The romantic notion that all satirists were frustrated in their original ambition, whether that
ambition was to write or not, is not borne out by
the facts. It is true that Voltaire's father was violently opposed to the idea of his son's becoming a
writer. But the family of Jane Austen urged her
to write, and Anatole France's parents made it easy
for him to do so. One reason for parental objection
is the fact that, as Morris Bishop remarks,
"Thomas Hood was the first English writer to
make a living chiefly by writing humor."

Although his father was quite wealthy, Molière
at twenty-one chose to become an actor, and for
a dozen years toured with his company, underpaid,
mistreated, and regarded as a social outcast in
seventeenth-century France. Gogol tried to be an
actor but was not successful. John Dryden recognized his limitations when he spoke of "the
stage (to which my genius never much inclined
me)." And Sinclair Lewis' success as an actor was
credited to force of personality rather than dramatic talent.

Among writers who abandoned law before taking up writing were Thackeray, Gilbert, and Washington Irving. Irving served in his family business and as a staff officer in the War of 1812 before becoming a professional writer and diplomat. Sydney Smith did not want to be a clergyman. He wanted to become a lawyer, but his father refused financial aid. Smith objected to going into the clergy because he felt that there was no future in it for an ambitious man; but since teaching was the only other alternative that his father offered, Smith chose the clergy.

Robert Benchley had planned to become a social worker. George Meredith and Anatole France worked for publishers as "readers." Arbuthnot and Mandeville were physicians. Charles Erskine Scott Wood was a colonel in the American army. John Gay left his hated job as a silk-mercer's apprentice, but was an astute man of business and eventually achieved financial independence. Ring Lardner had gone to the University of Michigan "to study football and dentistry." Fred Allen, working as a boy in the Boston Public Library, found a book on juggling and began practicing. W. C. Fields also juggled. Before Josh Billing could make a living as a humorist, he acted as an auctioneer in Poughkeepsie. Mark Twain was a pilot on the Mississippi and kept his job at times when other good pilots were laid off, so (in spite of Horace Bixby's reminiscences about Twain's lack of confidence) he must have been a good pilot.

Cervantes had been a soldier, a slave in Algiers, a civilian clerk in the naval office, and collector of revenue in Granada. He was not conspicuously successful in any of these occupations.

A strong interest in philology was shown by satirists Samuel Johnson, H. L. Mencken, Swift, Dryden, Lucilius, and Voltaire. When Voltaire was president of the Academy, he suggested the creation of a new dictionary and worked hard to get the project started. Samuel Johnson's dictionary is well known. Mencken's eventual fame may rest on his philological work rather than on his satire.

It may be that writers as a group are impractical and helpless in business matters. But few of the people who had to do business with Bernard Shaw, Somerset Maugham, Sinclair Lewis, Voltaire, Dickens, and Charlie Chaplin felt that they were dealing with incompetents. All of these writers were very successful in getting large sums for their work and in obtaining satisfactory contracts. Contemporary editors have paid reluctant but strong tribute to Maugham's business skill. Shaw was enormously successful in getting high rates for his work and in protecting his interests. Publishers had great respect for Sinclair Lewis' ability in negotiating contracts, and in promoting and advertising his books. Quevedo and Chaucer were skilled diplomatic negotiators. And John Gay had a high reputation as an honest business man; even Jonathan Swift entrusted his London affairs to Gay's hands.

At the other extreme was G. K. Chesterton, who, some of his friends suspected, was unable to make his way across town without assistance, and who might well have starved to death, either in the medieval period he loved or the industrial world he hated, without the managerial assistance of friends.

Enid Welsford compares Archie Armstrong, the last important English court fool, with L'Angely, the last famous French court jester: "Both fools were clever men, who made themselves feared and disliked at court and grew rich by their wit."

Voltaire invested the profits from his first play, *Oedipus*, in Low's Bubble, held his shares for a few weeks, then sold them at a profit before the venture collapsed entirely. Later in his life Voltaire was to loan money to princes, import grain from Africa, supply an army with rations, and become "the richest man of letters that ever lived."

Politics

Because they often criticize the *status quo*, satirists have been called "radicals" by some scholars. Other scholars insist that satirists are conservatives, who attack deviations from the norm (or the theoretical norm) of their society. Each theory is convincing, and would be even more convincing were it not for the fact that there have actually been radical, liberal, conservative, and reactionary satirists. Furthermore, there have been conservative satirists in liberal periods and in conservative periods; and there have been liberal satirists in liberal periods and in conservative periods.

The satirist is likely to be skeptical about most social institutions. Even satirists who are staunch partisans of specific political systems do not pretend that those systems are perfect. And from time to time satirists change their political affiliations, implying that they are not as profoundly convinced as some of their works indicate they are. Samuel Johnson was a Tory, Charles Churchill was a Whig; Swift, like them an eighteenth-century satirist, had been a Whig and became a Tory. Ben Franklin has been praised by conservatives and liberals. Some satirists definitely chose one political party or another; others vacillated among parties in and out of power; still others never committed themselves.

In discussing the politics of satirists it is well to remember that by his very nature the satirist is an attacker rather than a defender. Criticism functions by exposing the wrong, rather than by praising the right. For the satirist it is less a problem of morality than of temperament and technique. Satire specializes in incongruities and weaknesses and inadequacies. For that reason even when he takes the conservative position (as he often does), the satirist concentrates not on defending the *status quo* but on attacking critics of that *status quo*. When he takes the "radical" position, he criticizes the weaknesses of his society. Because every society offers innumerable opportunities for criticism, the satirist is more likely to seem liberal or radical than conservative or reactionary. In practice, however, few satirists have been sufficiently courageous, or sufficiently radical, to attack the basic economic or political organization of their society.

Since the satirist is often motivated by his feelings rather than by his reason it is not safe to assume that simply because he criticizes something he approves of the obvious alternative. It is quite wrong to suppose that because George Orwell ridiculed the excesses of totalitarianism, in *Animal Farm* and *1984,* he approved of capitalism; he was, in fact, an active Socialist. It is a mistake to think, as many critics did, that because Sinclair Lewis was a vociferous critic of middle class Americans he advocated some other way of life. Lewis himself repeatedly admitted that he liked middle class Americans and their way of life best of all. Nor should Aldous Huxley's criticism of the philosophic, scientific, and economic trends of the twentieth century be interpreted as approval of the logical alternatives. Huxley's mystic answers are quite different from the conventional ones.

The impetus that Voltaire gave to the revolution in France is widely recognized. But Voltaire himself accepted the theory of monarchy and, in Schilling's words, "was distrustful of popular movements, of sudden and violent changes in a social scheme of things that had treated him generously most of his life." G. K. Chesterton, who in 1899 had called England an imperialistic bully, in World War I supported England as a "heroic defender of Christian civilization against Prussianism." On the other hand, as Irvine points out, Bernard Shaw supported England in 1899 "as taking a necessary step toward world peace," and in 1914 criticized her "as sharing in the guilt and stupidity of an unnecessary war."

Satirists, like other men, have on occasion changed their political views, usually proceeding from an early liberalism to an elderly or middle-aged conservatism. The customary shift is from adolescent criticism of society to middle-aged defense of society. Among satirists who followed this pattern, Sydney Smith was for many years an aggressive liberal protestant against reactionary Tory procedures; but as he aged, Smith turned more and more toward a conservative position. W. H. Auden sympathized with Communism in the thirties, liberalism in the forties, and conservatism in the fifties. And John Dryden went through a number of changes which coincided with changes in the political climate of England after the Restoration.

Charles Dickens' politics have led critics to contradictory conclusions. Marxist T. A. Jackson insists that Dickens was practically a Communist; conservative G. K. Chesterton insists that Dickens was a conservative. George Orwell and Edmund Wilson find elements of both radicalism and conservatism in Dickens. Monroe Engel concludes that Dickens is a "radical" in the sense of going to the root of things, but definitely not a Marxist, being "anti-deterministic" and "opposed to any extremism." Dickens attacked Chartism, the radical political movement of his own time. Yet he sympathized with many of the Chartist objectives and exposed in his books the social evils of Victorian England.

Some satirists have avoided taking definite political positions. Edgar Johnson, contrasting Ovid to Byron, notes that Ovid's work "had none of those political overtones . . . no paeans to liberty, no blasts of indignation against oppression and tyranny." Analyzing Ibsen's opinions, Thompson writes, "It is characteristic of his ironic temper that in reading Cicero Ibsen sympathized with the object of the orator's invective, the rebel against order and respectability." Ibsen may have been sympathetic, but he never expressed any rebellion against the political systems of his own time. Max Eastman says of Artemus Ward that "many of his opinions were a mere, unimaginative standing-pat on the *status quo* . . . his attitude toward the Mormons was Philistine. Upon the subject of woman's rights he was an ordinary male bigot. . . . Politically he was vague." Eastman feels that Ward was telling the truth when he said, "I have only drifted with the current, which has carried me gaily on of its own accord." And Thackeray showed as a student at Cambridge "the same mistrust of extremes in political and religious questions that he showed in later life." When he stood for Parliament, it was as an Independent.

In an article on satirists in politics, Dr. Pannenborg notes that of the eleven satirists he classified as "extroverts," five were involved in political activity — Beaumarchais, Defoe, Kotzebue, Machiavelli, and Voltaire. Pannenborg suggests that politically active individuals are far more likely to make use of irony than the average man, that the typical politician tends to be ambitious, imperious, and unreliable, and that these five satirists were ambitious, imperious, and unreliable.

If Bergson's view (laughter is society's way of punishing nonconformists and keeping them in line) is correct, satire is basically conservative and satirists are conservatives. In support of this theory, Zucker points out that the hero who challenges the existing order and becomes the standard bearer of a revolt is likely to be the "protagonist of a tragedy." The criticism of the *status quo* by humorists and satirists is a safe one, says Zucker, "where the comedian ridicules some old institutions . . . the old hierarchy has already cracked up and the audience applauds its own victory." But it would be extremely difficult to prove that all of the objects of satiric criticism have actually "cracked up."

A related theory states that laughter at the expense of the *status quo* permits a healthy letting-off of steam; the laughers understand that they are indulging in a letting-off of steam, and that the criticized institutions will not be changed. In the Fool's Day celebrations popular during the Middle Ages, the Fools and their patrons took prominent part; "however," notes Enid Welford, "in France, as was natural, the royal fools were noted champions of orthodoxy." The newspapers and periodicals with the largest circulation in the United States and England are today the aggressively conservative ones, whose caustic ridicule of innovators and idealists seems to please their reading public.

"The satirist claims," says Robert Elliott, "with much justification, to be a true conservative. Usually . . . he operates within the established framework of society, accepting its norms . . . as the standard against which to judge the follies he sees. He is the preserver of tradition." Bernard Shaw once said, "In really contemporary situations, your genius is ever one part genius and ninety-nine parts Tory." Swift, Pope, Johnson, Gay, Arbuthnot, Dryden, Gilbert, and Canning are prominent English conservatives. "Orthodoxy is my doxy," announced Sam Johnson. Russell Kirk gives Chesterton and Belloc credit for nourishing the conservative impulse, although he limits his approval: "But Belloc and Chesterton were only auxiliaries of conservatism." Kirk praises James Russell Lowell's conservatism, disregarding his early radicalism and explaining that Lowell's deviations from tradition were due to special conditions in the North of his time. Lowell wrote in a letter, "I was always a natural Tory, and in England should be a staunch one." Roy Campbell, an avid disciple of Wyndham Lewis, was a militant fascist.

Sei-Shonagon's *Pillow-Book* is a classic example of Japanese satire. Her humor, R. H. Blyth says, "is peculiarly Japanese in that it springs from the genius she has for the perception of the fitness of things." French remarks that "it is idle to reproach Chaucer for the conservatism which is so pronounced a feature of his temperament," and to complain that he is not clearly aware of the rottenness of medieval institutions. And W. F. Taylor observes that during the nineteenth century the "native American humorists . . . customarily assumed the prudential code of the middle class, and often explicitly satirized violations of that code."

The inconsistency of a conservative satirist's position is recognized by Cazamian: Jonathan Swift "stirred up a deep and secret unrest in the minds of those in power during his time . . . despite the conformity of his declarations and principles." Yet the basic conservatism of Swift seems unquestionable. In his sermon on "mutual subjection," Swift warned the poor against committing the sin of "murmuring and repining, that God hath dealt his blessings unequally to the sons of man." Swift regarded the inferior position of most men a necessity in God's order. "For a person of Swift's conservative habits of mind," Louis Landa says, this theory seemed perfectly acceptable; Landa shows that although Swift was a strong supporter of the Charity School movement, he insisted that these schools train their pupils only for "the very meanest trades" and as domestic help. Swift warned against the economic danger of preparing people above their station in life.

As with Voltaire and Swift, there is evidence of inconsistency in the conservatism of Dr. Johnson. George B. Hill quotes a number of "radical" statements by Johnson which might have "scared the city Tories." Johnson's acceptance of the theory of subordination and his insistence on the fundamental principles of Tory philosophy made him a fairly safe man to be given a pension. Yet Johnson was unorthodox enough to write: "No scheme of policy has in any country yet brought the rich and poor on equal terms into the court of judicature." At another time he said, "a decent provision for the poor is the true test of civilization." His religious and ultraconservative father, a man similar to the father against whom Anatole France rebelled, became for Samuel Johnson a symbol of dignity and respect; Johnson remained a confirmed Tory and a devout layman. One of Johnson's early teachers, John Hunter, was a confirmed Jacobite, and the climate of opinion in Lichfield was strongly conservative. At Oxford, where Johnson went in 1728, the same tradition prevailed.

On the political continuum, a line between conservatives and reactionaries cannot be sharply drawn. If, however, we are to regard those who are most insistent on a return to the past as representative of the reactionary point of view, Juvenal is a reactionary. He complains about the privileges extended to former slaves, the impudence of actors and merchants and gladiators, the prevalence of Greeks and other foreigners in Rome, and the loss of respect for old families. Juvenal says nothing about the advantages of political freedom in the old republic, before the tyrannical emperors of his own day took power; he rants about moral decay, but carefully avoids direct criticism of cruel and degenerate kings.

If H. L. Mencken were judged solely by his writings, he too would have to be regarded as a reactionary. His espousal of the "superman" theory of Nietzsche, his acceptance in human society of the law of the jungle, his contempt for democracy, all put Mencken in the category of political reactionaries. He ridiculed Christianity, he hated socialism, and he despised "humanitarianism."

Aristophanes, colorful and vituperative, was also a reactionary. He was always fighting for the good old days, when families like his own were given proper recognition. A rich man and a landowner, he had personal as well as philosophic reasons for objecting to the political and economic policies of the democratic parties in power. He was courageous in expressing that objection, but it was the objection of a conservative critic.

Whether T. S. Eliot belongs in the conservative or reactionary grouping is debatable. Russell Kirk puts him in "the tradition of Burke." Eliot's desire for a graded society, his opposition to democracy, and his partisanship for the elite certainly put him far to the right of center.

Evelyn Waugh claims that "there is no political party in existence . . . sufficiently (in the strictly literal sense of the word) reactionary" for him to join. He maintains that he is at least two hundred years behind the times and in his comments on modern politics approves only of fascist governments. Waugh urges a return to the medieval way of life, with greater respect for the aristocracy and the Catholic Church. In a one-man war against modern civilization, he writes with a pen which has to be dipped in ink, refuses to learn how to drive a car, and sends letters to neighbors instead of using the telephone. Waugh is rebelling against a liberal society, liberal religion, and liberal politics.

In an essay called "The Socialist," Ambrose Bierce described the typical socialist as a stupid, often immoral, intellectually sick incompetent who wants to level society down to its lowest denominator. Bierce attacked all organized attempts of civilized society to care for its members. No system of political philosophy appealed to him, but inasmuch as he castigated liberal institutions far more vehemently than conservative ones it seems safe to call Bierce a reactionary.

Shortly before he died, Dean Inge remarked that he believed neither in "heaven, hell, nor the British socialists." And Mikes calls Stephen Leacock "a republican who genuinely approved of the monarchy."

Just as there is reason to doubt the consistency of conservative satirists, there are grounds for questioning the consistency of liberal satirists. They too have often contradicted themselves. Even the liberalism of Anatole France, who late in his career was lauded by communists, has been questioned. Marcel LeGoff says, "His socialism is not an urge of the heart, nor an organizing thought, it is but the manifestation of his irony." Chevalier dismisses the liberal activities of France (Dreyfus, socialism, pacifism) as peripheral. France, however, reverses the usual order of development, and proceeds from the conservatism of his early years to the liberalism of his later period. He said, before World War I, "I do not wish for socialism, but I do not fear it." During the war he expressed sympathy for Russian communism, but towards the end of his life he was, according to Shanks, completely disillusioned and disgusted with all revolutions.

Sydney Smith was an active and courageous Whig most of his life, especially when it was politically unwise to be one. But after 1830, when the Whigs came into power, he became more and more conservative, saying, "I find an utter inability of fighting for either party." By the time he died, Smith had expressed doubts about the wisdom of extending the franchise. Yet he had spent most of his life fighting for liberal causes, at the expense of his own promotion in the church.

Sinclair Lewis had never been very radical, and by the end of his life veered towards conservatism. As early as his Nobel Prize Address in 1929, he described himself, correctly, as "a writer whose most anarchistic assertion has been that America, with all her wealth and power, has not yet produced a civilization good enough to satisfy the deepest wants of human creatures." P. G. Wodehouse admits, "I never was interested in politics. I'm quite unable to work up any kind of belligerent feeling." And there is good reason to believe that Charlie

Chaplin's criticism of society is based less on Marxist political theory than on an individualistic, anarchistic revolt against all kinds of authority.

Among liberal satirists, covering a wide range of "liberalism," are Shaw, Hugh MacDiarmid, John Kendrick Bangs, H. G. Wells, George Orwell, and J. B. Priestley, who announced in 1951, "I am not a socialist." To these may be added Charles Churchill, John Wolcot, Lord Byron, Addison, and Steele, and, with some reservations, Hugo, Vondel, Franklin, Freneau, and Trumbull.

The radical of one generation becomes, it has been often observed, the conservative of the next. That wild radical of the early twentieth century, Shaw, is today dismissed as an old-fashioned Fabian socialist.

Religion

In their attitude toward orthodox religion, or the religion that their particular society accepted as "orthodox," satirists range from St. Jerome and pious Samuel Johnson to atheistic Sinclair Lewis. Evelyn Waugh and G. K. Chesterton and Roy Campbell were converted to Catholicism, and T. S. Eliot to Anglicanism, but all four wrote satire both before and after their conversions. Among the antireligious satirists, even Bierce, Mencken, Lewis, Twain, and Voltaire carefully distinguished between Christianity, which they criticized, and Christ, whom they respected. C. S. Lewis, Hilaire Belloc, Samuel Johnson, and G. K. Chesterton wrote satire in defense of religion. Mark Twain, H. L. Mencken, Samuel Butler the second, Sinclair Lewis, and Voltaire wrote satire against religion. All are good satirists.

Donne, Dryden, Swift, Pope, Addison, Gay, and Samuel Johnson were "religious" satirists. Chaucer is generally felt to have been an orthodox Catholic, although excerpts from his works were sometimes quoted by anti-Catholic reformers during the Reformation. Evelyn Waugh announced in 1954: "In my future books there will be two things to make them unpopular; a preoccupation with style and the attempt to represent man more fully, which to me means only one thing, man in his relation to God." Erasmus was apparently too liberal for fifteenth-century Catholicism, but not liberal enough for the Reformation. Vondel was genuinely devout.

Jonathan Swift made his position clear. Of Freethinkers he said: "Their intent is to overthrow all religion, that they may gratify their vices without any reproach from the world." And, "Let no man think that he can lead as good a moral life without Faith, as with it."

Although Washington Irving technically belongs with the believers, Stanley Williams expresses some doubts: "Despite Irving's ultimate union with the Church of England . . . there is often in his essays a half-pagan satisfaction in the pleasures of this world, and little disposition on the whole to seek compensation in another."

The religion of the Reverend Sydney Smith,

Hesketh Pearson thinks, was genuine but not doctrinaire. "To do good and to be happy — that was his creed. As to whether a certain saint had said or done this or that . . . what did it matter?" Elsewhere Pearson said of Smith, "No man was ever less of a fanatic than he. He believed that Christianity was made for man, not man for Christianity."

Lewis Carroll, in his way, was a believer in the orthodox religion of his society; Aeschylus and Sophocles, in their quite different ways, were believers in the orthodox religion of their society; and James Russell Lowell was an orthodox believer in the religion of his society.

C. S. Lewis' family was Church of England; as a schoolboy he rejected religion, with the feeling that he was being liberated from hypocrisy rather than from belief. He lived through his twenties, he says, a reasonably happy, amoral man. But a realization that he was experiencing only "pleasure, not joy," made him desire "joy" irresistibly. This "joy" could be achieved, he decided, only through religion. When at the age of thirty he came back to the church, he called himself "perhaps, that night, the most dejected and reluctant convert in all England."

Between the devout believers and the outright nonbelievers there stretches a long line of satirists; some were deists, some were religious at one time and unreligious at another, and some simply cannot be categorized. Shaw announced that for him Creative Evolution was a religion as well as a science, and maintained that a great artist who lacked religion would, like Shakespeare, become a pessimist. Because Thackeray's mother had forced him to attend evangelical services he developed an antipathy "for that sort of composition"; but even when he went through a skeptical stage at Cambridge, he never questioned the existence of a personal God and in discussions with FitzGerald always upheld doctrine against his friend's agnosticism.

Voltaire spent his life attacking the church; he is usually called a deist; and he died, or tried to die, a Catholic. Attempting to explain why, after a lifetime of attacking the church, he wanted so badly to die with its blessing, Voltaire said: "It is necessary for a man to die in the religion of his fathers. If I lived upon the banks of the Ganges, I should wish to die with a cow's tail in my hand." When another deist, Benjamin Franklin, brought his grandson to meet Voltaire and asked for a blessing for the boy, Voltaire said, "My child, God and Liberty, remember those two words." Thirty years earlier Voltaire had managed, in spite of his feud with the church in France, to get a blessing and two medals directly from the Pope. Voltaire opposed for forty years what he felt to be the injustices of the church and the superstitions fostered by it; but when he died the official Catholic Register admitted that Voltaire never seemed "to have contracted the stupid frenzy of atheism."

There is some doubt whether the "irreligion" of Voltaire was less Christian than the "religion" of Baudelaire, Huysmans, and Evelyn Waugh. Heine's "deism" had flaws; when Heine described Spinoza as "my fellow unbeliever Spinoza," he was not only denying an orthodox religion but implying the acceptance of an unorthodox yet genuinely spiritual one. And William Faulkner once remarked that, having found God, Hemingway became a good writer.

Tracing the stages of Auden's religious metamorphoses is not easy, even for Auden; he went through Anglicanism and skepticism, considered Catholicism, and paused at a special kind of existentialism. Ibsen was never able to return to the religion of his youth, and seemed disturbed by his inability to do so; Thompson suggests that, having failed to find a substitute for faith in his playwriting, Ibsen "grew disillusioned and bitter and at length desperate." Although critics are not sure of what Euripides did believe in, they agree that he did *not* believe literally in the numerous Greek deities which his contemporaries presumably worshipped. The deism of Benjamin Franklin neither hurt not helped the satires that he wrote. Ring Lardner and Aldous Huxley, from quite different unorthodox religious positions, were able to write successful satire. The mysticism of Huxley and Thoreau caused both men to ridicule man's attempt to substitute science for soul.

"I don't believe in hell — but I'm afraid of it," said Mark Twain. Twain's attitude towards God varied, but the dominant tone was skeptical pessimism. Parsons says: "When Clemens let his mind dwell on God, he was likely to be pessimistic, but when he contemplated a Newtonian-deistic creator . . . he swung towards optimism." Twain's championship of Satan is generally felt to be antireligious, but his consistent defense of genuinely Christian virtues (as distinguished from Christian practices) is religious. Mark Twain himself was never quite sure.

In the definitely antireligious group, Ambrose Bierce has a prominent place. He says in the essay "Religion" that he is not a Christian, but he calls Jesus the best, truest, and sweetest figure in literature, next to Buddha. Bierce attacks Christianity, never Christ, and like other satirists accepts many teachings of religious leaders as desirable; the failure to carry out those teachings by the professed followers of those leaders seems to him hypocritical. Bierce's definition of "Christian" is: "One who believes that the New Testament is a divinely inspired book admirably suited to the spiritual needs of his neighbor. One who follows the teachings of Christ insofar as they are not inconsistent with a life of sin."

H. L. Mencken made his atheistic position clear in his essays and the *Treatise on the Gods.* "It is impossible to avoid disgust," said Mencken, "in the presence of one who believes that he has an immortal soul of some vaguely gaseous nature and that it will continue to exist four hundred million years after he has been shoveled away." Mencken defined a "Clergyman" as "a ticket speculator outside the gates of heaven." "If the average man is made in God's image," he reasoned, "then such a man as Beethoven or Aristotle is plainly superior to God." Mencken could find no special condition during his formative years which would account for his atheism. The women in his family regarded churchgoing as a social function; his father was an agnostic. Mencken attended Sunday school, liked church music, and denied that any severe restrictions were placed upon him there. Yet some critics have interpreted the vigor of his attack on religion as proof of his rebellion against a puritan upbringing.

Kotzebue, Montesquieu, and Machiavelli expressed varying degrees of skepticism. The reminiscences of Anatole France's friends show that in his old age he was almost fanatical in the effort to disprove the historicity of Christ; France had been brought up in a devout Catholic family and had attended a Catholic college. Wilson Mizner said, "I respect faith, but doubt is what gets you an education." Samuel Butler fought throughout his adult life the orthodox Christianity of his hated father. And Sinclair Lewis, an admitted atheist, carried his aggressiveness so far as to challenge God, from a church pulpit, to strike him dead. W. A. White felt that God did strike Lewis dead, as an artist, at that moment.

Dr. Pannenborg believes that the phlegmatic type of person is least likely to mock at religion; conversely, the schizothymic satirist, the nervous type, is most likely to be antireligious. The average proportion of "deeply religious" people, he claims, is 30 per cent; for satirists it is 7 per cent.

Philosophy

In their personal philosophy, satirists appear to be somewhat more pessimistic than other writers. But Mencken openly avows enthusiasm. "I must confess, with sixty only around the corner, that I have found existence on this meanest of planets extremely amusing, and, taking one day with another, perfectly satisfactory." Speaking of George Orwell, Voorhees says, "Human life was a good thing, and the suffering was to be accepted. 'Ripeness is all' was one of his favorite quotations." H. G. Wells, who had long bubbled with optimism and had offered solutions to most of the world's problems as casually as the druggist in *Tono Bongay* sold patent medicine, became quite depressed over the world's prospects towards the end of his life. Alexander Pope, in spite of his illnesses and hump and social frustrations, wrote that "All partial evil is universal good" and "whatever is, is right." These optimistic statements may sound strange coming from a man who called his life "perpetual misery," but that is what Pope wrote.

Although some critics feel that Bernard Shaw's puritanism reflects a joylessness in life, the majority are convinced that Shaw was an extreme optimist, believing wholeheartedly in man's ability to help direct evolution toward a more perfect society. "I am prepared to back human society," Shaw said, "against any idea, positive or negative, that can be brought into the field against it." He accepted both the *elan vital* of Bergson and the categorical imperative of Kant, and reasoned that both of those concepts help prove that the universe is an evolving and purposeful organism. In the Preface to *Man and Superman* he wrote: "This is the true joy in life, the being used for a purpose recognized by yourself as a mighty one . . . being a force of Nature instead of a feverish selfish little clod of ailments and grievances complaining that the world will not devote itself to making you happy." The Life Force, Shaw thought, is not perfect and sometimes runs into temporary delays on its ascending journey. But the journey *is* ascending, and Evil does not really exist; it is folly which is often mistaken for malice. The strongest force in the universe is Creative Evolution — and it is a good force.

Whatever their philosophy, a number of satirists were hedonists in their personal lives, or tried as hard as they could to be hedonists. Mencken and Sinclair Lewis and Norman Douglas and Somerset Maugham, while showing in their writings the unhappiness of men, have themselves tried to find as much physical satisfaction and pleasure as they could. They shared the attitude of the famous French philosopher who, chided by a nobleman for being a gourmet, retorted, "And do you think God made all these good things for fools?"

Sydney Smith wrote: "My idea of Heaven is eating *pâté de foie gras* to the sound of trumpets"; before departing for heaven, Smith managed to attend an enormous number of parties and dinners, and to enjoy himself at most of them. In a letter to a friend, Smith listed, semijocularly, some rules for happy living. Included among these were: "Amusing books. . . . Short views of human life — not further than dinner or tea. . . . Be as busy as you can . . . Compare your lot with that of other people. . . . Don't expect too much from human life — a sorry business at the best. . . . Do good." These views are not nearly as original as Sydney Smith's humor was, but they are hardly an indication of cynical philosophy. In a letter to another friend, Sydney Smith warned against "the melancholy effects of temperance," adding, "Depend upon it, the wretchedness of human life is only to be encountered upon the basis of meat and wine."

From Horace to Anatole France many satirists found hedonism the most satisfactory method of dealing with the vicissitudes of life. And though in their books they ridiculed materialism and sensuality, they tried to get as much personal pleasure out of both as they could. They could have cultivated their gardens like Candide if they had really wanted to, but they preferred to enjoy the fruits of the garden and to work at writing instead.

Juvenal's praise of the Stoic philosophy would be more convincing if his satires did not reveal qualities somewhat difficult to reconcile with pure

Stoicism. His hatred of foreigners, his romantic escapism to primitive times, his tirades against the excessive freedom of those not nobly born, his contempt for humble occupations — all are less characteristic of a stoic than of a disappointed man.

Although most satirists have avoided an explicit statement of their philosophies, and have not been consistent, the majority of them can be fairly described as "skeptics." Not all of them would go as far as Anatole France when he said, "To die for an idea is to set a rather high price upon conjectures. . . . There is some impertinence in getting oneself burned to death for an opinion," but most of them shared his distrust of absolute criteria and permanent dogmas. France also believed that "life is made bearable only by illusions. . . . It is possible for art to play a role by fostering those illusions, the best of which is beauty."

A number of Sinclair Lewis' protagonists expressed a skeptical attitude very similar to his own. Doremus Jessup, the liberal editor in *It Can't Happen Here,* says: "What conceivable reason could one have for seeking after righteousness in a world which so hated righteousness? . . . He never did find any particularly good reason. He simply went on." Ann Vickers asks: "Were the statistics-stuffed and liberal-minded social workers . . . really capable of instituting a vastly better system of government than the greedy and cynical politicians of Tammany Hall and Republican headquarters?" And the following remark of

Doremus Jessup is one which Lewis himself had often made: "Well, gentlemen, I have listened to all your solutions, and I now inform you that I . . . have the perfect, the inevitable, the only solution, and that is: there is no Solution!" As one of the maxims for revolutionaries, Bernard Shaw listed the following: "The golden rule is that there are no golden rules."

Skepticism is as genteel a word as any to describe James Thurber's attitude when he wrote, "Man is born to the belief that he is superior to the lower animals, and . . . critical intelligence comes when he realizes that he is more similar than dissimilar. . . . He will not get anywhere until he realizes . . . that he is . . . less kindly than the dog, possessed of less dignity than the swan, and incapable of being as magnificent an angel as the black panther. I have become a little tired of the capitalization of man, his easy assumption of a dignity more apparent than real, and his faith in a high destiny for which he is not fitted by his long and bloody history." Mark Twain and Will Cuppy and Ring Lardner would have agreed with this point of view.

The skepticism of H. L. Mencken is summarized in his statement: "*Quod est veritas?* Simply something that seems to me to be so — now, and to me. It has no more objective character than the sweet and dreadful passion of love." This attitude has led many satirists, including Swift and Sinclair Lewis and Mark Twain, to a position which seems to be anti-intellectual. The satirist plays both ends against the middle; he uses logic to support his own arguments; he rejects logic when it supports arguments that he does not approve of. Like most men, the satirist accepts emotional evidence when it bolsters his position. Among writers, the satirist is in good company: Isaiah Berlin speaks of "Tolstoy's natural anti-intellectualism . . . and his deeply skeptical and pessimistic view of the strength of non-rational motives in human behavior."

Satirists-clergymen Jonathan Swift and Sydney Smith shared a belief more appropriate for satirists than for clergymen. Swift said, "Fear and hope are the two greatest motives of all men's action." And Sydney Smith wrote, "From what motive but fear, I should like to know, have all the improvements in our constitution proceeded? . . . If I say, give this people what they ask because it is just, do you think I should get ten people to listen to me?"

Satirists sometimes sound more bitter than they actually are. Charlie Chaplin once said, "The human race I prefer to think of as an underworld of the gods. When the gods go slumming they visit the earth." Dean Inge paraphrased Jonathan Swift when he said, "I do not love the human race. I have loved just a few of them. The rest are a pretty mixed lot." Mandeville believed that man's reason is defective because it is influenced by irrational passions. Mandeville was willing to accept this fact and to make use of it with what seems to the squeamish a cynical brutality, but which may have seemed to Mandeville simply candor. Fadiman offers as a possible explanation for Ambrose Bierce's interest in the supernatural the fact that "he was so obsessed by the horror of real life that he had to call in the aid of another dimension in order to express it." And Mencken wrote: "I know of no existing nation that deserves to live, and I know of very few individuals."

Samuel Johnson, like Mencken, was often more cruel in what he wrote than in what he did. There is no doubt that he was profoundly pessimistic. Yet in a mellower moment Samuel Johnson wrote, "Mutual benevolence is the great end of society," and "to receive and communicate assistance constitutes the happiness of human life." According to John Gay, civilized men casually betray friends in a fashion which no animal would permit. But Voltaire set up at Ferney a model society to show the world how a philosopher would rule. Voltaire had said, "A government which could provide for all would do more in a year than the order of preaching friars have done since their institution," and at Ferney he not only provided a decent living for all of the people working in his factory, but offered a refuge for the oppressed and persecuted from many lands.

Mark Twain suggested in *The Mysterious Stranger* that there are only two ways for man to achieve happiness — insanity and death. "Why is it that we rejoice at birth and grieve at a funeral?" he asked. "It is because we are not the person involved." And in *Pudd'nhead Wilson's Calendar* Twain wrote, "If you pick up a starving dog and make him prosperous, he will not bite you. This is the principal difference between a dog and a man."

The satirist is likely to be a skeptic. Because he suspects that values are relative, he distrusts dogmas. Because he knows that many beliefs which were unquestioningly accepted in the past have proved to be wrong, he is dubious about beliefs of the present. It is not so much longing for truth as suspicion of falsehood that stirs him. Like Aldous Huxley he is likely to believe that the principal difference between the educated and the uneducated is that the former are able to offer more scholarly evidence for precisely the same beliefs as the latter hold. He tends to see romantic love as a sign of overstimulated gonads; politeness as artificiality; the thief's work as illegal and the politician's as extra-legal; education and smuggling and advertising as businesses, conducted by equally self-interested individuals. The satirist is prone to giving flip replies because he suspects that our knowledge of Truth is extremely limited.

A number of questions about the relationship between satire and philosophy remain to be answered. Because few philosophers have been humorists, it has been generally assumed that profundity is inconsistent with humor. Conversely, it has also been assumed that humorists are superficial observers, and that only such men as Socrates and Montaigne and Schopenhauer could raise irony to the level of significant philosophy. Most scholars think that the cynicism of La Rochefoucauld and Bierce constitutes too narrow a view of life, that the philosophies of Voltaire and Shaw are unsystematic, and that the element of playfulness in humorous writing is definitive proof of its immaturity. Irwin Edman felt that the inadequacy of existentialism stems from making "a cult of anxiety and despair," and finding "a kind of wry comfort in saying, 'Since the world is absurd, let absurdity and irony be our standards.'"

In defense of the satirist, however, it may be maintained that far from being too superficial an observer to differentiate reliably between the real and the apparent, the profound and the superficial, he is one of the few observers who do see the truth — and that he reports on its operations in the daily actions of men, instead of speculating on its theoretical existence in library cubicles. The fact that the satirist's manner is casual or flippant does not necessarily mean that what he is saying is untrue. Indeed most satirists, like Leacock and Thurber, for example, communicate their ideas most effectively not when they make serious expository statements but when they write satiric sketches, stories, fables, and parodies.

Ambiguous Ideology

The satirist's business is to criticize and to attack; his special talent, his technique, and his attitude are not suitable for defending or praising. But because unrestrained criticism and indiscriminate attack are frustrating and socially undesirable, the satirist needs to believe in something — or to pretend to believe in something. That "something" usually proves to be a vague ideal or an abstract principle which he uses as his criterion for judging men's actions.

The ideal most frequently adopted by great satirists is "freedom" — freedom in a form so general that even its enemies usually pretend to accept it. Freedom from religious persecution, from conformist restrictions, from stupid customs, from unfair politics has been vehemently defended by Voltaire, Byron, Mencken, Sinclair Lewis, Anatole France, Heine, and many other satirists.

This belief in some vaguely positive ideal acts as a rudder for the satirist and superimposes a measure of consistency into his work. The ideal itself is rarely offered openly as an alternative. Its function is to help guide the reactions of the satirist, reactions which are often impulsive and sometimes contradictory. In essence, the satirist does what Heine said a nation does: "As once every nation, in adopting Christianity, altered it according to its own needs and disposition, so each will now adopt of the new religion, liberty, only that which fits its local requirements and national character."

In addition to the concept of freedom, the satirist sometimes chooses for his ideal a hazy notion of a society more beautiful, or more logical, or more pleasant, or more interesting than the one in which he lives. From Horace to Marquand satirists have suspected that there is no utopian solution to man's problems. But they have usually been reluctant to confess that suspicion. It is advisable for satirists to restrain themselves from offering positive alternatives to the conditions which they criticize; when satirists do offer alternatives, those alternatives usually prove to be either so abstract as to be useless, or so banal as to be childish. The social alternatives of Sinclair Lewis and Nikolai Gogol are superficial; the mystic alternatives of Huxley and Thoreau seem, to most human beings, impractical.

Also contributing to the vagueness of satirists' ideals is the fact that satirists are seldom radical in their metaphysics or politics or social philosophy. Since they are essentially conservative, in that they do not really object to the way in which their society is *fundamentally* organized, they are not likely to offer a revolutionary alternative to that society.

This ambiguity is clearly apparent to the scholar who tries to summarize the specific beliefs of the satirist whose work he is studying. The difficulty stems not from the critic's inadequacy but from the satirist's vagueness. "George Orwell is the conscience of his generation," says V. S. Pritchett. But precisely in what way this conscience functioned is not very clear: Orwell was a socialist who satirized socialism, a liberal who was skeptical about the ability of liberals to solve society's problems. E. B. White likes life in the country and Don Marquis' ideal man seems to have been the pioneer of the frontier. But in the township and on the frontier still remains the discontent which White and Marquis had found in the societies they had rejected. Thurber was either wise enough or cynical enough not to offer any ideal, vague or specific; he made it clear that neither the frontier of Marquis nor the country-side of White satisfied him.

When he was asked shortly before his death whether he had discovered any meaning in life, Logan Pearsall Smith said: "Yes, there is a meaning. At least, for me, there is one thing that matters — to set a chime of words tinkling in the minds of a few fastidious people." Word-tinkling is hardly an ideal likely to convince most people that the satirist's work is significant. In this sense Smith resembles Max Beerbohm, of whom Kronenberger wrote, "when he savors it is not to make converts, any more than when he satirizes it is really to protest."

Carl Van Doren criticized Ring Lardner who had great comic gifts and created typically American characters but, Van Doren thought, lacked stature because he was "not passionately upset by vulgarity or stupidity"; he was simply amused. The notion that being passionately, or dispassionately, upset by vulgarity or stupidity is an adequate ideal for a satirist is open to question. But there is no questioning the fact that Lardner had no program for improving society.

Nor is the ideology of Artemus Ward especially original: "I have always meant the creatures of my burlesques should stab Error and give Right a friendly push." Marquand satirizes New Englanders' excessive interest in tradition and businessmen's excessive interest in money, but he admires the New Englanders and the businessmen, so it is difficult to see what alternative he prefers to the conditions he criticizes. Van Wyck Brooks felt that the measure which Mark Twain held up against his own society was not much different from that society; after Matthew Arnold's criticism of American materialism, Twain jumped to its defense by glorifying the American mechanic in *The Connecticut Yankee.*

T. K. Whipple saw in Sinclair Lewis' "series of postures" an attempt to find a genuine positive belief, and Spears thinks that W. H. Auden's philosophic metamorphoses are a similar quest for certainty. "Since . . . Auden . . . needs common standards to serve as norms . . . for his satire, his whole career may be described as a search for beliefs." Spears concludes that Auden "advocates no panacea . . . and he has little faith in programs." Eric Bentley suggests that Oscar Wilde's "solution to . . . the problem of finding a vantage point for satire in an unaristocratic age . . . was the solution of Bohemianism." Bohemianism may have been a solution, and a mask, for Wilde, but it is not the highest possible ideal for a satirist nor a satisfactory solution for social problems.

In summing up the philosophy of Evelyn Waugh, Joan Griffiths feels that his ideals are "too limited and partisan to suggest any profound concern with the human dilemma. Waugh's values are dead things." And William L. Miller, ridiculing moral claims made for humorists, says that Benchley "did strike a blow for freedom from the merci-lessness of a hostess intent upon her guests having a good time, but that's about the extent of it."

When Edgar Johnson summarizes the positive beliefs of satirists, in his *Treasury of Satire,* he is compelled to use generalizations and abstractions. The best that he can say about Thomas Love Pea-cock's ideology is: "The two things he truly loves and takes seriously are classical scholarship and comfortable living." In defense of Ben Jonson he says, "He does believe in men's capacity for shame and sanity . . . let them reform themselves. They can." The positive teaching of Horace is summed up as "keep to the golden mean, admire nothing too heartily, and enjoy each day as it comes." That of course was also Candide's conclusion, hardly a startlingly original solution of man's problems. "Like Rabelais, [Molière] has confidence in the health and soundness of human instincts." And Rabelais teaches, says Professor Johnson, that "virtue lies in a free choice of what is good; not in blind obedience . . . only free men and free women . . . can be really courteous and well bred, have generous hearts and loving spirits." The best he can say of W. S. Gilbert's idealism is: "Though Gilbert cares nothing for virtue and hardly seems to grant its existence, he has a hatred of pretense, a rough loyalty to fact." Chesterton's virtue consists of the fact that "to modern chi-canery . . . he opposed medieval chivalry." Norman Douglas "has no desire to change the world, little faith in change save as novelty." And of Addison, Johnson says, "Nothing he said would ever disturb the most deep-seated convictions of commercial respectability."

Jonathan Swift's criticisms of society are specific and concrete. But his alternatives to that society are not nearly so clear. William Ewald says: "The values he appeals to most frequently are permanent ones — the belief . . . that fraud, war, and madness are bad and that truthfulness, reason and humility are good." There isn't much doubt that these qualities do seem "bad" and "good" respectively, to most people; but that admission does not really lead to the elimination of man's troubles. And Cazamian's remark about Swift — "his preferences lie in the observance of a golden mean" — limits the satirist to a fairly safe ideal.

When Stuart Sherman summed up the positive values of Sinclair Lewis he could only say: "He has . . . a generalized conception of the Good. . . . Everything that is candid, crisp, fresh, alert, clean, supple . . . he likes." The adjectives are pleasant but none of them is convincing. Robert Cantwell felt that Lewis "recognized the mechanics of capitalist control, and satirized them, without . . . visualizing any alternative except an escape . . . into reverie and day-dreaming." And Rebecca West found Lewis lacking "the quality the lack of which he is deriding in others." Specifically, she finds his satire (of those who misuse religion) in *Elmer Gantry* inadequate because Lewis himself "has no vision of the use they ought to make of it."

Mencken's statement, "The things I esteem most in this world . . . are truth, liberty, tolerance, and common-sense," seems impressive until one realizes that the liberty Mencken defends is usually the liberty for Mencken to say what he wants to say. A more accurate statement of his position is the following, also by Mencken: "The fact that I have no remedy for all the sorrows of the world is no reason for my accepting yours. It simply supports the strong probability that yours is a fake."

Anatole France's ideal is usually identified as "beauty." And it is true that France frequently praised beauty. But it is difficult to rely on the sincerity of a man who insisted that to die for any idea is to place too much value on one's judgment. Voltaire's reply, when asked what he would substitute for religion, was an indignant, "What? I help you destroy a noxious monster, and you ask me what I would put in its place?" Voltaire was being truthful; his specialty was destruction; but people do need a substitute when religion is taken away from them.

What did Pope believe in? Dyson can find nothing higher than "the ideals of Augustan culture, a culture which was not democratic . . . its ideals . . . were definitely aristocratic, the ideals of leisurely good breeding." Of the first Samuel Butler, Cazamian says, "It is doubtful whether he himself has a very clear conception of the limits of his denials, and of the positive affirmations at which his thought may still snatch." And the best that the other Samuel Butler could offer in *Erewhon* was a reversal of every modern trend.

Jane Austen suggested no satisfactory alternative to those incongruities of middle class domesticity which she ridiculed. "Sydney Smith believed in freedom; it was probably the only thing he did believe in," says Hesketh Pearson. "John Gay recognized that his power of remedying . . . evils was negligible," says Armens, "but he did feel it his duty . . . to imply . . . the existence of a moral code and a way of life much preferable to the one operative in his own day." Clifton Fadiman stresses the lack of positive alternatives in Charles Dickens, who hated the injustices and cruelties of the institutions of his time. "But he would have hated even more fiercely the institutions . . . Marx wanted to substitute for them. His position is Rousseauist, even anarchistic." When Gogol, with delusions of grandeur, turned from being a satirist to publishing sanctimonious moralizing, he became the laughing-stock of Russia.

Before he became disillusioned, H. G. Wells did offer, in his specific blueprints of Utopian society, what he felt were adequate alternatives. And Kronenberger credits Shaw with a positive program: "Shaw does deal in absolutes; in spite of snarling them up in paradoxes, he does offer solutions."

In general, satirists are much more skillful at pointing out weaknesses than in defending. They are wise when they follow H. L. Mencken's advice: "I am a diagnostician; I do not practice therapeutics." When satirists go in for therapeutics, they usually botch up the job. The kind of skill required in observing incongruities is very different from the kind of skill required to eliminate them. Rarely does the same person possess both skills; in only a very few satirists is the ability to visualize sensible alternatives as strong as the capacity for spotting incongruities, weaknesses, and contradictions. The satirist may not be intentionally refusing to offer alternatives in his writing, but it is a sound instinct that leads him to avoid them and to leave such projects to other men.

Nor is the lack of satisfactory alternatives limited to satirists. In his brilliant essay, "The Hedgehog and the Fox," Isaiah Berlin suggests that Tolstoy's writing was devoted to annihilating what he regarded as false beliefs — including all previous systems of history, philosophy, and sociology — but that Tolstoy lacked positive beliefs himself, and justified his attacks by the rationalization that he was searching for the truth.

The final reason for the vagueness of the satirist's ideal is simple: he has had experience in disillusionment. Even an immature adult knows that there is imperfection around him — and learns some of the practical reasons for that imperfection. The longer he lives the less likely he is to postulate a perfect alternative to any existing condition.

Most scholars do not share the view expressed here. In general, they accept the traditional concept that the successful satirist expresses a sincerely held standard of judgment, just and moral and conventional, and that he is genuinely eager to communicate that judgment to other people.

Pose As Nonsatirist

People who write poetry call themselves poets; people who write novels call themselves novelists; people who write plays call themselves playwrights. But satirists often refuse to admit that they are satirists. There have been, of course, some who proudly announced that they were satirists: Juvenal, Joseph Hall, Pope, Byron wrote satire and admitted that they were writing satire. But many satirists have either genuinely believed that they were doing some other kind of writing, or pretended to believe that they were.

Some writers whom everyone regards as satirists, such as Bernard Shaw and Sinclair Lewis and Evelyn Waugh, insist that they are not satirists but realists. Again we face a semantic problem. The satirist who claims that he is a realist believes, or pretends to believe, that his perspective may *seem* different from that of most people, but that it *is* the real world at which he is looking and that he sees it more clearly than other people do. The satirist feels that he is dealing with the real world, as much as a grain broker who never leaves New York is dealing with the real world; both handle symbols, and the symbols of both represent concrete materials.

To support his claim that he is not a satirist but

"a recorder of natural history" with exceptionally good vision, Bernard Shaw recalled that he had gone to see his oculist and had been told that he had "normal" vision. Inasmuch as normal vision is possessed by only about 10 per cent of the population, Shaw triumphantly concluded that this explained why he saw things differently from the way most people did. He insisted that he "dealt in natural history sincerely," in spite of the fact that in his authorized biography he mentioned numerous parallels between himself and other great satirists. Huxley described himself as "by nature a natural historian" of human society. James Thurber felt that his peculiarly distorted vision, the blurred image he got from part of one eye, gave him a perspective which was not only unusual but in many ways more accurate than the indiscriminate reliance on objective facts that most people depend upon. "Such are most human actions that to relate is to expose them," wrote Edward Young in the eighteenth century; satirists still feel that way. And the satiric belief that all a satirist has to do is accurately record the ridiculousness of life was expressed by Heine in a letter: "You could ridicule hollow liberals, bone-headed Republicans. . . . It was easy game. You only need to portray these individuals exactly; Nature had anticipated you by presenting your pen with caricatures, already finished."

Other satirists who call themselves realists are Evelyn Waugh, who claims that his books are not meant to be satirical, and Carlyle, who wrote, "Sarcasm I now see to be, in general, the language of the devil; for which reason I have, long since, as good as renounced it." Horace called his poems "sermons," not satires; Spencer did not regard his *Mother Hubberds Tale* as satire; and Mandeville did not call his *Crumbling Hive* a satire. Bierce defined a cynic as "A blackguard whose faulty vision sees things as they are, not as they ought to be." Melville did not regard himself as a cynic, but felt that he had to exaggerate his pessimism in order to counteract the "inflated optimism of nineteenth century America." Pirandello regarded life as too painful for simple entertainment.

Sinclair Lewis wrote of himself: "He who has been labeled a 'satirist' and a 'realist,' is actually a romantic medievalist of the most incurable sort." On another occasion Lewis wrote, "I don't make exposés. If I happen to write things as I see them, and people don't like it, that's not my fault. Why doesn't someone call *The Bridge of San Luis Rey* an exposé of Peruvian bridge builders?" Lewis was convinced that American life is more grotesque than his literature, and that its intensity is so pronounced that it is difficult to report it, let alone to exaggerate it. He insisted that he was showing the real world to people who had been deluded by romantic falsifiers so long that they no longer recognized the real thing when they saw it.

Relation To Environment

John Dryden traced the origin of satire back to the Garden of Eden. Having grudgingly admitted that hymns of praise may have come first, he assumed that criticism followed soon after. "After God had cursed Adam and Eve in Paradise, the husband and wife excused themselves, by laying the blame on one another."

The satirist appeared very early. Professor Robert Elliott offers considerable evidence to "establish the central point: in its early manifestations in Greece, Arabia, and Ireland satire is intimately connected with magic and the satirist hardly distinguishable from the magician." Elliott accepts the theory of Jane Harrison and F. M. Cornford that the original phallic rituals in ancient Greece had two parts: the invocation of good through the magic influence of the phallus, and the "expulsion of evil by means of the magic power of satire, invective, lampoon — this last im-

> *Satire flourishes in a homogeneous society with a common conception of the moral law . . . and in times of relative stability and contentment.*
> — Evelyn Waugh

provised by the leaders of the songs." Satire was assumed to have magic powers against the individuals named in the songs. The power of that magic is suggested by the legend that Archilochus, in the seventh century B.C., composed a satiric poem which forced Lycambes and his daughter (who had betrayed Archilochus) to hang themselves. G. L. Hendrickson mentions a similar legend about Hipponax, whose satiric poems drove two sculptors to suicide. At one time Arabs regularly sent professional satirists into battle with them, to hurl insults and curses at the enemy during the battle. And ancient Celtic poet-satirists were sometimes sent to collect taxes when other means had failed.

When, at a later stage, the satirist lost his claim to magical or religious powers (having been superseded by magicians or priests), his satire changed, reflecting the new relationship between the satirist and his society. Professor Elliott traces the shift from magic incantation to aesthetic effect. The satirist made the climb, or the descent, from prophet to poet. That he sometimes had doubts about the eminence of his new status is implied by Horace's remark: "The poet is of use to the state, if you grant that even by small things great ends are helped."

Obviously the satirist, dealing as he must with contemporary material, is dependent for that material on the society in which he lives. But it is dangerous to assume dogmatically that some periods are far more conducive to satire than others, or that great satirists flourish only in favorable environments. There have been satirists, and great satirists, in all kinds of environment. The milieu limits the satirist's material and technique to the extent that the milieu limits all artists; it may force him to use subtle satire in a tyrannical society, or permit him to be outspoken in a free society, but it does not keep him from being a satirist.

Today it is easy to see how wrong Gilbert Cannan was in 1914 when he said that the time was ideal for satire since English life offered only two interests — money and sex. Cannan's thesis, briefly, is this: When a community reaches a stage of extreme dullness and stagnation, as a result of exaggerated respect for contemporary individuals and contemporary morality, some of the community genius "goes to the making of an individual who will have no respect for these things." That individual will be a satirist. His ideal environment is neither a society which is in actual danger, for danger brings out men of action, nor a society which is flourishing, for a healthy society brings out genuine poets. Satirists appear "when the second-rate rises to the surface and brings about the degradation of all standards." But the period Cannan describes did not produce great satire.

Certainly society affects the satirist and his art in obvious ways. The court jester in medieval times could say aloud, by pretending to be a fool or a madman, many unpleasant truths. In a democratic society today satirists may say aloud, without pretending to be fools or madmen, many unpleasant truths. Distasteful conditions exist in all societies; it is the methods of expression which are different. But, in spite of Hippolyte Taine's effort to prove the contrary, there is no simple cause-and-effect relationship between a particular society and the satirists of that society. In the twentieth century, for instance, Sinclair Lewis and H. L. Mencken remained atheistic satirists, whereas Evelyn Waugh, G. K. Chesterton, Roy Campbell, Hilaire Belloc, T. S. Eliot, and C. S. Lewis became religious satirists. Yet they all wrote satire in the same environment.

Nevertheless, satire does not exist in a vacuum. It is an expression of critical opinion by specific writers, at specific times, concerning specific persons or institutions. But before we can determine the degree of influence a particular satirist's environment has on his work — whether, as Carlyle believed, the writer dominates his time or, as Taine and Plekhanov insisted, the environment is responsible for the writer — we must examine what we mean by environment.

We accept an enormous amount of cursory generalizing about "milieus." The most common error is to speak of a whole nation as if it consisted of a single group of homogeneous, classless, equal individuals. No such society has ever existed. There may be a vast difference between the one section of society which is likely to be observed by literary critics and academic observers, in relative isolation from other groups, and the actual conglomeration of dissimilar elements which make up a complete "society." For example the description of late nineteenth-century society as "skeptical" is correct — as far as many late nineteenth-century intellectuals of Western Europe are concerned. That description is, in varying degrees, incorrect for the bourgeoisie and the proletariat of the same period. Writers sometimes look only at those aspects of society which interest or concern them, and fail to report on other important elements in their society.

Writers and critics are not the only ones guilty of generalizing about all of society on the basis of a single literary segment, or a single social class, or a single philosophical group. Sociologists and pollsters make the same mistake. Surely the sanctimonious assumptions about the "humanitarianism" of the twentieth century, its tolerance and liberalism and concern for human beings, have been refuted by the brutality of Fascists, Nazis, and Communists. Neo-fascist and post-Stalinist governments have shown the same inhumanity as their prototypes. The use of nuclear weapons is difficult to defend on humanitarian terms. Nor is the fight over segregation in the South and in Africa definitive proof of the growth of tolerance.

The tendency to make sweeping generalizations is not limited to conclusions about the twentieth century. Historians like to call the year 1300 "typically medieval"; Carl Becker speaks of the medieval climate of opinion as if it were one in which all men lived for eternity rather than for the moment, and everyday actions were motivated only by the soul's desire for salvation. Yet Dante's Inferno and Purgatory are full of his contemporaries who had clearly *not* been living by any such values or in any such climate of opinion as Professor Becker assumes. Dante's victims were being punished for precisely the same physical and social excesses which our society still recognizes as basic motivations of human beings, in the climate of opinion of the sophisticated and nonmystic twentieth century. And Professor French tells us: "No institution of fourteenth-century England was so often the object of satire as the Church." The habitual behavior of medieval laymen and clergy certainly does not indicate excessive spirituality.

Cazamian recognizes the danger of generalizing. "Almost every quality," he says, "can be safely ascribed to the Middle Ages. Shall we say that they were chiefly epic and chivalrous; or tragic and somber; or mystic and dreamy; or again, quiet, happy, and sane; or lastly, bubbling over with fun? Yes, indeed, all five separately, or together." Cazamian adds that this kind of mixture is likely to occur in "a relatively new culture" where "the tones and values of life . . . had not yet been sorted, classified, and assigned their proper places." He assumes that those tones and values are eventually classified — but whether society itself recognizes those classifications, as the literary historian does, is not at all certain.

To label any age is to oversimplify. Note how

misleading is the familiar designation for eighteenth-century England, "the Age of Reason," as Kronenberger's analysis demolishes the notion of a homogeneous society. He calls it an "era of consolidation" between the violence of the seventeenth century and the activity of the nineteenth, and he finds the following characteristics: growth of individual liberty, religious tolerance, and convention; decay of authority; presumably "reason," "restraint," "golden mean"; "enthusiasm" despised, common sense respected; period of "style." *But:* The Aristocratic Ideal was more dream than reality; men showed more desire for Reason than exhibition of it; the age "frequently made a beast of itself," producing many unbalanced men, among them Swift, Collins, Cowper, Blake, George III. There is a long list of contradictions — excesses and extremes, the rich are very rich and the poor very poor; scholars fight duels over Greek accent; men drink prodigiously, the wealthy port, the poor gin. The Age of Reason is also the age of brutal and widespread crime, and of harsh punishment; there is profligacy in high life and in low; scandal and corruption are commonplace; the "worst excess of all . . . was the gambling" — for high stakes and unusual ones, such as wives, homes, children, and lives. The repressed emotion of "The Age of Decorum" bursts forth in numerous riots — over wages, popery, gin, Wilkes, and in personal quarrels — Pope-Addison, Addison-Steele, Lady Montagu-Pope. The deism of the upper classes and the skepticism of Gibbon and Hume is overwhelmed by the passion and faith of Wesley and Whitefield; the sentimental novels of Richardson are the most popular reading matter of the age.

We need not stop with the eighteenth century; every age has its multiple facets. The Restoration produced not only the cynical comedy of manners but also *Pilgrim's Progress*. The early nineteenth century gives us the prince of romantic novelists, Sir Walter Scott, and the antithesis, Jane Austen. The *Canterbury Tales* and *Piers the Plowman* appear at the same time, one cosmopolitan, unconcerned with political unrest, good-natured, the other provincial, propagandistic, revolutionary. Frances Russell stresses the role that the growing democracy played in creating Victorian satire, but democracy was certainly not a strong force in the satire of the Restoration or of seventeenth-century France or of Rome.

The ages of great tragic drama — in Sophocles' Athens and Shakespeare's England — are usually described not as tragic periods but as eras of power, exuberance, renascence. The usual explanation for this paradoxical condition is that man suddenly became aware of the dignity and significance of the individual, and consequently was able to write great tragedy. But what explains the writing of great satire, by Aristophanes and Ben Jonson, during these same periods? In seventeenth-century France, Racine and Corneille were writing great tragedy — and Molière was writing great satire. Nor would a simple inversion of values solve our problem. Certainly it is not correct to say that if tragedy is written in "happy" periods, then satire is written in "unhappy" periods. Much satire was written in England in the last decade of the sixteenth century and the first decade of the seventeenth, contemporaneously with the flowering of Elizabethan tragedy. How then does one explain the concurrent appearance of two different reactions to the same society?

In America, too, the problem of accurate interpretation has not been resolved. De Voto in *The Literary Fallacy* criticized such writers of the twenties as Lewis, Sherwood Anderson, and Dreiser for creating a false picture of American life which led Europe to believe that Americans were weak and materialistic and indifferent to spiritual values. In 1949 Gerald W. Johnson complained that American society was denigrated by contemporary American novelists. But Granville Hicks in *The Great Tradition* said that all of America's nineteenth-century writers were guilty of sugar-coating the society they lived in.

Generalizations about the character of American society lead to other difficulties. Sinclair Lewis had one opinion of his contemporaries, most of the academic critics had another. By the time Lewis died it was fashionable to say that he no longer understood America or interpreted it correctly. It is possible, however, that Sinclair Lewis was an accurate representative of the middle class in his own Philistinism, his skepticism about improvement, his suspicion of radical change, his insistence on personal freedom, his nostalgia for the tradition of rugged individualism. On the other hand, Lewis has not presented accurately the values and attitudes of the working class of America, nor of its other classes. He knew the middle class; that does not mean that his picture was an accurate portrait of our entire society.

To understand the relationship of the satirist to his environment we have to resist the temptation to make generalizations about that environment. This is extremely hard to do. In her excellent book, *The Fool,* Enid Welsford says casually, "to the child of the Renaissance, man was essentially great. . . . To the Medieval thinker, man was essentially vain." But, judging from the literature of the Renaissance, to many writers man was essentially vain; and there are many examples in popular medieval literature which hint that man is essentially good. Correct analysis of environment is something that even Freud failed to make; recent sociologists have shown that the social organization of Germany and Austria (from which most of Freud's patients came) at the turn of the century is not the only kind of environment available to civilized human beings. Anthropologists have illustrated, for instance, that in matriarchal societies and in certain other communities the Oedipus complex and related psychoses are not present to the same extent as in Freud's milieu. It is tempting to assume that our own environment is everyone's environment, or should be everyone's environment, but this assumption is not true.

*　*　*

The theory that the ideal environment for satirists is a changing, unstable society is logical and persuasive. It has been convincingly stated by a number of scholars. The main objection to this theory is the persuasive statement, by a number of other scholars, that the ideal environment for satirists is an unchanging, stable society.

"Satire is inevitable as it is necessary in an age of rapid change when concepts of culture and moral codes in the advanced group outrun the conventional bound minds of those from whom the vanguard has escaped," wrote Harlan Hatcher. Edgar Johnson agrees: "An age of change is always one of intellectual ferment. . . . Altering social institutions and conventional beliefs leads to criticism, and criticism begets satire. That is why the great periods of historical change have always been marked by a flowering of satire."

Dr. Kanzer believes that in discontented societies the repressed social protest finds outlet in the work of satirists like Voltaire and Gogol. Professor Cazamian feels that the controversies of late seventeenth-century England bred the skepticism out of which developed the proper milieu for Augustan satire. And Enid Welsford points to the "popularity of the fool as a vehicle for satire and comedy" in late medieval society as "a symptom that ominous cracks were appearing" in the structure of that society.

Wyndham Lewis insists that modern society has little moral dignity and Eric Bentley's analysis of modern drama supports the thesis. "Modern comedy," says Bentley, "belongs to no homogeneous group. The modern satirist rests on no rock of generally granted assumptions." But contemporary drama is, in Bentley's view, both a mature and a realistic art. "Modern comedy reflects not only the surface but the structure of modern society."

Professor French adds eloquent support to the changing-society thesis. He feels that the literature of fourteenth-century England is "so pervaded with a questioning spirit as to make this a great age of satire." The revolt of the peasants, the heresies of Wycliffe and the Lollards, the decay of feudal institutions, had resulted in a "society in which medieval ideals had become so old fashioned that only a few quixotic persons any longer allowed them to interfere with their materialistic purposes." French concludes that satire was inevitable when "An age of Faith was passing into an age of skepticism, and authority of every sort was losing its grip upon the English public."

But Evelyn Waugh emphatically disagrees. Satire, he says, "flourishes in a stable society and presupposes homogeneous moral standards." He regarded eighteenth-century England as such a society. Auden agrees with Waugh: "Satire flourishes in a homogeneous society with a common conception of the moral law, for satirist and audience must agree as to how normal people can be expected to behave, and in times of relative stability and contentment, for satire cannot deal with serious evil and suffering. In an age like our own it cannot flourish except in private circles as an expression of private feuds; in public life, the serious evils are so importunate that satire seems trivial and the only suitable kind of attack prophetic denunciation." Waugh and Auden choose to ignore the popularity of their own satires in the unstable twentieth century.

Kenneth Burke implies support of this theory when he says that dramatic irony, a high form of satire, "flourishes best when a scheme of orientation is comparatively firm." Enid Welsford accounts for the decay of the conventional fool with the remark "the fool in cap and bells can only flourish among people who have sacraments, who value symbols as well as tools, and cannot survive the decay of faith." And Dr. Ernst Kris adds a psychologist's support: "Enjoyment of the comic entails a feeling of complete security from danger."

"Where all is known and acknowledged," theorizes J. B. Priestley, "one set of ideas ruling every mind, there may be wit in plenty . . . but there will be little humour. The mind must be free to play to be humorous. The doctrinaire, just because his mind is so completely made up and he has standards that he can apply instantly, may enjoy considerable power of wit and satire but he has no humour, and such laughter as he has will be savage and fully condemnatory."

George Meredith was convinced that for great comic writers "a society of cultivated men and women is required. . . . Feverish emotional periods repel him; and also a state of marked social inequality of the sexes." When Meredith generalizes about "society" he is actually referring only to a particular level of that society, and a particular kind of humor which he happens to regard as most desirable. And William Hazlitt, like Meredith, thought that man becomes truly ridiculous only in "a highly advanced state of civilisation," when he imitates "the extravagances of other men."

Both Cazamian and Waugh cite early eighteenth-century England as a flourishing satiric period; but Cazamian calls it an age of change, Waugh a stable age. And Edgar Johnson, who accepts the age-of-change thesis, nevertheless admits that the freedom Pope enjoyed is "one demonstration more of how stable was the social order, how firmly based the cosmos on its foundations." Obviously, the contending parties are either misinterpreting the period or accepting a single segment of the period's culture as typical. Pope did write much of his satire for a select, isolated, wealthy and secure group. But whether that group typified all of England is not certain.

There is still another subject for scholarly dispute — the effect of censorship on the satirist. Satire flourishes in a strictly censored society. Unless, that is, it flourishes in a free society. Both theories have their supporters. The Earl of Shaftesbury believed that censorship stimulates satire. " 'Tis the persecuting Spirit has raised the bantering one," he wrote. "The greater the Weight is, the bitterer will be the Satire. The higher the Slavery, the more exquisite the Buffoonery."

Kenneth Burke agrees. He believes that conditions for satire are more favorable "under censorship than under liberalism — for the most inventive satire arises when the artist is seeking simultaneously to take risks and escape punishment for his boldness." Dr. Kanzer suggests that repressive governments make "deliberate as well as unconscious use" of such methods for channelizing discontent as permitting carnivals and circuses, where protest can be symbolically but harmlessly discharged. Professor Müller, speaking of writers in general rather than just satirists, rejects Longinus' premise when he says, "Much of the world's great literature has *not* been written in an atmosphere of freedom." (Italics mine.) And Scheffauer concludes that "the futility of satire appears particularly pronounced in republics."

Professor O. J. Campbell believes that the censorship edict of the English bishops in 1599 drove satire into the drama, which offered more opportunities for indirect criticism. But Professor John Peter disagrees, arguing that the shift toward satiric drama had begun before 1599 and that "the efflorescence of satiric plays about the turn of the century" can be better explained by other reasons. What the ban did accomplish, Peter suggests, was to make the writers modify or disguise their work, stop using the word "satire," clean up pornography and obscenity, and turn away from "the outlandish and crabbed vocabulary" that English satirists, in imitation of Roman satire, had affected and made a characteristic element of satiric style.

Montesquieu, a fine satirist himself, differentiated subtly among kinds of repression. He wrote: "Satirical writings are hardly known in despotic governments. . . . In democracies they are not hindered, for the very same reason which causes them to be prohibited in monarchies; being generally leveled against men of power and authority, they flatter the malignancy of the people, who are the governing party.

"In monarchies they are forbidden, but rather as a subject of civil animadversion than as a capital crime. They may amuse the general malevolence, please the malcontents, diminish the envy against public employments, give the people patience to suffer, and make them laugh at their sufferings.

"But no government is so averse to satirical writings as the aristocratic. There the magistrates are petty sovereigns, but not great enough to despise affronts. . . . The prince . . . is placed on such an eminence that it (a satirical stroke) does not reach him; but an aristocratic lord is pierced to the very heart. Hence the decemvirs, who formed an aristocracy, punished satirical writings with death."

Other scholars, however, speak up on behalf of liberty. S. Diana Neill suggests that a satiric insight, like Thackeray's, "for its full expression required an atmosphere of freedom." Horace Kallen stresses the importance of the comic spirit in achieving man's freedom, and Kenneth Burke, having said previously that satire flourishes best in a tyrannical society, qualifies his remark with the limitation that "skepticism requires a considerable amount of security before it can be developed in any systematic form." Burke suggests that the ideal milieu is "an adequate productive and distributive system which is decaying but has not yet decayed. Hence, skeptics were happier in the nineteenth century . . . than they can be in the twentieth."

The notion that democratic societies are necessarily free of censorship has been pretty much exploded. In the mass media, such as movies, television, and radio, absurd objections have been made to the slightest criticism of any occupation, food, drink, institution, or house pet. As long as art is subject to mass audiences and commercial sponsorship, that kind of censorship may be even more effective than political censorship in totalitarian countries.

What it finally comes down to is that censorship determines not whether satire is written but the form of satire that is written, by requiring varying degrees of subterfuge. Sinclair Lewis needed little ingenuity to conceal his criticism of social and religious and political elements in a society which permitted social and religious and political criticism. Branch Cabell did have to exercise a great deal of ingenuity, as in *Jurgen,* when writing about sex, a topic which was censored in his society.

Jonathan Swift had to be ingenious in his political and religious satire because his society prohibited direct criticism of those institutions. It is likely that all three would have written satire in whatever society they inhabited, but they would have had to choose different techniques to cope with the restrictions of that society.

Hippolyte Taine popularized the theory that the "milieu" is the most important element in determining the shape of a writer's art. (In actual practice, when Taine applied his theory to specific writers, he sometimes found that they did not react to the milieu as they were supposed to.) G. M. Plekhanov, the pioneer Marxist literary critic, carried the theory even further, insisting that the artist writes in direct, measurable reaction to the society in which he works, and great art can appear only when the artist is in sympathy with the basic values of his society.

The indisputable fact is that the same environment has produced very different kinds of satirists. This makes it rather difficult to account for the satirist entirely in terms of his environment. Neither Plekhanov's nor Taine's theory adequately explains why one person turns out to be a writer, while other persons in the same environment do not. They fail to explain why the same environment, such as a rigidly totalitarian society, or an orphan home, produces very different individuals and temperaments. Granted that society influences its products, it is the difference in those products which the environmentalists fail to account for.

Not all the products of tyrannical prep schools become satirists, as Anatole France and George Orwell and Thackeray and C. S. Lewis did. What was the environmental effect on the other individuals, and the other writers who went to those schools? Not all satirists who had a strict religious upbringing became antireligious; Samuel Johnson didn't, and Voltaire's older brother became a religious fanatic. A village in Minnesota produced the rough satiric style of Sinclair Lewis, and a village in Wisconsin produced the sophisticated ironic style of Glenway Wescott. What of the other boys in these Minnesota and Wisconsin villages who did not become writers? The Marxist oversimplification does not account for the artist. It is not enough to say that he rebels against his bourgeois environment, for like Lewis and Wescott, James Branch Cabell was a product of a small town, this time in Virginia, and developed a third kind of writing. Cabell's *Jurgen,* published in 1919, and Lewis' *Main Street,* which appeared in 1920, were two very different satires; *Main Street* proved enormously popular, whereas *Jurgen* achieved only a limited success. It is possible that if *Main Street* were published today it would not be nearly as popular; it is possible that if *Jurgen* were first published today it would be more successful. But those are idle speculations. Those two very different forms of satire did appear almost simultaneously in the United States.

Within the same environment, writers and satirists have taken opposing points of view. In the 1920's, Sinclair Lewis and Ring Lardner and H. L. Mencken and T. S. Eliot were criticizing certain aspects of American society from the individualistic point of view. But at precisely the same time, American society was being defended by Irving Babbitt and Paul Elmer More, and attacked for very different reasons by a third group in the persons of John Dos Passos and Art Young and Max Eastman and other Marxist writers.

Dryden recognized a paradoxical element in the satirist's relation to his society when he said, "Horace had the disadvantage of the times in which he lived; they were better for the man but worse for the satirist." Eric Bentley suggests that Oscar Wilde's solution to the problem of "finding a vantage point for satire in an unaristocratic age was . . . the solution of Bohemianism . . . Bohemianism was for Wilde a mask." It was, but Bohemianism was not the attitude towards the same society that Hardy and Kipling and Shaw and Gissing chose at that time.

The contrasting reactions to the same environment by Shaw and Chesterton have been summarized by Maisie Ward. They agreed only about science, and only in the sense that both were critical of science, "Chesterton because it tried to be a genuine religion, and Shaw because it failed to be a genuine religion." Shaw, Maisie Ward contends, recommends eugenics and the separation of sex and marriage, whereas Chesterton defends the tradition of the family; Shaw proposes creative evolution, Chesterton, Christian ethics; Chesterton does not accept Shaw's Fabian democracy or Fabian socialism, opposing a romantic notion of democracy to the former and a peasant-proprietorship in a medieval society to the latter.

Eric Bentley calls Shaw the "comedian of a revolutionary period. . . . And Pirandello's point of vantage . . . was that of an outcast." A. R. Thompson contrasts the reactions of Hardy and Housman in a period when both poets were torn between the need for faith and the inability to accept faith: "Hardy expressed his sense of this dilemma with tragic gravity. Housman . . . turned against his own passion with ridicule." At the same time, Pirandello decided that the only escape from unbearable knowledge of the real world was offered by a fictitious world.

The same environment produced satirists who opposed each other in the Restoration: Dryden was writing pro-Stuart satire and Marvell was writing anti-Stuart satire; Oldham was attacking Jesuits and Butler was attacking Puritans and Rochester was attacking everything. A few years later, Swift, Pope, Gay, and Arbuthnot wrote satire on behalf of the Tories, Addison and Steele wrote satire on behalf of the Whigs, and Defoe wrote for both sides. Juvenal and Martial were describing Rome at the same time, but Juvenal took the point of view of an indignant reformer, whereas Martial wrote as if he found the material simply a useful source of comic pleasure. Juvenal is indignant,

Martial is indifferent. While the romantic spirit was presumably running wild, Jane Austen and Thomas L. Peacock were writing antiromantic novels. During the period which Anatole France found perfectly suited for irony, the Goncourts and Zola were writing naturalistic novels. And Thompson feels that Shaw, "unlike most thoughtful men of his time — Hardy and Ibsen are notable examples — had not suffered disillusionment, and hence . . . felt none of their bitterness." Because of his emotional detachment, Thompson suggests, Shaw "could be amused" by the same defects of western civilization which shocked other writers.

Furthermore, a satirist may lose his public because its interests or tastes change. Mencken's point of view remained belligerently consistent, but the Nietzschean individualism which delighted solvent, peaceful, and superficially cynical Americans during the twenties proved to be inadequate for the following decades, when depression and war disturbed men more than social hypocrisies, and the struggle for survival was too intense, too personal, and too terrifying to be laughed at. Many Englishmen were so exasperated with Puritanism in the 1660's that the first two parts of *Hudibras* were greeted with immense approval; but by the time Butler published the third part in 1678 the climate of opinion had changed, and the new poem and its author were virtually ignored.

In support of his theory (society channelizes its discontent into humorous expression) Dr. Kanzer suggests that in three separate cultures latent revolutionary forces were responsible for the appearance of three major humorists: Cervantes in Spain, Voltaire in France, Gogol in Russia. But Dr. Kanzer says nothing of such major humorists as Mark Twain and Chaucer and Bernard Shaw and Charles Dickens and Jonathan Swift and Rabelais and Terence, whose appearance did not precede revolutions. Nor does he account for revolutions which were not preceded by major humorists. Environment is important, but environment alone does not make great satirists.

Finally, there is no convincing evidence that there is at some stages less satire than at others, only evidence that there is less *great* satire at some periods than at others. And if, as I will demonstrate, the difference is accounted for by the appearance of great satirists rather than by the milieu itself, then the relationship of satire to its environment is not as easily analyzed as might appear. It is true that different *forms* of satire are stimulated by certain environments and prohibited by others. But that is another problem entirely. The adaptation of a satirist, in his choice of methods and material is one thing; the existence of the satirist is another.

Since Taine, most literary historians have favored the theory that certain social conditions are especially conducive to satire. They assumed that because a satirist was successful at a particular time, that particular time was the only correct one for him. So George Meredith reasoned when he wrote that the court of Louis was the perfect one for a comic poet like Molière. "He had that lively quick-silver world. . . . A simple bourgeoisie circle will not furnish it, for the middle class must have the brilliant, flippant, independent upper for a spur and a pattern; otherwise it is likely to be inwardly dull as well as outwardly correct."

Dryden wrote that "Juvenal was as proper for his time, as [Persius and Horace] for theirs; his was an age that deserved a more open chastisement. . . . Horace was a mild admonisher, a court satirist, fit for the gentle times of Augustus." Professor Ashby feels that Congreve and Noel Coward are especially representative of their milieus. Quevedo made use of his experience as a professional politician at the Spanish court. Joseph Addison, a gentleman himself, adjusted to the changing environment by offering the rising middle class a model of aristocratic manners, as well as approval of middle-class virtues. Margaret Marshall suggests that Thurber's particular kind of madness is so acceptable because "it is an authentic species of the genus of humor Americans have always demanded and created." Professor Spears accounts for W. H. Auden's metamorphoses with the remark: "Auden's successive positions — radicalism, liberalism, religion — represent extreme versions of fairly wide-spread changes in the contemporary *Zeitgeist*." Rice thinks that "it was easy for the sentimental to recognize [Byron] as a child of their age." And Steve Allen believes that comedian

Bob Hope's popularity is due to the fact that "his personality is . . . peculiarly representative of the civilization in which he functions. . . . Perennial wise-guy."

Thackeray's "current emotional experience" was immediately reflected in his writing, says Gordon Ray, and when the novelist withdrew "from the give-and-take of intense personal relationships" his writings became more quiet and detached. Professor Ennis interprets the change somewhat differently, concluding that Thackeray's "whole literary career since *Vanity Fair* was a retreat from his satirical position under pressure of the Victorian mistrust of satire." And V. F. Calverton vehemently denies that Thackeray had at any time made a serious attack on the fundamental premises of his society.

Chevalier feels that Anatole France was peculiarly fit for his times, and his times peculiarly fit for his "ironic temper." The disillusionment of the late nineteenth century (science having presumably eliminated absolute values) created a reading public especially suitable for the melancholy detachment and aloof irony of Anatole France. He was conservative in his early years, liberal in his middle period, radical for a while, then disillusioned again at the end. He ridiculed war up to 1914; during World War I he wrote patriotic pamphlets; later he resumed his criticism of war. He wrote for socialism and against it. For a chaotic time France was ideally suited, and in *La Vie Litteraire* he wrote, "never has there been an age more interesting to the curious mind, except perhaps the age of Hadrian."

According to Walter Lippmann, Sinclair Lewis' personal mood of disillusionment coincided, by chance, with the American postwar temper. Calverton thought that Lewis was so successful in describing the Babbitts because he was so close to them in spirit and in philosophy. Lewis remained popular with audiences long after he had lost his popularity with the critics, although there is evidence that he continued to reflect middle-class opinions as accurately in the 1930's as he had reflected them in the 1920's. When the attitudes of literary critics are different from those of the middle class, the critics are likely to assume that any writer who expresses the middle-class point of view is misrepresenting it. It may not have been Lewis who was wrong. Robert Cantwell felt that Lewis was describing not America's coming of age but America's catastrophic going-to-pieces. But Stuart Sherman prophesied that Lewis would become the most important American novelist because he correctly mirrored his period's aspirations. Lewis himself insisted that he was describing realistically an extraordinarily intense society.

It was fashionable in the 1930's to say that Lewis was losing his popularity because he limited himself to social criticism. But John P. Marquand was becoming a popular American satirist in the 1930's while he was ignoring the same economic and political problems which Lewis was criticized for ignoring. Marquand was writing about even more special social conditions than the ones Lewis concerned himself with, yet he was well received. And, to refute the Marxist oversimplification further, most of the proletarian literature of the depression period is dead, whereas Marquand's noneconomic literature has survived.

Jane Austen limited her observations to her immediate environment. Ignoring all of the contemporary political and economic problems, wars, and Napoleon, she concentrated on her specialty — the middle class. On the other hand, Dryden dealt in his time with precisely such political, economic, and religious issues as Jane Austen ignored. "He speaks to his contemporaries," says Nichol Smith, "or for them, on the things about which they are thinking."

Of Alexander Pope, Dyson writes that "no poet has more completely identified himself with his age." But Kronenberger observes that Pope "was enormously sensitive, and the age was coarse; incredibly vain, and the age was cruel." The society within which Pope functioned, says Edgar Johnson, "was a close-knit society . . . everybody knew everybody else. . . . All Pope's poetry was written for it."

Dr. Kanzer, we have seen, believes that the critical spirit of the Russian people found expression in the writings of Gogol, whose "success as a wit stemmed from a paranoid empathy with the Russian masses. He was able to give voice to this unrest despite the curbs established by the government." This theory is a modern extension of

Taine's monumental attempt to analyze the relationship between a writer and his milieu. Kenneth Burke is in essential agreement, accepting Chevalier's interpretation of Anatole France as a writer who was instinctively expressing irony long before he realized that the issues of his time were especially encouraging to irony. "Hence France," says Burke, "like a kind of Leibnitzian monad, could be obeying wide social patterns while obeying his own."

Furthermore, Burke suggests, this condition explains why the nineteenth century, "a century inferior in great drama, should be so concerned with a device so integral to drama" — dramatic irony. "Dramatic irony arises from a relationship between the audience and the play. The audience knows that certain tragic events are destined to take place. It also hears some figure on the stage boasting of the good times to come. And in the audience, as *spectator,* arises dramatic irony." In the nineteenth century, Burke continues, men like France, Renan, and Henry James saw their contemporaries eagerly accepting contemptible but irresistible values. These writers "became *spectators,* with the divided ironic attitude that comes of seeing people headed with confidence towards desolate ends."

Chevalier develops the case for environmental influence in great detail. "There have been moments in history particularly favorable to an attitude of mind which we characterize as Ironic," he says. "Irony will grow only in certain soils. It flowers fully only in sensitive, refined, highly intellectual individuals. It is found in sophisticated societies, in societies that are to a high degree sociable. It has for several centuries been particularly at home in France."

David Worcester also accepts the environmental theory and suggests that, lacking the positive alternatives that earlier satirists implied, "the irony of the modern hero serves no ulterior purpose and reveals no creative thought. It is irony for its own sake; a manner worn as a protective device by a dissociated and neurotic personality."

If the critics just quoted are correct, some writers became satirists because the critical spirit was a powerful force in their environments. But other writers became satirists in environments which were hostile to the satiric spirit, and the usual explanation is that they were rebelling against their surroundings. Both kinds of environment — favorable for satire and unfavorable — have given us satiric writers; both kinds of environment have also given us nonsatiric writers.

Many satirists were distinctly out of tune with their times. "Sheridan did not so much reflect the taste of his time," says Professor Ashby, "as lead a revolt against it." Sheridan may have been admitting, by writing *The School for Scandal*, that he was born a century too late, suggests Andrew Schiller: Sheridan "did not, in any proper sense of the term, write a Restoration comedy, but he did succeed in translating . . . that comedy into terms that were significant and acceptable to his own times."

When Aristophanes, during the disastrous Peloponnesian Wars, realized that he could not change conditions, he changed his plays, suggests Katherine Lever, in order to "offer . . . escape through imagination. The pattern of his plays changed from fight to flight. This change heralded the Middle Comedy." Professor Stoll observes that Ben Jonson was in conflict with his times: "It is a striking fact that Jonson, who, in the respect discussed, most closely approximates the comic art of the Continent, was not highly acceptable to the London public." Jonson continued to write the same kind of play during the different milieus of Elizabeth and James. Ashby concludes that "Wilde represented nothing so much as he represented Wilde." Morris Bishop notes that the English humorist Robert Brough, who died in 1860 at the age of thirty-two, "at a time when most humorists made their butt of the ill-read, the lowly-born, the badly-dressed, dared to mock the aristocracy. If he had lived, Brough might have become a major satirist."

Certainly G. K. Chesterton was out of tune with his environment. And, as Fadiman remarks, he profited by the disjunction. "Chesterton was born at exactly the right time, by which, of course, one means exactly the wrong time. From his point of view the times were out of joint, but had they not been, he might have had no viewpoint at all. . . . It was 'modernism' that converted him to Catholicism." Evelyn Waugh's relation to society is similar. Rolo suggests that as a writer "who repudiates the realities of his time," Waugh must offer either satire or constructive alternatives to the *status quo*. When he attempts the latter, the result has been work that is "often distressing and sometimes disastrous."

Charles Dickens, says Edmund Wilson, "of all the great Victorian writers . . . was probably the most antagonistic to the Victorian Age itself." Bernard Shaw agrees, claiming that both Marx and Dickens were revolutionaries; but the former knew it, the latter never suspected it. Calverton, however, insists that Dickens was a timid conformist, and Monroe Engel's analysis of Dickens' political views reveals a basic conservatism and resistance to fundamental change.

The effect of his environment on Mark Twain has been disputed. Constance Rourke calls Twain a typical example of the American tradition. "The talent of Mark Twain was consistently a pioneer talent. He showed touches of that abysmal melancholy. . . . Emotion he seldom revealed except in travesty. . . . His obscenity was also of the pioneer piece." Twain shared the inadequacies of his milieu. "In a sense, the whole American comic tradition has been that of social criticism: but this has been instinctive and incomplete, and so it proved to be in Mark Twain." But Van Wyck Brooks insists that Twain was thwarted and stunted by the genteel nineteenth-century environment, his Victorian wife, and his fear of the respectable conformists who surrounded him. Delancey Ferguson and Bernard De Voto disagree categorically with Van Wyck Brooks, and are convinced that Mark Twain dominated his environment. Ferguson says, "Far from being repressed, he succeeded all his life long in doing the things he most wanted to do."

Dixon Wecter, trying to explain Mark Twain's genius, says, "It might be said that a humorist by temperament, for example Benjamin Franklin, is a man serenely adjusted to his environment, while a wit like Jonathan Swift is not. Clemens himself . . . partook of both natures." Since Wecter's continuum provides for all varieties of satire and humor, and leaves Twain in the middle, it is not a formula very helpful in categorizing satirists. But that is not Wecter's fault. There really is no satisfactory formula for categorizing satirists.

Not everyone, of course, has surrendered to the environmental theorists. Evelyn Waugh takes his stand with Carlyle. "The statesman who damned the age with the name 'the century of the common man' neglected to notice the simple historical fact," says Waugh, "that it is the artist, not the statesman, who decides the character of a period. The Common Man does not exist. He is an abstraction invented by bores for bores." And Andrew Schiller, analyzing the decline of comedy during the bourgeois-dominated eighteenth century, says, "It is undemocratic, if you like, to point out that the brilliant comic spirit of the theater died as soon as its patronage shifted down to a broader base, but the statement is nevertheless true, and there is, anyhow, nothing democratic about art."

When we examine the satirist's own attitude toward society we find that for him all times are out of joint. No matter when he is born he can be a satirist, for society always provides satiric material. The conflict between ideal and practice in civilized society is always present; it transcends the limited degree of harmony that society may at a particular period temporarily attain. That degree fluctuates betwen dissatisfaction and resignation. But even in the most congenial period there exists an enormous amount of pretense, hypocrisy, and artificiality in society — and the satirist concentrates on that material.

The *kind* of satirist a man becomes is determined to a large extent by his environment, in the sense that the development of his craft may offer new or encourage old techniques at certain periods. But the environmental theories of Taine and Plekhanov underestimate the importance of individual personality. Had James Thurber chosen to be a blunt satirist he could have followed the Franklin-Twain tradition. Had Sinclair Lewis chosen to be a sophisticated stylist he could have taken as his model Addison or Washington Irving or Jane Austen or Oscar Wilde. *The satirist imposes himself*, by strength of personality and temperament, *upon his environment.* And the great satirists — Swift, Rabelais, Voltaire, Chaucer — were unique literary forces. Lesser satirists, like Ben Jonson and Sam Johnson, also had this power; and even of H. L. Mencken, Walter Lippmann said, "Mencken is bigger than his ideas."

Taine himself, the proponent of the "milieu" theory, was unable to fit Shakespeare into his environmental system and confessed, "All comes from within — I mean from his soul and genius; circumstances and externals have contributed but little to his development." And Chevalier, propounder of the "ironic-age" theory, admits, "A few individuals impose themselves: Socrates, Erasmus, Voltaire, Heine." In the centuries before and after Chaucer, no English satirist matched his skill or originality. Voltaire overwhelmed a reluctant France with Locke's political and Newton's scientific ideas. Byron's choice of a classical style in a romantic period is evidence that a great satirist can overcome limitations of his environment. Dryden imposed himself on the literary milieu by establishing the heroic couplet as the basic medium of satiric verse. And Gilbert Seldes says of Charlie Chaplin, "It is a miracle that there should arrive in our time a figure wholly in the tradition of the great clown — a tradition requiring creative energy, freshness, effectiveness — for neither the time nor the country in which Chaplin worked is exceptionally favorable to such a phenomenon."

Paying tribute to the timeless popularity of Swift, Hilaire Belloc notes a number of paradoxes: Swift is a satirist, and satire is not popular today. The specific objects of Swift's satire are gone. He is a Tory in a predominantly liberal England. He is attached to dogmatic religion. He cannot create characters. Belloc concludes that it is Swift's individual style which accounts for his permanence. And if style is a reflection of personality, it is Swift's personality that is responsible.

On the other hand, very different attitudes toward Swift are expressed by three other critics. Herbert Davis is convinced that Swift's writings in the later years of Queen Anne's reign "have their origin in the circumstances of the time. They may even have little to do with the expression of the individual genius of the artist; his spirit is subdued and bent to a purpose beyond his control." Cazamian believes that, had he been born a century later, Swift would have been an ardent romantic; as it was, he repressed his temperament and wrote as a classicist. And Aldous Huxley scathingly suggests that if Swift were alive today he would write *Peter Pan* instead of *Tale of a Tub*.

The relative importance of heredity and environment (or the writer and his milieu) has not been determined yet. The pendulum of critical opinion keeps swinging. Its precise position at the moment is not important; one may safely assume that it will continue to swing.

Although, as we have seen, he developed in great detail the theory that Anatole France's particular milieu was remarkably suited to his ironic temperament, Chevalier is fair enough to admit that France's milieu was also the milieu of Zola and the Goncourts, and that "the group which delighted in the graces and subtleties of the former was hardly as considerable as that which thrilled to the enormities of the latter." Chevalier goes even further in recognizing an apparent contradiction of his thesis when he quotes with approval T. S. Eliot's remark that there are no "disillusioned ages," only disillusioned individuals.

Professor Harry Levin complains that psychology "has treated literature too often as a record of personal idiosyncrasies, too seldom as the basis of a collective conscience. Yet it is on that basis that the greatest writers have functioned." The "collective conscience" has been stressed by Jung also, and Walter Bagehot believes that significant writers are able to "seize on the public mind." But *the public mind" of one section of the public is sometimes very different from "the public mind" of other sections,* as Arnold Toynbee has laboriously demonstrated. Great satirists usually express their personal views, which may or may not coincide with "the public mind." The fact that satirists like Swift and Addison, Dryden and Marvell, Johnson and Churchill, Campbell and Auden, proclaimed opposing views at the same time, makes it difficult to be sure of just what the public mind is.

Satirists have appeared in what were called "stable" societies (Molière, Swift, Dickens, Thackeray), in "decadent" ones (Juvenal, Martial, Congreve), in "renascent" ones (Rabelais, Cervantes, Jonson), in "restrictive" ones (Dante, Chaucer, Gogol, Voltaire), and in "free" ones (Twain, Lewis, Shaw). The satirist is, in some respects, bigger than his environment.

Part Four 🦎

Established Writers
and Novices

11

Writers of Satire

When we consider satirists purely as artists we find numerous problems in trying to classify them. First, if we were to limit our scrutiny to "full-time" satirists we would have very few writers to discuss. Aristophanes, Juvenal, Swift, and Voltaire may be called "complete" satirists. Frances Russell listed as "completely satiric" but "of smaller mold and less capacity" Skelton, Smollett, Churchill, and Gifford among English satirists. There is also some justification for regarding as total satirists such writers as Euripides, France, Rabelais, and Molière.

There are many writers for whom satire was an important but not the only form of literary expression. The fact that some writers are only intermittently satiric raises a problem for those critics who equate the satiric urge with neuroticism, for if the satirist is a neurotic he ought to be writing satire all the time and not just part of the time. Dr. Bergler's answer to this objection is that "flashes" of satiric writing come at that point "when the person has been at his lowest ebb in

In every wit there is something of a poet.
— Henri Bergson

his defensive efforts against the reproaches of the super-ego accusing him of psychic masochistic enjoyment. The frantic pseudo-aggressive defense in these people is — satire."

Disregarding for the moment Dr. Bergler's explanation, we might look at some "partial" satirists. Henry Fielding wrote nonsatiric literature and semisatiric novels, but his *Jonathan Wild* is one long sustained piece of irony. There is satire as well as allegory in Bunyan's *Pilgrim's Progress,* and more satire in *The Life and Death of Mr. Badman.* There is some satire in Shakespeare's plays but most critics agree that the satiric tone is not dominant. Cervantes wrote sentimental plays. Heine, Voltaire, France, Orwell, Thurber, Swift, Dryden, Washington Irving were proficient in many kinds of writing. While Heine is not necessarily typical, neither is he an unusual satirist in this respect: he wrote poems, plays, travel reports, literary reviews, fables, biographies, political essays, history, fairy tales, pamphlets, songs and ballads and hymns.

Many writers of satire were also, or predominantly, poets. Even the nonpoetic satirist is similar to the poet in his frequent use of metaphors, similes, and analogies, and in the concentration of material. Henri Bergson observed, "In every wit there is something of a poet. . . . Instead of treating his ideas as mere symbols, the wit sees them, he hears them, and, above all, makes them converse with one another like persons." And Gilbert Cannan recognized the relationship when he wrote: "It is precisely through its delving into the gross stuff of humanity that the intensive imagination of satire leads back to the extensive imagination of poetry."

To some critics the combination of poetry and satire seems incongruous. In his tribute to Heine, Gautier wrote: "No other writer has had, at the same time, so much poetry and so much wit, two things which usually destroy one another." But when Scheffauer claimed that Heine was the first to blend the satirical with the lyrical note, he was ignoring Burns, Byron, Horace, Pope, Goldsmith, and dozens of other satirists who had tried to do precisely that. Meredith did not feel that there was any necessary conflict: "The comic spirit is not hostile to the sweetest songfully poetic. Chaucer bubbles with it; Shakespeare overflows . . . Pope has it, and it is the daylight side of the night-half obscuring Cowper." And Professor Blyth praises the great Japanese poet Basho because he was able "to retain the humor while increasing the poetical content."

To begin one's writing career with poetry is not at all unusual; among French writers, for instance, de Maupassant, Maeterlinck, and Rostand wrote poetry before they turned to other forms. This poetic season for most prose writers usually ends in the early twenties. But for Anatole France it lasted much longer. He wrote poetry, off and on, most of his life. Robert Burns said, "A little before my sixteenth year I first committed the sin of rhyme." Voltaire was chosen school poet and assigned to write verses for a crippled soldier who was petitioning the king for a pension;

the petition was granted. E. B. White, C. E. S. Wood, John Gay, Arbuthnot, Hemingway, Mencken, Thoreau, and Victor Hugo wrote poetry. Constance Rourke felt that Emily Dickinson "was not only a lyric poet; she was in a profound sense a comic poet in the American tradition." Spears says, "Auden is dominantly a satirist, and his poetic strategy is more like that of Dryden and Pope than like that of Yeats or Eliot." Yeats and Eliot, as well as Chaucer and Pope and Shakespeare, may be called writers who are, as Rice puts it, "primarily poets and also not secondarily humorists." Other satirists who wrote poetry, or poets who wrote satire, are Dante and Pushkin, Byron and Swift, Langland and Spenser and Dryden, Burns and Hardy and Housman, Juvenal and Horace and Persius and Martial and Leopardi, Villon and Boileau, Samuel Butler the first, Samuel Johnson and Ben Jonson, John Donne and Skelton and Dunbar, Robert Frost, E. A. Robinson, James Russell Lowell, Kenneth Fearing, E. E. Cummings, Stephen Spender, William Carlos Williams, E. L. Masters, Karl Shapiro, Robinson Jeffers, Roy Campbell, Carl Sandburg, Dorothy Parker, Emily Dickinson, Louis MacNeice, Hugh MacDiarmid, and Langston Hughes.

If one agrees with E. B. White that "almost every good humorist is a critic of sorts," the number of satirists can be extended considerably. Among them would be Lewis Carroll, Lawrence Sterne, Twain, Saki, Thurber, White, Lardner, Sydney Smith, Thorne Smith, Max Beerbohm,

Jane Austen, Addison, Steele, Charles Dickens, Goldsmith, P. G. Wodehouse, and Max Shulman. There is satiric content in the work of Fu Hsuan, Theocritus, Ben Franklin, Ch'eng Hsiao, John Milton, La Fontaine, Baudelaire, Rimbaud, Erasmus, Alexander Blok, Daniel Defoe, Edward Young, William Blake, Robert Browning, Freneau, Campenella, and Stephen Crane. There is more in Norman Douglas, Gogol, Shaw, Pirandello, Evelyn Waugh, Aldous Huxley, Meredith, H. G. Wells, George Orwell, La Rochefoucauld, Ambrose Bierce, the two Samuel Butlers, Thackeray, Nathaneal West, Dorothy Parker, Sinclair Lewis, John P. Marquand, T. L. Peacock, John Erskine, C. S. Lewis, Vercors, Oscar Wilde, Ionesco, Marcel Aymé, Vladimir Nabokov and Jean Giradoux. And writers whose work is not usually called "satire," but in whom the ironic or satiric attitude is strong are Ivan Bunin, Andreyev, Par Lagerkvist, Maugham, Socrates, Gibbon, Montesquieu, La Bruyere, Maupassant, Sterne, Thomas Carlyle, James Branch Cabell, George Eliot, Boris Pasternak, Ernest Hemingway, O. Henry, Steinbeck, Thornton Wilder, Irwin Shaw, John O'Hara, William Faulkner, Karl Capek, Eugene O'Neill, Ernst Toller, Georg Kaiser, Franz Kafka, James Joyce, Samuel Beckett, Philip Wylie, Mary McCarthy, Ilya Ehrenburg, and Jules Feiffer.

The attempt to identify satirists with classicism is traditional but not wholly satisfactory. Byron's material is "romantic" but his technique is "classical." Sinclair Lewis' work includes both romantic and realistic elements; Lewis remarked that though H. G. Wells' *Tono-Bungay* is called realistic, Uncle Ponderevo is a romantic character. Anatole France alternates between realistic commentary on the contemporary world and romantic flights to the past. Heinrich Heine mixes fantasy and realism to a degree that makes him difficult to classify. And how could one place Dickens or Twain in the classical tradition?

The conventional designation of "classical" is applied to Horace and Persius and Lucian and Martial, and "neoclassical" to Boileau, Dryden, Pope, Johnson, Swift, and Gay. But if Juvenal and Persius are both classicists, we get realistic classicism from the former and academic classicism from the latter. And Cazamian sees even in Swift "the latent powers of a virtual Romanticism."

As to romanticism, such "romantic" writers as Byron, Heine, and Goldsmith have too many differences among themselves and deviations from romantic criteria to be conveniently pigeon-holed. Sylvan Barnet suggests that if we accept as an essential characteristic of romanticism the belief that the universe is an evolving organism, then Shaw is a romantic. His "fundamental biological ideology, creative evolution, like his fundamental economic ideology, a watered-down Marxist view of a necessarily evolving society, is ultimately rooted in romantic thinking." In more traditional terms, Washington Irving and Heinrich Heine and Leopardi and Byron are called "romantics"; but they express individual varieties of romanticism.

Most satirists cannot be easily fitted into any one conventional category. Some satirists David Worcester calls "cosmic": James Thompson, Thomas Hardy, A. E. Housman, Eugene O'Neill, and the Mark Twain of *Mysterious Stranger*. We are struck by the "realism" in the work of Shaw, Maugham, John Erskine, Jane Austen, Voltaire, Montaigne, Samuel Johnson, Molière, Mandeville, Edgar Lee Masters, Thackeray, Juvenal, Sinclair Lewis, Mencken, France, Heine, H. G. Wells, George Orwell, Samuel Butler, and Charles Dickens. And we note "surrealism" in Kafka, Pirandello, Beckett, Ionesco, Giradoux, Genet, and Joseph Heller.

As far as style and technique are concerned, there are perhaps two extreme groups: "rough" and "smooth" satirists. Again, there is no definitive agreement as to the precise line between roughness and smoothness. Nor is it necessarily true that a smooth technique is invariably superior to a rough one. Although much great satire depends on the satirist's technical skill in contrasting shocking matter and calm manner, many satirists have raised invective and vituperation to a high level without attaining, or trying to attain, detachment. Among "rough" satirists we would be likely to list Juvenal, Bierce, Lardner, Twain, Sinclair Lewis, H. G. Wells, Rabelais, and Aristophanes. Among the "smooth" satirists we might include John Marquand, Irving, Addison, Jean Anouilh, Christopher Fry, Maugham, Vladimir Nabokov, Horace, France, E. B. White, Thurber, Hemingway, O'Hara, Lucian, Norman Douglas, Peter DeVries, Mary McCarthy, Evelyn Waugh, and Oscar Wilde. But precisely where we ought to put Jonathan Swift, Voltaire, Petronius, Fielding, Huxley, Gogol, Orwell, and James Joyce is uncertain. They are in some respects smooth but often are not detached, and they make subjective comments. Such judgments as "polished" or "coarse" are, above a certain minimum level of satiric competence, pretty much personal evaluations. The fact remains that great satires have been written by rough satirists, smooth satirists, and mixed satirists.

To the extent that their writings can be classified, it is true that there are savage satirists — like Swift, Juvenal, and Bierce, and mild ones — like Addison, E. B. White, and Charles Lamb. Whether the savage satirist differs from the milder one in kind or only in degree has never been satisfactorily determined. For instance, although Dr. Pannenborg concludes that a "schizothymic" satirist is not likely to exhibit lightheartedness in his work, there is considerable playfulness in the work of such schizothymes as Byron, W. S. Gilbert, Heine, Pope, and Swift.

There is no denying that some satirists have been personally bitter men. It is also true that they have been maligned, though probably not to the extent that David Worcester claims: "How easily satirists acquire a bad name! Lucian, the Anti-Christ, deservedly torn to pieces by dogs; Rabelais, the filthy mocker; Swift, the human misanthrope. . . . How little humanity, how little study, are needed to show that these and many other ill-treated satirists are the cleanest, and brightest, and merriest-minded of men." It is doubtful that all of these pleasant adjectives are applicable.

Certainly there is tremendous vehemence in the satire of Pope and Byron and Juvenal and Bierce and Twain and Swift and Voltaire and Mencken and Victor Hugo. William Inge justified his nickname as "the gloomy Dean"; he once said that "preaching is similar to throwing a bucket of water over a row of narrow-necked vessels. A drop or two may find its way in here and there," and he left the unmistakable impression that he was pessimistic about his life-work. Bolitho called Ring Lardner "the greatest and sincerest pessimist America has produced." To achieve that distinction, Lardner would have had to be more pessimistic than Ambrose Bierce, not an easy feat to accomplish.

On the other hand, Chaucer, France, Fielding, and part-time satirist Shakespeare are not usually regarded as bitter writers. Nor is there much vitriol in the satire of Addison and Lamb and Washington Irving and John P. Marquand and Horace and E. B. White.

Among satirists who seem to be less aggressive personalities, writers like Leacock and Benchley and Thurber are likely to be self-deprecating in their work. This protective laughter is, some biographers think, a defense for timid men such as Gogol, Heine, and Anatole France. But Chesterton, who was in some ways helpless in society, expressed his opinions with ferocious vehemence.

Two types of satirists are neatly balanced in Hesketh Pearson's comparison of Richard Sheridan and Sydney Smith: "Sheridan's wit was dry, Sydney's wit sparkled; Sheridan never laughed, Sydney was always laughing; Sheridan prepared his *bon mots* and adroitly led up to their delivery, Sydney was spontaneous. . . . Sheridan's wit was savage and saturnine, Sydney's was jovial and kindly." Alva Johnson contrasted Will Rogers and Wilson Mizner: "Will Rogers, a good man who liked everybody and humored the entire population, wrote hundreds of thousands of words and is remembered for little except 'All I know is what I read in the papers.' Mizner, a bad man who despised nearly everybody, wrote almost nothing, and put hundreds of lines in circulation."

Aldous Huxley, comparing Rabelais and Swift, says that there is as much dung in the former as in the latter but the spirit of Rabelais transfigures it to fun. Rabelais is in a joyful mood, a loving mood, and accepts reality in its entirety, whereas Swift childishly rejects it. Clifton Fadiman contrasts Dickens and Fielding: "The difference is plain: Fielding is at bottom a healthy man,

Dickens is not." And George Mikes writes: "Thurber is annoyed and angered by all humanity and consequently loves all human beings; Waugh is annoyed and angered by humanity and has consequently developed strong misanthropic tendencies; Chaplin seeks the grim Absolute, Wodehouse sticks to the gay Particular." Mikes means well but Thurber didn't really love all human beings.

Dr. Greenacre's comparison of Swift and Carroll stresses certain fundamental similarities and differences: "both were theologians, unmarried, and passionately disliked babies. . . . Both were secretive men and humorists, but their humor was of different textures. . . . Both wrote stories of adventurous travel in imaginary lands. . . . Swift was a man of the world. . . . Carroll lived at Oxford. Swift used his gift of satire to fight political and moral issues. Carroll developed his nonsensical fantasies to amuse little girls of whom he was fond. Swift was a man among men, attractive to women, but frequently distrustful of them and repelled by their bodies . . . a spasmodically convivial man whose sensitivity and irascibility sometimes alienated him from those for whom he cared most. . . . Carroll, by contrast, was temperate or abstemious . . . withdrew somewhat from men . . . preferring little girls of eight or so. He was fussily pedantic but was singularly lacking in ordinary shows of temper or direct aggressions. . . . Both men were somewhat compulsive walkers, and fearful regarding their health."

Aldous Huxley criticizes Swift for the intensity

of the latter's hatred of the body; Edgar Johnson criticizes Aldous Huxley for the intensity of Huxley's hatred of society. Kronenberger contrasts the importance of the body in Swift's work with its insignificance in the work of Shaw, and their careers — Swift's "one of the most tragically mishandled" and Shaw's "one of the most perfectly managed." Thackeray was appalled by Swift's bitterness, calling him "the unhappiest man in the world"; Thackeray much preferred Fielding and Steele, who were obvious sinners but lovable men. Savage satirist Swift differs in a number of important respects from savage satirist Mencken: Swift maintains a semblance of objectivity, Mencken is always obviously partial; Swift often calmly understates. Mencken usually exaggerates openly, flippantly, dogmatically; Swift imagines new worlds and situations, Mencken limits himself to contemporary journalistic issues; Swift deals with tragedy, Mencken with foolish customs.

The emphasis in the work of some satirists is tragic, in others comic. Somber is the mood of Thomas Hardy and Juvenal; frequently playful is the mood of Voltaire, Byron, and Pope. There are striking similarities between Euripides and Bernard Shaw, and a fundamental contrast — Euripides sees the world as a tragedy, Shaw as a comedy. Other "tragic" ironists are Sophocles, Ibsen, John Webster, Swift, Joseph Conrad, and Hemingway. Eugene O'Neill and Samuel Johnson, John Marston and A. E. Housman see the world as essentially tragic. Primarily comic is the philosophy of

Rabelais, Shaw, Jane Austen, Molière, Lucian, Martial, Terence, Menander, Aristophanes, Meredith, Sydney Smith, Chaucer, and P. G. Wodehouse. And there is a tragi-comic mixture in the work of Evelyn Waugh, Melville, Horace, Sinclair Lewis, Dickens, Shakespeare, Byron, Heine, and Oscar Wilde.

R. A. Knox feels that Mark Twain is seldom at his best when he attempts to be a satirist, but that he is a great humorist. Friedrich, on the other hand, thinks that Thurber is not at his best as a humorist but is fundamentally a serious satirist. Benchley's lighthearted writing lacks the significant implications of Thurber's. Macaulay called Sydney Smith "the greatest master of ridicule who has appeared in England since Swift." James Russell Lowell wrote some satire but devoted most of his efforts elsewhere; Ben Franklin wrote many clever satires for propaganda purposes but they were not his major interests; and P. G. Wodehouse has written an enormous amount of humor without getting much satire into it.

To complicate the problem of classification still further, a number of writers have distinguished between the humorous talker and the humorous writer. "Humor," Delancey Ferguson suggests, "is a form of self-dramatization. . . . The reason why many people who are humorous *talkers* cannot write acceptably is simply their inability to achieve this self-dramatization. In talk their total personalities supply the background and color; in writing all this color is lost."

Dr. Edmund Bergler goes much more deeply into the subject. He distinguishes sharply between the story teller (clown, comedian) and the story writer (humorist, satirist), and insists that they represent two completely different neurotic types. Both are fighting what Dr. Bergler calls "the battle of the conscience," and trying to compensate for an early frustration. But the raconteur's conflict is more superficial than the writer's, and his likelihood of achieving satisfaction greater. The raconteur is trying to compensate for the failure of his parents to recognize his importance when he was a little boy; he is "the life of the party" now because he was excluded from the family "party" as a child, and he is now an exhibitionist before a group most of whom he knows. He is a "show-off" who uses material *created by others,* and his gift is essentially that of "presentation and repartee." "It is remarkable," Dr. Bergler observes, "how many raconteurs are convinced that they are ugly or unattractive, and that their compulsive exhibitionism is an attempt to compensate for this real or imaginary deficiency."

But the writer's problem, according to Dr. Bergler, is altogether different. He feels guilty over rejecting Mother in infancy, and he tries to overcome that guilt by pretending that Mother never existed. What does exist is a world he creates through his own imagination, which is really only a symbolic exhibition of his inner defenses before an audience (readers) mostly unknown to him.

Although some satirists show much more creative imagination than others, it is difficult to draw a sharp line between the "imaginative" satirists and the "commentators." Gilbert Cannan believes that all satirists are poets with an inferior imagination. But Haakon Chevalier, praising irony as the highest form of satiric art, calls Voltaire an ironist *because* he belongs to that group which observes the incongruities of the existing world instead of inventing satiric material.

Nor is there agreement among critics as to what "imaginative" satire consists of. Sinclair Lewis has often been criticized for the lack of "imagination" in his work, and his own definitions of the word are not stimulating: "That power of childish make-believe which is called 'imagination,'" and "I guess imagination is partly wanting to be places where you aren't." Nevertheless, as imaginative a writer as James Branch Cabell credits Lewis with having created a whole new world in his books; an unimaginative writer could hardly have created such a world. Cannan believes that "the satirist is one who, passing beyond, or escaping, the lyrical impulse, cannot yet reach up to the dramatic . . . and so turns upon the world to break the insensibility that has infected him with its paralysis. It is not spite nor a spirit of personal revenge that is the motive force, but a necessity as natural as that of water."

To complicate the problem still further, Carolyn Wells suggests that "humor is creative, while the

sense of humor is merely receptive and apprecia-
tive. . . . Many great humorists have little or no
sense of humor. . . . Such was the case with Dickens,
with Carlyle, with many renowned wits." James
Thurber admits that the fecundity of Agatha
Christie is "a marvel to a writer (like myself) who
is hard put to invent two or three small plots in
a year and a half." And E. E. Stoll says that Shakespeare's "genius . . . is synthetic, not analytic,
and his thought concrete, not abstract— both being
different from Jonson's and Molière's."

If creating in their literature a "special world"
is a sign of imagination, then writers such as Oscar
Wilde, James Thurber, Lewis Carroll, Branch
Cabell, Sinclair Lewis, Charlie Chaplin, Pirandello, Evelyn Waugh, Charles Dickens, P. G.
Wodehouse, and Giradoux, having created such
worlds, presumably possessed imagination. So do
the creators of Li'l Abner and Peanuts and Pogo.

The unfairness of rigid classification becomes
apparent when we see that such "commentators"
on the incongruities of society as Aldous Huxley,
Jane Austen, Voltaire, Anatole France, Montesquieu, Goldsmith, John Erskine, Ring Lardner,
and Bernard Shaw are very different from such
direct satiric commentators as Mencken, Socrates,
Finley Peter Dunne, Montaigne, Juvenal, Addison,
Pascal, Will Rogers, Steele, and Fletcher Knebel.

In summary, there have been some writers who
wrote primarily satire, some who wrote a good deal
of satire, and some who wrote only a little satire.
There have been classical, romantic, realistic,

cosmic, expressionistic, and impressionistic satirists. There have been savage satirists and mild ones, rough stylists and smooth ones. There have been satirists who specialized in oral satire, and there have been those who concentrated on written satire. Finally, some satirists used their imagination much more than others. But, one way or another, they all achieved the same effect — a humorous criticism of individuals, society, or the universe.

The Amateur

Although there have been only a few great satirists, there are a great many people with satiric temperaments. Swift, Voltaire, Cervantes, Gogol, Juvenal, Heine appear at rare intervals, but millions of men and women who never create satire on paper or stage are, in attitude and personality, satirists. Many of them in the ordinary activities of their lives see things from the perspective of satiric criticism or comic distortion; lacking the technical skill to make written literature out of their reactions, they express themselves orally instead. Their colleagues regard them as either humorists or "grouches." By inclination, by attitude, and by behavior there are far more humorists and satirists than are listed in histories of literature, and most large social groups contain easily recognizable amateur clowns.

The number of enduring contributions to satiric literature is small. Aldous Huxley reduced to absurdity many pretenses of modern science

*There are far more humorists
and satirists than are listed
in histories of literature.*

when, in *Brave New World,* he substituted test tubes for human mothers, hypnosis for education, and conditioned reflexes for individual differences. Jonathan Swift in *A Modest Proposal* suggested that since Englishmen had consumed the adults of Ireland economically they might as well eat the infants of Ireland physically — and he recommended a number of ways to serve baby meat most appetizingly. Evelyn Waugh accentuated the commercialization of death by having a funeral director in the *Loved One* remark, "We usually recommend the casket half-exposure for gentlemen because the legs never look so well." Ambrose Bierce defined revolution as "in politics, an abrupt change in the form of misgovernment." H. L. Mencken identified conscience as "the inner voice which warns us that someone is looking." Oscar Wilde felt that "In this world there are only two tragedies. One is not getting what one wants, and the other is getting it." When Irvin S. Cobb heard that his hated boss was ill, he exclaimed, "My God, I hope it's nothing trivial." And Mark Twain made the logical observation, "Familiarity breeds contempt — and children."

These images and witticisms were recorded by professional satirists. But thousands of similar images and witticisms occur daily to amateurs. When a satirist's commentary on society proves sufficiently entertaining, he is rewarded by the encouragement of others. If he is rewarded often enough, he becomes a professional or semiprofessional satirist. There are more latent satirists in almost every group than there are officially recognized ones; many individuals are to some degree, and a few individuals are to a very considerable degree, satirically inclined, in the sense that they react with comically-critical attitudes towards commonplace incidents and remarks. Satire, in the form of "kidding," exists in almost every society, from the most primitive to the most sophisticated. And there is no convincing evidence that the motivation of a neighborhood mocker is different from that of the literary satirist who has perfected his technique.

According to the popular notion, the satirist is a maladjusted, abnormal personality type. In a sense, he is; but only in the same sense that other personality types can also be called abnormal or maladjusted. It depends entirely on the standards of "normalcy" that one chooses to apply. For instance, a *Fortune* magazine study of young presidents (men under forty who were heads of million-dollar companies) concluded that the majority of these young presidents were neurotics who had compensated for their "maladjustment" by devoting their entire lives to business. Such a total adjustment may be quite as unnatural as the adaptation of the satirist, but a society which regards business success as its highest achievement admires this particular form of maladjustment.

The term "maladjusted" carries far less unpleasant connotation now than it did at the beginning of the century. One need not go as far as the Freudians, who insist that everyone is maladjusted, and that only the *degree* of neuroticism separates the ordinary man from the psychotic. Even John Dewey accepts the principle of relative maladjustment, if Lawrence Kimpton is right: "Dewey is really saying that thinking begins in the maladjustment to the environment and continues as an active, tough, and difficult process."

In the twentieth century men are less certain of what ideal adjustment to society is than they have been in previous periods. Modern psychology, sociology, and anthropology reject Victorian morality as the only yardstick for normality. Precisely what kind of deviation is desirable, though, is not clear. William Bolitho described Mohammed as a man who "throughout his supernatural expedition, kept quite sane, even a little stupid, which is the quality of robust sanity." The idea that stupidity may be helpful is unconventional; the idea that callousness may be helpful is familiar, sensitive people being the ones most likely to break down under pressure. Sydney Harris suggests that those who create fantasies are not the only ones who are trying to escape from reality; so are those who accept nothing but physical facts. Excessive literal-mindedness, he feels, excessive dependence on concrete fact, is as abnormal as reliance on fantasy and imagination.

Furthermore, the sentimental notion that tramps and hobos are actually the ones best adjusted to society has been pretty well refuted by sociologists. Interviews with skid-row inhabitants reveal that far from being happy and carefree they are acutely dissatisfied. Adjustment is a far more complex problem than was formerly assumed. And neither the hobo at one extreme, the schizophrenic at the other, nor Babbitt in the middle seems to be contented.

The popular belief that a comic view of life is somehow abnormal is based on the assumption that there is a "normal" attitude toward life. But, the humorist asks, what is the normal attitude toward life? Is it the sham geniality of the outer-directed conformist? The ruthless ambition of the executive? The quasi-resigned acceptance of the Hindu philosopher? Until one is convinced that there is a particular point of view which is "normal," the humorist can make out a good case for his position that the comic view of life is at least as defensible as any other, and perhaps preferable to the cynical, the ruthless, the pessimistic, or the tragic.

There are those who feel that the humorist's attitude toward life, far from being objectionable, is a healthy and desirable one. The evaluators of recent psychological experiments at Yale concluded that a sense of humor "is the best part of a cheerful and tolerant attitude toward life." Charlie Chaplin said: "I look upon humor as a kind of gentle and benevolent custodian of the mind which prevents one from being overwhelmed by the apparent seriousness of life." Randolph Bourne went so far as to affirm that the ironic life is better than the religious life.

At the other extreme, there are those who dislike both humor and the humorous attitude as a way of life. A. M. Ludovici, insisting that nowhere in the New Testament is there any humor, and warning against confusing humor with tolerance, maintains that a smile is actually the baring of teeth in a vicious expression of triumph. Heywood Broun wrote: "Humor is the coward's livery, and there is great wisdom in the popular challenge 'laugh that off.' For generally we laugh at the things which we are afraid to face and fight." And Hubert Pierlot said, "Mockery is the weapon of those who have no other."

Like everyone else, the satirist is the product of two forces: heredity and environment, the sources of and the limitations on his development.

The primary force is an innate or early developed *talent for distortion*. It may seem imprudent, in an age dominated by physical scientists, to speak of something as ambiguous as "talent." And it may seem presumptuous, in an age statistically measured by sociologists, to conjecture that this talent may be innate. But physical scientists admit their uncertainty about the nature of matter, and sociologists should admit their uncertainty about the nature of instinct, talent, and genius; so men have had to make hypotheses on the basis of available knowledge. And observers as diverse as Socrates, Ouspensky, and Freud have speculated that men do possess certain special innate talents. It is possible that the satirist is born with a talent for distortion, a talent as spontaneous as the talent for music with which Mozart was born, or the talent for art with which Michelangelo was born, or the talent for analysis with which Pascal, Newton, and Einstein were born.

In his youth, the satirist develops and sharpens his talent for distortion until he learns how to make it *comic* distortion. At first he does this instinctively, spontaneously, aware only in a vague way of what he is doing to adapt himself to his environment. He evolves an attitude toward life and a technique of reacting to individuals and institutions. His attitude is strengthened by a growing recognition of the discrepancy between the real and the apparent, the actual and the ideal. This recognition leads to disillusionment, and the satirist's critical attitude has usually been explained on the grounds of his disillusionment. But surely the cause is insufficient to account for the result. Most human beings above the level of morons learn, sooner or later, that both individuals and institutions are less kind, generous, honest, and altruistic than they pretend to be; yet most human beings do not become satirists as a result of this realization. Most people develop, instead, an attitude euphemistically called "maturity." They say to themselves, in effect, that this is the way things are; it may be regrettable but it is inescapable. The sensible thing to do, the "practical" thing, is not to try to change society as reformers do, or to fight it as criminals do, or to make fun of it as satirists do, but to concentrate on getting ahead personally, by conforming and approving and pretending.

The satirist, however, does not react as most men do. Instead of accepting society he makes fun of it. His reasons for making fun of it, his motivations, have been discussed. The point is that the satirist applies his particular skill, his talent for comic distortion, to ridiculing the affectations of individuals and institutions, and the apparent inconsistencies of the universe. Even objective analysis of individuals (their rationalizing, sublimating, pretending, repressing) and of institutions (their pose of altruistic dedication to public welfare) reveals considerable hypocrisy and charlatanism. But the satirist is never satisfied with an objective report (although he often pretends that that is all he is doing) and he distorts, usually by exaggeration, the conditions he is criticizing. That such exaggeration is abnormal is debatable. Satirists themselves have usually maintained that it is the conventional apologists for the *status quo,* the majority pretending that things are better than they really are, who are guilty of distortion and should be charged with abnormality.

Reading List

Reading List

Addison, Joseph. *Spectator*. December 15, 1711. No. 249.

Allen, Steve. *The Funny Men*. New York, 1956.

Anderson, Sherwood. "Four American Impressions," *New Republic*. October 11, 1922. 11.

Angoff, Charles. *H. L. Mencken*. New York, 1956.

Armens, Sven. *John Gay, Social Critic*. New York, 1954.

Auden, W. H. "Notes on the Comic," *Thought*, Spring 1952. 27:57.

Bald, R. C. "Huxley As Borrower," *College English*. January 1950. 183.

Barnet, Sylvan. "Bernard Shaw on Tragedy," *PMLA*. December 1956. 889.

Baudelaire, Charles. *The Essence of Laughter*. New York, 1956.

Bentley, Eric. *The Playwright As Thinker*. New York, 1955.

———. "Shaw's Politics," *Kenyon Review*, Summer 1946. 8:368.

Belloc, Hilaire. "On Swift," *Conversation With a Cat*. New York, 1931.

Bergler, Edmund. "Anxiety, 'Feet of Clay,' and Comedy," *American Imago*. 1949. 6:97.

———. "A Clinical Contribution to the Psychogenesis of Humor," *Psychoanalytic Review*. 1937. 24:34.

———. "Dislike for Satire at Length," *The Psychiatric Quarterly Supplement*. 1952. 26:198.

———. "Does 'Writer's Block' Exist?" *American Imago*. 1950. 7:53.

———. *Laughter and the Sense of Humor*. New York, 1956.

———. "Myth, Merit, and Miracle," *American Imago*. 1950. 7:287.

———. "Story-tellers and Story-writers," *American Imago*. 1949. 6:53.

———. *The Writer and Psychoanalysis*. New York, 1954.

Bergson, Henri. *Laughter*. London, 1911.

Berlin, Isaiah. *The Hedgehog and the Fox*. New York, 1957.

Bishop, Morris. *A Treasury of British Humor*. New York, 1942.

Blair, Walter. *Native American Humor*. San Francisco, 1960.

Blum, G. S. *Psychoanalytic Theories of Personality*. New York, 1953.

Blyth, R. H. *Japanese Humor*. Tokyo, 1957.

Bolitho, William. *Twelve Against the Gods*. New York, 1929.

Bourne, Randolph. "The Life of Irony," *Atlantic Monthly*. March 1913. 357.

Bredvold, L. I. "A Note in Defense of Satire," *English Literary History*. December 1940. 253.

Brooks, Van Wyck. *The Ordeal of Mark Twain*. New York, 1933.

———. "Twain's Satire," *Dial*. April 1920. 424–443.

Brown, James. "Swift As Moralist," *Philol. Q.* 1954. 33:368.

Bullitt, John M. *Jonathan Swift and the Anatomy of Satire*. Cambridge, 1953.

Burke, Kenneth. *The Philosophy of Literary Form*. Baton Rouge, 1941.

Calverton, V. F. *Sex Expression in Literature*. New York, 1926.

Campbell, Oscar J. *Shakespeare's Satire*. New York, 1943.

Camus, Albert. "Art and Revolt," *Partisan Review*. May 1952. 268.

Cannan, Gilbert. *Satire*. London, 1914.

Cazamian, Louis. *The Development of English Humor*. Durham. 1952.

———. *The History of English Literature*. New York, 1940.

Chesterton, G. K. *Charles Dickens: The Last of the Great Men*. New York, 1942.

———. *George Bernard Shaw*. New York, 1956.

———. "Pope and the Art of Satire," *Twelve Types*. London, 1906.

Chevalier, Haakon. *The Ironic Temper: Anatole France and His Time*. New York, 1932.

Cooper, Lane. *An Aristotelian Theory of Comedy*. New York, 1922.

Daiches, David. "GBS," *Saturday Review*. July 21, 1956. 9.

Davis, Herbert. *The Satire of Jonathan Swift*. New York, 1947.

Deutch, H. "Don Quixote and Don Quixoticism," *Psychoanalytic Q*. 1937. 6:215.

De Voto, Bernard. *Mark Twain at Work*. Cambridge, 1942.

———. *Twain in Eruption*. New York, 1940.

Dooley, Lucille. "A Note on Humor," *Psychoanalytic Review*. 1934. 21:49.

———. "The Relation of Humor to Masochism," *Psych. R*. 1941. 28:37.

Dryden, John. "A Discourse . . . of Satire," *Dryden: Poetry and Prose*, ed. by D. Nichol Smith. London, 1925.

Eastman, Max. *Enjoyment of Laughter*. New York, 1948.

———. *Sense of Humor*. New York, 1922.

Elder, Donald. *Ring Lardner*. New York, 1956.

Elliott, Robert C. *The Power of Satire*. Princeton, 1960.

Ellmann, Richard. *Yeats: The Man and the Mask*. New York, 1948.

Engel, Monroe. "The Politics of Dickens' Novels," *PMLA*. December 1956. 945.

Ennis, Lambert. *Thackeray: The Sentimental Cynic*. Evanston, 1950.

Erskine, John. "Humor," *Century*. February 1928. 115:421.

Ewald, William Bragg. *The Masks of Jonathan Swift*. Cambridge, 1954.

Fadiman, Clifton. "Portrait of a Misanthrope," *Saturday Review of Literature*. October 12, 1946. 29:61.

————. *Party of One.* New York, 1955.

Fatout, Paul. *Ambrose Bierce and the Black Hills.* Norman, 1956.

Feldmann, S. "A Supplement to Freud's Theory of Wit," *Psychoanalytic R.* 1941. 28:201.

Ferguson, John Delancey. *Mark Twain: Man and Legend.* New York, 1943.

Ferenczi, S. "Gulliver Phantasies," *International Journal Psych.* 1928. 9:288.

Findlater, Richard. *Grimaldi, King of Clowns.* London, 1955.

Forster, E. M. *Abinger Harvest.* New York, 1936.

Fowler, Gene. *Minutes of the Last Meeting.* New York, 1954.

Frederick, J. G. *The Psychology of Writing Success.* New York, 1933.

Friedman, Paul. "The Nose," *American Imago.* 1951. 8:339.

Friedrich, Otto. "James Thurber: A Critical Study," *Discovery.* No. 5, March 1955. 158–201.

Freud, Sigmund. "Humor," *Int. J. Psych.* 1928. 9:2.

————. *Wit and Its Relation to the Unconscious.* London. (n.d.)

Greenacre, Phyllis. *Swift and Carroll.* New York, 1955.

Ghiselin, Brewster, *The Creative Process.* Berkeley, 1952.

Griffiths, Joan. "Waugh's Problem Comedies," *Accent.* Spring 1949. 170.

Grotjahn, Martin. *Beyond Laughter.* New York, 1957.

Harding, D. W. "Regulated Hatred," *Scrutiny.* 1940. 8:347.

Heine, Heinrich. *Works of Prose,* ed. by Hermann Kesten. New York, 1943.

Highet, Gilbert. *Anatomy of Satire.* Princeton, 1962.

Hoffer, Eric. *The True Believer.* New York, 1951.

Hopkins, Kenneth. *Portraits in Satire.* London. 1958.

Hooker, E. N. "Humour in the Age of Pope," *Huntington Library Q.* August 1948. 11:379.

Huff, Theodore. *Charlie Chaplin.* New York, 1951.

Hungerland, H. "Psychological Explanations of Style in Art," *Journal of Aesthetics and Art Criticism.* 1946. 4:160.

Huxley, Aldous. "On Swift," *Do What You Will.* London, 1929.

Irvine, William. "Shaw and Chesterton," *Virginia Q. R.* 1947. 23:274.

Johnson, Edgar. *A Treasury of Satire.* New York, 1945.

Johnston, Alva. "How To Become a Great Writer," *Subtreasury of American Humor,* ed. by E. B. and Katharine White. New York, 1941.

———. "Legend of a Sport," *A Treasury of Laughter,* ed. by Louis Untermeyer. New York, 1946.

Jones, Alexander. "Twain and Sexuality," *PMLA.* September 1956. 613.

Kanzer, Mark. "Gogol — A Study on Wit and Paranoia," *Journal Amer. Psychoanal. Assoc.* 1955. 3:110.

Kao, George. *Chinese Wit and Humor.* New York, 1946.

Kemler, Edgar. *The Irreverent Mr. Mencken.* Boston, 1950.

Kernan, Alvin. *The Cankered Muse.* New Haven, 1959.

Kirk, Russell. *The Conservative Mind.* Chicago, 1953.

Knox, Ronald A. "On Humour and Satire," *New and Old Essays.* London, 1937.

Koestler, Arthur. *Insight and Outlook.* New York, 1949.

Kris, Ernst. "Ego Development and the Comic," *Int. J. Psychoanalysis.* 1938. 19:77.

Kris, Ernst and Ernst Gombrich. "Principles of Caricature," *British Journal of Medical Psychology.* 1938. 17:341.

Kronenberger, Louis. *The Republic of Letters.* New York, 1955.

Ladell, R. "The Neurosis of Dr. Samuel Johnson," *British J. Med. Psych.* 1929. 9:314.

Landa, Louis. "Jonathan Swift and Charity," *JEGP.* 1945. 44:347.

LeComte, Edward S. *Dictionary of Last Words.* New York, 1955.

Lever, Katherine. *The Art of Greek Comedy.* London, 1956.

Levin, Harry. "Literature As an Institution," *Accent,* Spring 1946. 159–168.

Levine, Jacob. "Responses to Humor." *Scientific American.* February 1956. 24.

Lewis, C. S. *Surprised By Joy*: *The Shape of My Early Life*. New York, 1955.

Lewis, Grace Hegger. *With Love From Gracie*. New York, 1955.

Lewis, Sinclair. "Mr. Lorimer and Me," *Nation*. July 25, 1928. 81.

———. "Self-Conscious America," *American Mercury*. October 1925. 129–139.

Lewis, Wyndham. *Men Without Art*. London, 1934.

Leyburn, Ellen. *Satiric Allegory*: *Mirror of Man*. New Haven, 1956.

———. "Swift's View of the Dutch," *PMLA*. 1951. 66:736.

Lippmann, Walter. *Men of Destiny*. New York, 1927.

Lucas, F. L. *Literature and Psychology*. Ann Arbor, 1957.

Mack, Maynard. "The Muse of Satire," *Yale Review*. 1951. 41:90.

Manchester, William. *Disturber of the Peace*: *Life of H. L. Mencken*. New York, 1951.

Marshall, Margaret. "Notes By the Way," *Nation*. November 14, 1942. 515.

Marx, Arthur. *Life With Groucho*. New York, 1954.

Matson, Floyd. "Aldous and Heaven Too," *Antioch Review*. September 1954. 293.

Mead, Margaret. *Sex and Temperament in Three Primitive Societies*. New York, 1939.

Mencken, H. L. *Happy Days*. New York, 1940.

Meredith, George. *An Essay on Comedy*. London, 1913.

Mikes, George. *Eight Humorists*. London, 1954.

Miller, William Lee. Review in *Reporter*. January 12, 1956. 39.

Monro, D. H. *Argument of Laughter*. Melbourne, 1951.

Moore, John P. "Was Swift a Moderate?" *South Atlantic Q*. April 1954. 53:260.

Mudrick, Marvin. *Jane Austen: Irony As Defense and Discovery*. Princeton, 1952.

Mumford, Lewis. "The Mood of Satire," *Freeman*. November 14, 1923. 224.

Oberndorf, C. P. "Kidding — A Form of Humor," *Int. J. Psych*. 1932. 13:479.

Orwell, George. *A Collection of Essays*. New York, 1954.

Pannenborg, W. A. *Satirische Schrijvers: Karakter en Temperament*. Assen, 1953.

Parsons, C. O. "The Devil and Samuel Clemens," *Virginia Q. R*. 1947. 23:586.

Pearson, Hesketh. *Charles Dickens*. New York, 1949.

———. *G.B.S*. New York, 1950.

———. *Gilbert and Sullivan*. London, 1935.

———. *The Man Whistler*. New York, 1952.

———. *The Smith of Smiths*. London, 1948.

Peter, John. *Complaint and Satire in Early English Literature*. Oxford, 1956.

Piddington, Ralph. *The Psychology of Laughter*. London, 1933.

Potts, L. J. *Comedy*. London, 1948.

Priestley, J. B. *English Humour*. London, 1929.

Quintana, Ricardo. *Swift: An Introduction*. London, 1955.

Rank, Otto. *Art and the Artist*. New York, 1932.

Reich, Annie. "Structure of the Grotesque-Comic Sublimation," *Bulletin of Menninger Clinic*. September 1949. No. 5, 160.

Reik, Theodor. "Our Lady's Juggler," *Complex*. 1950. 1:14.

———. "The Pyschology of Irony," *Complex*. 1950. 1:18.

Repplier, Agnes. *In Pursuit of Laughter*. Boston, 1936.

Rolo, Charles. "Waugh," *Atlantic Monthly*. October 1954. 80.

Rosenberry, Edwin H. *Melville and the Comic Spirit*. Cambridge, 1955.

Rourke, Constance. *American Humor*. New York, 1953.

Rudwin, M. J. *The Devil in Legend and Literature*. London, 1931.

Runyon, Damon Jr. *Father's Footsteps*. New York, 1954.

Russell, Frances. *Satire in the Victorian Novel*. New York, 1920.

Scheffauer, H. "The Death of Satire," *Living Age*. July 12, 1913. 82.

Schiller, Andrew. "School for Scandal," *PMLA*. September 1956. 698.

Schilling, Bernard N. *Conservative England and the Case Against Voltaire*. New York, 1950.

Schorer, Mark. *Sinclair Lewis*. New York, 1961.

Schwartz, Delmore. "Lardner," *Reporter*. September 9, 1956. 54.

Seldes, Gilbert. "The Death of Satire," *New Republic.* January 5, 1927. 193.

———. *The Seven Lively Arts.* New York, 1924.

Shand, John. "Satire and Cynicism," *Living Age.* May 30, 1925. 472.

Shanks, Lewis P. *Anatole France: The Mind and the Man.* New York, 1932.

Sheldon, William H. *The Varieties of Temperament: A Psychology of Constitutional Differences.* New York, 1942.

Smith, David Nichol. *Dryden.* London, 1925.

Smith, Logan Pearsall. *Trivia.* New York, 1917.

Spears, Monroe K. "Late Auden: The Satirist As Lunatic Clergyman," *Sewanee Review.* 1951. 59:56.

Sutherland, James. *English Satire.* Cambridge, 1958.

Tarachow, Sidney. "Clowns and Circuses," *Psychoanalysis and Social Sciences.* New York. 1951. 171–185.

Tave, Stuart M. *The Amiable Humorist.* Chicago, 1960.

Thackeray, W. M. *The English Humourists of the Eighteenth Century.* London, 1949.

Thaddeus, Victor. *Voltaire.* New York, 1928.

Thompson, Alan R. *The Dry Mock: A Study of Irony in Drama.* Berkeley, 1948.

———. "Shaw: Ironist or Paradoctor?" *Pacific Spectator.* 1947. 1:113.

Toynbee, Arnold. *A Study of History.* New York, 1946.

Untermeyer, Louis. *A Treasury of Laughter.* New York, 1946.

Voorhees, Richard J. "George Orwell: Rebellion and Responsibility," *South Atlantic Q.* October 1954. 53:556.

Walker, Hugh. *English Satire and Satirists.* London, 1925.

Warren, Austin. "The Mask of Pope," *Sewanee Review.* 1946. 54:23.

Watkins, W. B. C. *Perilous Balance: The Tragic Genius of Swift, Johnson, and Sterne.* Cambridge, 1960.

Waugh, Evelyn. "Fan-fare," *Life.* April 8, 1946. 53.

Wecter, Dixon. *Sam Clemens of Hannibal.* Boston, 1952.

Wells, Carolyn. *Outline of Humor.* New York, 1923.

Welsford, Enid. *The Fool: His Social and Literary History.* New York. (n.d.)

West, Rebecca. *The Strange Necessity.* New York, 1928.

Whipple, T. K. *Spokesmen.* New York, 1928.

Wilson, Colin. *The Outsider.* New York, 1956.

Wilson, Edmund. "Dickens: Two Scrooges," *The Wound and the Bow.* Boston, 1941.

Winterstein, Alfred. "Contributions to the Problem of Humor," *Psychoanalytic Q.* 1934. 3:303.

Wolfe, Humbert. "Satire," *Criterion.* October 1929. 7.

Worcester, David. *The Art of Satire.* Cambridge, 1940.

Zucker, Wolfgang M. "The Image of the Clown," *Journal of Aesthetics.* 1954. 12:313.